The Skills
of Helping

The Skills
of Helping

Richard D. Parsons
West Chester University

Allyn and Bacon
Boston • London • Toronto • Sydney • Tokyo • Singapore

Series Editor: Ray Short
Editorial Assistant: Christine Shaw
Cover Administrator: Linda Knowles
Manufacturing Buyer: Louise Richardson
Editorial-Production Service: Walsh Associates
Cover Designer: Suzanne Harbison

Library of Congress Cataloging-in-Publication Data

Parsons, Richard D.
    The skills of helping / Richard D. Parsons.
       p.   cm.
    Includes bibliographical references and index.
    ISBN 0-205-14713-5
    1. Helping behavior. 2. Helping behavior—Case studies. 3. Counseling.
  4. Counseling—Case studies. I. Title.
  BF637.H4P37   1994
  158—dc20   94-6038
                                                   CIP

Printed in the United States of America

10 9 8 7 6 5 4 3 2   99 98

To Bob Wicks—
a helper, a scholar, a colleague . . . but
most importantly, my friend

Contents

Exercises

Preface

In a society which prizes competency and independence, needing and asking for help are often looked down upon as if evidence of a person's personal immaturity or perhaps that person's inadequacy. Contrary to that opinion, the position taken within this text is that both seeking and providing help are truly rich and special gifts of our humanity.

As we enter the 21st century, it is clear that even with the increasing numbers of mental health specialists and professional helpers, the need for helping outpaces the professional resources available. As a result of this imbalance, more non-professional helpers, such as community workers, educators, clergy, paraprofessionals, and students (e.g., peer counselors) are being called on to provide help. *The Skills of Helping* has been designed to help meet the training and skill development needs of these individuals.

The Skills of Helping is not a book on pathology or theories of psychotherapy. It is a book designed to

1. increase the reader's awareness and appreciation of the various components of the helping process;
2. assist the reader to begin to develop the facilitative attitudes necessary for effective helping;
3. help the reader to develop the fundamental helping skills, and perhaps most importantly,
4. assist the reader to begin to identify his or her own attitudes, biases, and expectations, and to understand that it is perhaps his or her "person" more than his or her "skills" which is key to effective helping.

As you read *The Skills of Helping*, you will not only be introduced to the theories, techniques, skills, and processes employed in helping, but you will also be introduced to a model of helping which prizes and respects the genuine, unconditional valuing and care which are the hallmarks of human helping.

In this text, you will find extensive discussion and attention given to the specific nature and process of helping, as well as the unique attitudes and skills required of the effective helper. Yet throughout the book, the reality highlighted is that helping another human being at a time when he or she needs our support is much more than theory or skill application, it is an experience of deep personal responsibility and satisfaction.

Perhaps you are reading this book as part of your first course or experience as you begin your journey to becoming a helper. Or, perhaps you are reading this text as part of a renewing experience after years of being involved either formally or informally with helping. Whatever your status and experience, as you proceed through the text, it is important to stop and reflect on your level of understanding and skill development, as well as on yourself as helper: your motives, your characteristic style, and your values as they come to bear on the helping process.

The chapters are designed to include case illustrations, practical exercises, and thoughtful suggestions for future direction. This approach is offered in hopes that the reader will gain:

1. Cognitive clarity. It is important that you not only read the material presented, but discuss the concepts described with your teacher, classmates, or colleagues. Memorization of terms is not the end goal; rather, it is hoped that the theories, the constructs, and the concepts presented become part of you, integrated into your own approach to helping.
2. Behavioral clarity. Practice the skills described by completing the exercises, modeling and role playing, and requesting corrective feedback from your classmates or colleagues. Practice probably won't make it perfect, BUT it will certainly lead to improvement.
3. Affective clarity. Helping is not a mechanical, sterile process. As you move through the various chapter examples and case illustrations, as well as the exercises provided, you will soon come to appreciate that helping is an emotional experience for both the helper and the person seeking help. Begin to clarify your feelings as a helper, identifying those feelings which are facilitative and those which may be inhibitory to your helping endeavors.

Finally, what is presented within this text is one author's conceptualization of the helping process. Even though the material presented is culled from extensive research and experience, it is not THE definitive approach to helping. The fact remains that no such definitive model exists. Therefore, it is essential that the reader approach this experience as but the first step on a long, continual journey of professional development—a journey which I hope will be successfully and satisfyingly initiated as you read *The Skills of Helping*.

Acknowledgments

While many researchers and theorists provide the foundation for the material to be discussed, the real substance and "life" of the book has been extracted from the many courageous clients and supportive colleagues with whom I have been privileged to work.

The illustrations which are presented throughout the book reflect a composite of the various individuals with whom I have worked. All the names and significant identifying information about the actual cases have been modified in order to insure confidentiality.

In addition to the many individuals who have invited me, as their helper, to become part of their life's journey, I have also been fortunate to have the encouragement and support of many professional colleagues. A special "thank you" goes to Dr. Patricia Kelly for her ever-present energy and enthusiasm for life, as well as her valuable suggestions for this text. Thanks also goes out to the faculty at West Chester University—particularly, Carol, Angelo, Wally, and Bill, for their support and excellent modeling of the skills of helping.

Finally, to my wife, Karen, and my children, Kristian, Drew, and Jonathan, for providing me the love and joy that everyone should know.

► 1

Being a Helper

The process of helping another or being a helper seems perfectly natural.

> "Well, you go down two blocks, until you see the AM/PM Minimart. Take a
> left at that light and travel to the next stop sign. The address you are
> looking for is on the left."
>
> "No, don't turn the knob to the right, turn it to the left!"

Most of us have found ourselves in situations like one of the two above, a situation in which one individual turned to us for some form of assistance. It is not so unusual for any one of us to find ourselves in the role of a helper. In fact, it would appear that the process of helping or being a helper is perfectly natural to the human condition. If this is true, then you might ask, So what is this chapter all about? What is so difficult about being a helper?

Helping may be perfectly natural, but it is NOT done perfectly, naturally. As you will see, helping another person to cope with an issue or concern is a very responsible process, one which should be approached with as much sensitivity and skill as possible. In this chapter you will begin to increase both your sensitivity and skill as a helper. Specifically, you will learn

- to define helping as a unique interpersonal process;
- to identify the salient characteristics of the effective helper, and;
- to identify the degree to which you currently possess the characteristics of an effective helper.

Before giving formal definitions and descriptions of what is involved in the helping process, it may be useful to identify your own expectations and biases about the helping process and the role of the helper. Exercise 1-1 is designed to help you begin to identify your personal view of helping.

But first a brief note: Throughout the text you will be invited to participate in a variety of exercises. The purpose of these exercises is twofold. First, it is hoped that the exercises will help to clarify the points under discussion. Secondly, and perhaps more importantly, it is hoped that the exercises will help you to personalize the material presented and assimilate it into your ongoing helping style. To facilitate this personalization process, it is recommended that you keep a personal journal as you perform the exercises. In the journal, you should identify your insights, reactions, and general expe-

---

EXERCISE 1-1
Your Personal View of Helping

Directions: Expectations and perspectives will impact the way you approach a situation. It is helpful, therefore, to be critical of your expectations and perspectives in order to insure their usefulness. Consider a recent situation or experience in which you served in a helping capacity. With that event as your focal point, answer each of the following questions. It would be useful for you to share and discuss your responses with a colleague or a classmate. It may also prove useful to keep your responses for this exercise and those to follow in a journal or copybook, so that you can reflect on them after you have completed this text.

1. What is helping? Your view:

   _____

   _____

   _____

2. What does it mean to be a helper? What do you do/say/feel?

   _____

   _____

   _____

3. What do you expect from those you help?

   _____

   _____

   _____

4. What is your view of your degree of responsibility, control, authority, and power in a helping relationship?

   _____

   _____

   _____

5. What do you feel you should NOT do as a helper?

   _____

   _____

   _____

riences as a result of each exercise. Further, as you proceed through the text, you may find it useful to review your previous journal entries to see if, with the additional information presented, you gain further personal insight into your role and style as a helper.

HELPING: A SPECIAL KIND OF INTERPERSONAL PROCESS AND RESPONSE

Helping is a process by which one person interacts with another in such a way so as to facilitate this other person's movement toward some specific outcome. The expected outcome of this interaction would be for the person receiving the help to take some constructive action on his or her own behalf, utilizing his or her own resources for coping with life.

Consider the following helping exchange which takes place between a crisis hotline worker and a woman whose child is choking. The exchange demonstrates the elements of *interaction, utilization of resources,* and *movement toward specific outcome.*

> Crisis Intervention Worker: Yes, ma'am. I can hear that you are very upset. I know it seems scary. Yes, ma'am, I am here, I am listening. Could you describe what is happening?
>
> Voice on the Phone (screaming): My baby is turning blue! Oh, my God! My baby . . . My baby . . .
>
> Crisis Worker (interrupting): Ma'am! Ma'am!
>
> Voice (trying to catch her breath): Yes?
>
> Worker: It is important for you to try to focus on what I am telling you. Can you hear me?
>
> Voice: Yes . . . but my . . .
>
> Worker (interrupting): I know it's hard for you, but keep listening to my voice. You must try. Roll your baby over on her stomach, place your left hand under her belly, and lift her stomach off the floor. Now with your right hand give her a gentle yet firm slap in the middle of the back, between her shoulder blades. Go ahead. You do that and tell me what's happening. I can hear you. (the worker continues talking as she listens to the mother) Good. I can hear the baby now, the baby is crying. That's good. Open the baby's mouth, put your finger in, and clear out anything that may be inside her mouth.
>
> Great. Her cries are clear and strong.
>
> Voice (sobbing): She . . . she is looking better, she coughed up a plastic grape. Thank you, thank you. You saved her life.

Implicit in this example is that helping is a *process* involving at least two people. While many names and labels can be applied to the person providing the help (e.g., psychologist, counselor, advocate, etc.), we will refer to this person simply as the *helper*. Similarly, the person receiving the help may be called a client, a patient, or some other such term, but for consistency we will simply identify him or her as the *helpee*. The operational elements of this special process are:

- the helping dynamic: Helping is a process, not a product
- the helping participants: Helping involves at least two people (one seeking help—the helpee; and one willing and capable of giving help—the helper)
- the helping relationship: Helping occurs through a process of interpersonal exchanges
- the helping focus: Facilitation of the helpee's utilization of resources is targeted
- the helping outcome: Helpee moves toward specific goals

The helping relationship is *first and foremost* exactly that—a very unique and special relationship. This point must be highlighted and will be discussed in greater detail in Chapter 2. But for now, it is important to note that too often in our eagerness to be of assistance, we rush in with our answers, our directions, our solutions, trying desperately to do something, to "solve the problem." We must remember that helping is *realized* in the context of a helping relationship. The quality of the relationship is therefore the keystone to the helping process, and thus needs to be of primary concern to all seeking to develop their helping skills. Even in the case of the choking baby, the helper needed to focus on establishing a working relationship with the mother, by listening, affirming, and calming *before* movement toward the desired outcome could occur.

THE NATURE OF EFFECTIVE HELPING

As with any relationship, the quality of a helping encounter, or the effectiveness of the helping, will depend upon the unique personal characteristics—traits, skills, attitudes and values—of those involved (i.e., the helper and the helpee), as well as the reasons for their being involved (i.e., the specific problem under discussion). Now while it may appear logical to assume that it would be the helper's technique or skill which would determine the ultimate effectiveness of the helping, such is not the case. Research (Combs, 1986) suggests that effective helpers do not differ significantly in their techniques or approaches when compared to less effective helpers. This same research, however, suggests that effective and ineffective helpers can be distinguished based on their personal beliefs and personal characteristics.

While the research fails to produce one single cluster of traits, a significant body of research (Carkhuff, 1969; Rogers, 1980; Combs, 1986; Combs & Avila, 1985; Claiborn, 1982) outlines characteristics or values which consistently and universally characterize the effective helper, and supports the notion that the effective helper is one who has a sense of self-awareness, facilitative attitudes and values, emotional objectivity, an investigative approach to helping, and a desire to strive for competence.

CHARACTERISTICS OF EFFECTIVE HELPERS

A Self-Awareness

One of the essential elements of being an effective helper is self-awareness. Effective helpers generally have a grasp of who they are, what is important to them, what unique gifts and limitations they possess, and which values guide their decisions and their actions.

Motivation

Helping requires that the helper be there for another. In the process of helping another, it is the helpee's issues, concerns, and needs which should take precedence. It is important to understand—to become aware of—where the helper's needs, values, and concerns begin and end, and where the helpee's begin. For example, while most people seek to become helpers because of their care and concern for others, quite often individuals find the role of helper to be one of power, control, and influence, and thus open to use for their own self-serving ends. Consider the negative effect of helper motivation for the scenarios presented in Exercise 1-2.

As Exercise 1-2 illustrates, helper motivation can sometimes be destructive to the helping relationship and helping outcomes. It is important for the effective helper to

---

EXERCISE 1-2
Self-Serving Helper Motivation

Directions: It is important to be clear about our motives when helping another, or else our interaction may be directed in service of our needs, rather than in service of the needs of those seeking help.

The possible damaging effect of self-serving motives of a helper can be demonstrated by reviewing each of the following examples of helper motivation. Review each helper's primary motive for engaging in the helping process, and consider and discuss how these motives can negatively affect both the process and outcome of helping.

Helper A: Engages in helping to feel needed by others.
Helper B: Is involved in helping because it can be a lucrative profession.
Helper C: Is primarily motivated by the need to feel powerful and in control in interpersonal relationships.
Helper D: Enjoys hearing the deep, dark "secrets" of other people.
Helper E: Wants to parent others in a very nurturing, and somewhat smothering, way.
Helper F: (Can you generate other motives which would prove negative and destructive to the helping process?)

engage in an ongoing process of self-reflection and clarification of his or her own needs, values, and motives as they engage in the helping process. Exercise 1-3 asks you to reflect on the motives which have stimulated your interest in becoming a helper, as well as the possible positive and negative effects such motives may have on the helping process and helping outcomes. Reflection upon one's motives is one of the elements of self-awareness.

Biases

In addition to increasing our self-awareness by reflecting on our motives for helping, we need to become increasingly clear about the expectations, biases, and even values

---

EXERCISE 1-3
Awareness of Personal Motives

Directions: To begin to identify the needs which motivate your interest in becoming a helper, and which may be operating within the helping encounter, reflect on each of the following. If you are working with a colleague or are in a classroom setting, share your reflections and discuss their potential positive and negative implications for helping.

1. List three things that you will get or gain from being a helper.

   _____

   _____

   _____

2. What do you experience in the process of helping?

   _____

   _____

   _____

3. What about the experience of helping do you like?

   _____

   _____

   _____

4. What about the experience of helping do you dislike?

   _____

   _____

   _____

5. What would you lose or miss if you no longer served as a helper?

   _____

   _____

   _____

---

which we bring to the helping relationship. The fact that our biases, expectations, or values are active in the helping process may run contrary to your belief that helpers must be totally objective, totally value-free. Many professional helpers (e.g., counselors, therapists, and social workers) present themselves as totally objective, totally value-free. Such is not the case.

We enter a helping relationships as we enter all relationships: full of personal expectations, biases, and values. Further, as with any of our encounters, these expectations, biases, and values influence our interactions. As part of the effective helper's self-awareness, he or she must be aware of his or her values, and those circumstances wherein his or her values may interfere with helping another effectively.

Exercise 1-4 identifies a number of professional helpers with very clear and strong values. For each of the helpers listed, identify a type of helpee problem with which they may have trouble remaining objective and value-free. For example, imag-

---

EXERCISE 1-4
Identifying Areas of Helper Value Conflict

Directions, Part 1: For each of the following situations, review the characteristics and experiences of the helper and assume that his or her unique experience may be biasing them in a particular direction. Next, identify a type of helpee problem for which the helper will have very strong feelings (for or against), and thus may have difficulty remaining non-judgmental and objective. Discuss, with your colleagues or classmates, the impact such bias may have on the helping process.

1. **Counselor A:** A female professional who had to pay for her own college and post-baccalaureate education, even as her family objected that a place for women is in the home.
   Someone on financial aid

2. **Counselor B:** A divorced professional who experienced, and continues to experience, a bitter dispute over child custody.
   Opposite gender, who is going through a child custody, dead-beat Dad or Mom

3. **Counselor C:** A very strict religious fundamentalist.
   Atheistic different religion behavior violates what they believe

4. **Counselor D:** An overachieving, highly successful, somewhat driven, almost workaholic helper.
   Someone who is lazy, government aid or funding workaholic who isn't successful

   Continued

EXERCISE 1-4   *Continued*

Directions, Part 2: Identify the values or biases which, if held by a helper, may interfere with the ability to remain objective when working with each of the following helpees.

1. **Helpee A:** A person considering an abortion
   _religious beliefs_____ _Someone who can't get pregnant_
   _anyone opposed to abortion_____

2. **Helpee B:** A person considering suicide
   _lost loved one to suicide_____
   _parent_____

3. **Helpee C:** A child abuser
   _someone who was abused_____
   _parent_____

4. **Helpee D:** A person having an extramarital affair
   _____
   _____

---

ine that as a helper I had seen my father, mother, and older brother all die of alcoholism. As a result, I have a very strong belief in the evils of drugs and alcohol. How objective or value-free would I be trying to help someone determine if their use of alcohol was problematic or recreationally and socially appropriate?

Exercise 1-4 demonstrates that values and biases can interfere with effective helping. This is not to suggest that each of the helpers identified in Exercise 1-4 should quit being a helper. Rather, the goal of self-awareness is to enable the helper to try to place his or her biases aside and be present for the helpee. Where this is not possible, the helper should recognize that referring the helpee to another less biased helper is the most effective and ethical thing to do.

While it may be hard for you to anticipate the type of helpee problems you will be invited to work with, and thus hard to determine how your values may help or hinder your effectiveness, Exercise 1-5 is provided to assist you to at least begin this process of self-awareness of values and bias. As with each of the exercises, it is suggested you respond to the scenario presented and discuss your response with your colleagues or classmates.

As you will see later, helping another requires that we can value or prize that person. As evidenced by the two previous exercises, the values and behaviors of the person seeking help may conflict with our own values in such a way as to make it hard for us to prize the helpee. Under these circumstances, helping is best done by assisting the helpee to find another source for receiving the needed help.

EXERCISE 1-5
Areas of Personal Bias

Direction, Part 1: For each of the following, identify your belief, your attitude, or your value about the issue presented.

1. Equality of genders

_____

_____

2. Fidelity in marriage

_____

_____

3. Children's rights

_____

_____

4. The recreational use of drugs

_____

_____

5. Date rape and the responsibility of the person raped

_____

_____

6. Cheating in school

_____

_____

7. The Horatio Alger viewpoint: pulling yourself up by your bootstraps

_____

_____

8. The sanctity of marriage

_____

_____

9. A woman's right to choose an abortion

_____

_____

10. Alternative lifestyles

_____

_____

Directions, Part 2: Through personal reflection and discussion of your responses to Part 1, identify those items in Part 1 for which you have strong opinions, attitudes, or values. Identify types of helpee problems where some these values might hinder your ability to remain objective and non-judgmental.

Cultural and World View

A very powerful, yet extremely subtle, bias to which every helper must become sensitized is the bias of culture. The effective helper appreciates that his or her view of life, and more specifically his or her view of a helpee and a helpee's problem, is highly influenced by his or her own world or cultural viewpoint. To be an effective helper, therefore, one must become sensitive to his or her own cultural framework and the way it biases his or her attitudes, values, behaviors, and approach to helping, and also to the helpee's cultural makeup and the role this cultural element plays in the creation and resolution of the problem presented.

This is not to suggest that each helper must become an expert on every culture encountered. It is important, however, that each helper attempts to understand and value the world view of his or her culturally different helpee. Specifically, it is important for the helper to consider the unique cultural circumstances which impact the experience of each helpee and to employ culturally sensitive approaches to the helping process. In keeping with this line of thinking, Sue, Arredondo, and McDavis (1992) have suggested that the culturally sensitive and effective helper should be

- knowledgeable about communication style differences and about how his or her style may clash or facilitate the helping process with culturally different helpees;
- aware of and respectful of the indigenous helping practices and intrinsic help-giving networks found in various cultures and communities;
- understanding of the institutional and cultural barriers that may interfere with the helpees' use of particular strategies and interventions.

The importance of cultural awareness and sensitivity cannot be overemphasized. It is highly recommended that the reader truly interested in becoming an effective helper learn more about the skills and attitudes required of the culturally sensitive helper. Two excellent sources for such information are: 1) D.W. Sue, *Counseling the Culturally Different: Theory and Practice (1990),* and 2) Allen Ivey, Mary Bradford Ivey, and Lynn Simek-Morgan, *Counseling and Psychotherapy: A Multicultural Perspective (1993).*

Facilitative Attitudes and Values

A second characteristic of the effective helper is that he or she possesses a number of attitudes and values which have been demonstrated to be facilitative to the helping process. Therefore, in addition to increasing our self-awareness of the limiting and potentially negative impact our biases may have on the helping process, it is also clear that we, as helpers, need to develop a number of values and attitudes which facilitate helping.

Facilitative Attitudes

Exercise 1-6 identifies a number of attitudes and values which have been found to be characteristic of the effective helper and facilitative to the helping process.

EXERCISE 1-6
Facilitative Attitudes

Directions: For each of the following, identify the degree to which you feel you possess that particular attitude or value. Also identify those areas where an increase in a particular value or attitude would be useful as you continue to develop your helping skills.

	Need Improvement	*Acceptable*	*Superior*
1. Co-equality	_____	_____	_____
2. Flexibility	_____	_____	_____
3. Respect for others	_____	_____	_____
4. Genuineness (real)	_____	_____	_____
5. Openness	_____	_____	_____
6. Focus on person rather than product	_____	_____	_____
7. Acceptance of another's values/perspectives	_____	_____	_____
8. Able to see situations from another's viewpoint	_____	_____	_____
9. Interest and willingness to grow	_____	_____	_____
10. Patience	_____	_____	_____

Personal and Professional Ethics

In addition to these facilitative attitudes and values, the effective helper will also allow his or her actions to be guided by values shared by the profession and articulated within the professional standards and ethics of practice. These specific standards and values will be discussed in more detail in Chapter 15.

Ability to Maintain a Degree of Emotional Objectivity

The effective helper places the concerns and needs of the helpee as top priority. As previously noted, the focus of the interaction is on the helpee, not the helper. Top priority on the helpee's concerns (i.e., altruism) rather than on the concerns of the helper (i.e., narcissism) demands that the effective helper distinguish feelings as a reflection of his or her issues and his or her emotional needs from what the helpee is presenting. Such emotional objectivity is often difficult to maintain and can be distorted or destroyed in certain types of relationships. The effective helper must be aware of the various forms such a loss or lack of emotional objectivity can take, and take steps to challenge that loss in order to increase his or her emotional objectivity. Where this is not possible, the helper should refer the helpee to one who can maintain objectivity.

Loss of emotional objectivity may occur in a number of different ways. However, four forms—direct personal involvement, simple identification, theme interference, and transference—can be particularly troublesome and as such are presented below.

Direct personal involvement occurs any time a helper has a personal relationship, in addition to the helping relationship, with the helpee. For example, consider Tom, who is attempting to help his girlfriend, Elaine, make a decision about either moving away from their hometown to spend four years in the Peace Corps, or staying at home and continuing in graduate school. Clearly, while Tom may truly want to assist Elaine in making the best decision (for her) he may have difficulty keeping his own strong desire, to keep her close to him and at home, out of the equation. Thus, his recommendations may be aimed more at meeting his needs for a personal relationship than at Elaine's need to make the best vocational choice.

Under such circumstances where a friend or family member desires an ongoing helping relationship, it is better to have that person find another helper who can be more emotionally objective.

A second somewhat more subtle form of loss of emotional objectivity is *simple identification.* Simple identification occurs when the helper identifies him- or herself with the helpee. This typically occurs when the helper relates the helpee's story, or life experience, to his or her own, thus tending to view the helpee as him- or herself.

This was made very clear by the case of Mr. Peepers. Mr. Peepers was a helper who worked with elementary school students. One student he was particularly concerned about was Joseph. He felt Joseph needed his help because the other fifth grade boys "always teased Joseph and pushed him and took his things." According to Mr. Peepers, the other boys were always so mean to Joseph, and Mr. Peepers was absolutely sure that Joseph was devastated by all of this. Well, the reality was that Joseph was fine. He teased the other boys as much as they teased him, and the fifth graders generally liked Joseph and included him in their activities. The problem was that Mr. Peepers was "seeing" himself in Joseph's experience. Joseph looked like Mr. Peepers. He was small and somewhat frail-looking. He wore thick glasses and appeared non-athletic. Because Mr. Peepers "identified" with Joseph on the basis of physical similarity, his emotional objectivity was destroyed and he assumed that what happened to him as a fifth grader was most likely happening to Joseph. Clearly, such loss of emotional objectivity needs to be identified and confronted if one is to be an effective helper.

The next two forms of loss of emotional objectivity, theme interference and transference, often occur at a level below conscious awareness. Thus, the assistance of a colleague may be needed to help point out their occurrence.

The third form of loss of emotional objectivity is called *theme interference* (Caplan, 1970). Theme interference occurs when a particular theme which is raised by the helpee—for example, a problem with authority or family or their sexuality—is also an unresolved personal problem for the helper. Under these conditions, the helper may be more motivated to cope with his or her own emotional upset than assisting the helpee.

The final form of loss of emotional objectivity is called *transference.* Transference is a more complex form of identification and distortion where the helper forces the story of the helpee to fit some aspect of his or her own life. This is a major distortion of reality and occurs below the helper's conscious level. However, transference results in the helper's expressing feelings, beliefs, or desires belonging to some other significant person in his or her life which are buried in his or her unconscious—in the context of this helping relationship. The ability to be sensitive to the possibility of transference is essential to effective helping, and it is discussed in more detail in Chapter 11.

While the helping relationships which most entry-level helpers encounter may not be of the length or the intensity to stimulate distortion of emotional objectivity to the degree characterized as transference, it is clear that all helpers run the risk of losing emotional objectivity in the form of direct personal involvement, simple identification, and perhaps even theme interference. Exercise 1-7 is presented to help you begin to identify how loss of emotional objectivity may manifest itself in your helping encounters.

EXERCISE 1-7
Threats to Emotional Objectivity

Directions: After considering each of the following, share your response with your colleagues or classmates in order to identify ways of preventing such loss of objectivity.

1. Identify one person with whom you have a personal relationship and discuss how that relationship could block your emotional objectivity and thus interfere with your being an effective helper.

_____

_____

_____

2. How might your own social roles (e.g., son, daughter, mother, father, ex-boyfriend, girlfriend, struggling student, etc.) be the source of simple identification?

_____

_____

_____

3. Identify a number of themes or issues which arouse an emotional response in you (e.g., themes of emotional dependency, victimization, authority, and power, etc.) and which might prove too close to your own emotional experience for you to remain objective.

_____

_____

_____

▷ *Investigative Approach to Helping*

The fourth characteristic of the effective helper to be discussed is that he or she approaches the helping encounter as an investigator. In this role, the effective helper is open to all information and is flexible in speculating about cause and course of action.

Helping is both an art and a science. As you will see in later chapters, the helper is called upon to absorb all the data presented by the helpee and then assist the helpee to make sense of the information and develop a course of action. For many new helpers, the amount of information given them by the helpee, as well as the speed with which it comes, often leads them to feel overwhelmed. Questions such as, What is important here and what's not? How does this piece of information connect with another piece of information? or more simply, What am I do to do with all of this? are most often asked by beginning helpers.

Imagine having someone take a novel, a biology textbook, a anthropology text, and a family album and cut them up in small little sentences, paragraphs, words, or images and then ask you to put them together. That is how it sometimes can feel when a helper begins to become overwhelmed by the amount and speed of information presented.

Consider the case of Cynthia, Exercise 1-8.

EXERCISE 1-8
What's It All About?

Directions: As you read the following case data, ask yourself, What is it all about? What does each piece of information mean and how can you weave all of this information into some meaningful whole? Discuss your responses with a colleague or your classmates looking for similar and dissimilar conclusions.

Cynthia

Cynthia is a college freshman. During her first week of school, she asks to speak to her residence assistant (who is a upperclassman) with a "minor complaint."

> Cynthia: I know school has just started, and I am just a naive, little helpless freshman, but I (looks down on to the floor) . . . well, I . . . (voice becomes quiet) have a kind of . . . well, a . . . I guess you could call it a small, but not real small, problem with my roommate. Look, I don't want to seem like a complainer—I'm not, am I? But (fidgeting a little), gads, this is kind of embarrassing to talk about, I mean, you're a guy (giggles), of course you know that, but . . . oh, HELL, I'm just gonna say it. I think my roommate . . . is . . . well, she . . . let's say, is nothing like me. No, what I mean to say is . . . I really like guys (smiles flirtatiously), even though I haven't had a

---

EXERCISE 1-8   *Continued*

chance to meet anyone here, except the freshman boys, but anyway . . . I don't think she does, if you know what I mean.

As an investigator, the effective helper needs to be open to all of the information provided, while at the same time remembering that his or her conclusions are tentative. It is necessary to find further support in additional material.

What meaning did you make of all of the varied verbal, nonverbal (looking
down, flirting, etc.), and para-verbal (intonation in her voice, volume, etc.)
messages. What did you pay attention to? All of it? How about your colleague
or classmate, did he or she focus on other data? Does it all fit nicely together? Is
there only one message being sent, or are there several messages? If there is
more than one message, which is primary? These are the types of questions the
effective, investigative helper asks him- or herself.

Use of Theory and Models

When given information that appears somewhat disjointed and disconnected, we need
to weave a thread of consistency of theme through the information so that we can
understand what is really going on and how best to approach the situation. Most
helpers find that making sense out of the information provided by the helpee is aided
by the use of a theoretical model or framework. Counseling theories such as behavioral theory, psychoanalytic theory, cognitive theory, and the like are frameworks for
attempting to understand the meaning of a person's actions, as well as offering pre-
scriptions for how to help the person function more effectively. These theories are
discussed more fully in Chapter 13. However, the interested reader is referred to a
number of good textbooks written on theories of counseling, which are listed at the
end of each chapter.

A more generic approach, or model, for gathering data will be presented in later
chapters. This model connects the information provided and draws hypotheses and
tentative conclusions about the meaning of that data. The approach presented by
this text is to view helping as a process of hypothesis testing. As data is provided,
the effective helper needs to hazard a tentative guess about what it means and how
it connects to previous data. Once these hypotheses have been established, the
helper needs to go about the process of finding more information to validate or
revise these hypotheses. This hypothesis-testing model of helping will be developed in later chapters.

As you develop your own experience and competence as a helper, you will most
likely develop your own counseling style and model. This is good. However, like all
models, yours and mine must be evaluated and tested for its validity. Models are
useful to understand reality, but should not be imposed on reality in order to shape it
to our expectations.

Striving for Competence

The final characteristic of the effective helper to be discussed is that the effective helper continually strives for increased competence. As noted earlier, helping is both an art and a science. It may be considered perfectly natural, yet clearly it is not done perfectly, naturally!

An effective helper strives to increase his or her competence by continuing to develop his or her skills and understanding of the helping process. The effective helper needs to be knowledgeable about the process of helping and also have a desire to continue to learn, both about the helpee and about the various ways the helper can assist the helpee. The competent helper will search for data to make informed decisions about the helpee's problem and ways to assist. But most importantly, the competent and effective helper will seek out ongoing opportunities for skills development and evaluative feedback on his or her knowledge and skill.

The information and exercises provided within this text are all aimed at increasing your competence as a helper. The hope is that you take your training, your skills development, seriously, and be willing to risk sharing your knowledge and your skills with those who can provide growth-filled feedback. This openness to suggestions which can provide increased competence is a characteristic of the competent helper, one which continues throughout his or her career.

WHAT NEXT

As has been implied, if not explicitly noted, helping is a serious, powerful process and being a helper an awesome, responsible, and yet satisfying role. It should also be evident from this chapter that while helping skills, techniques, and theories are important, helping is a personal, human endeavor. Thus, the person of the helper is more important than the techniques employed.

The purpose of this chapter was not only to introduce the reader to the definition and elements of effective helping, but also to have the reader think about him- or herself in the role of helper. Being in touch with what you bring to the helping encounter is essential to effective helping. Therefore, it is suggested that before proceeding through the next chapter you should take time to reflect on the following:

1. Review your responses to this chapter's exercises. Were you honest? Did you invest energy in responding? What did you learn about yourself as a helper?
2. What specific elements of helping, as presented within this chapter, excite you or concern you?
3. Which particular characteristics of the effective helper do you feel you possess most strongly, and which do you feel you need to focus on developing?
4. How might you approach the reading, the exercises, and the reflections in the next chapter to maximize your development as a helper?

This book, like any other text, can be an impersonal, factual disseminator of information. Hopefully, the case illustrations and the exercises will help to make it less impersonal. The real key, however, is you, the reader. As you read this book, make it personal. Invest yourself in the exercises. The more of yourself that you place into the text, the more the material will be able to stimulate your growth as a helper, beyond simply filling you with more facts and data.

REFERENCES AND RECOMMENDED READINGS

Aponte, H.J., & Winter, J.E. (1987). The person and practice of the therapist: Treatment and training. In M. Baldwin & V. Satir (Eds.), *The use of self in therapy* (pp 85–112). New York: Haworth Press.

Baldwin, M., & Satir, V. (Eds.) (1987). *The use of self in therapy.* New York: Haworth Press.

Brammer, L.M. (1988). *The helping relationship.* Engelwood Cliffs, NJ: Prentice-Hall.

Caplan, G. (1970). *The theory and practice of mental health consultation.* New York: Basic Books.

Carkhuff, R.R. (1969). *Helping and human relations,* Vols. I & II. New York: Holt, Rinehart & Winston.

Claiborn, C.D. (1982). Interpretation and change in counseling. *Journal of Counseling Psychology, 29,* 439–453.

Claiborn, C.D. (1987). Science and practice: Reconsidering the Pepinskys. *Journal of Counseling and Development, 65(6),* 286–288.

Combs, A.W. (1986). What makes a good helper? A person-centered approach. *Person-Centered Review, 1,* 51–61.

Combs, A.W., & Avila, D. (1985). Helping relationships: Basic concepts for the helping professions. Needham Heights, MA: Allyn and Bacon.

Corey, G. (1991). *Theory and practice of counseling and psychotherapy,* 4th edition. Belmont, CA: Brooks/Cole Publishing Company.

Ivey, A.E., Bradford Ivey, M., & Simek-Morgan, L. (1993). *Counseling and psychotherapy: A multicultural perspective.* Needham Heights, MA: Allyn and Bacon.

Kanfer, F. and Goldstein, A. (1986) *Helping people change,* 3rd edition. New York: Pergamon Press.

Parsons, R. (1992). The counseling relationship. In R. Wicks, R. Parsons, & D. Capps (Eds.), *Clinical handbook of pastoral counseling.* Mahwah, NJ: Paulist Press.

Parsons, R., & Wicks, R. (1994). *Counseling strategies and intervention techniques for the human services.* Needham Heights, MA: Allyn and Bacon.

Patterson, C.H. (1989). Values in counseling and psychotherapy. *Counseling and Values, 33,* 164–176.

Rogers, C. (1980). *A way of being.* Boston, MA: Houghton Mifflin.

Satir, V. (1987). The therapist story. In M. Baldwin & V. Satir (Eds.), *The use of self in therapy* (pp 17–26). New York: Haworth Press.

Sue, D. W. (1991). A conceptual model for cultural diversity training. *Journal of Counseling and Development, 70,* 99–105.

Sue, D.W., & Sue, D. (1990). *Counseling the culturally different: Theory and practice.* New York: Wiley.

Sue, D.W., Arredondo, P., & McDavis, R.J. (1992). Multicultural counseling competencies and standards: A call to the profession. *Journal of Counseling and Development, 70,* 477–486.

▶ 2

Helping: First and Foremost a Relationship

The helping relationship—be it called counseling, psychotherapy, or simply helping—has been the focus of many dramatic representations. When placed in the arena of therapy, the helping relationship is sometimes presented as the whimsical, superfluous indulgence of the rich. When taken more seriously, the helping process is often presented as something which is both deeply mystifying and magical. In this light, helping becomes an art, not a science, a special talent rather than a set of learnable attitudes and skills. From this perspective, helping appears to be a process which is beyond the comprehension of most uninitiated individuals.

Although helping is a very special type of relationship, it is, **first and foremost,** exactly that—a relationship. Helping shares many of the same elements experienced in our other relationships. Like our other relationships, the helping encounter involves at least two individuals, generally requires communication and interaction, and goes through a series of developmental changes. However, unlike most of our other relationships, the helping encounter is somewhat unique in its power and potential for facilitating growth in one or both of the participants.

In this chapter we will discuss the nature of the helping relationship and ways of increasing its effectiveness. Specifically, the chapter will

- provide a review of the current research and perspective on the role and value of the relationship in helping;
- discuss the steps to be taken to initiate a working alliance in the context of a helping relationship; and,
- present those attitudes and behaviors which appear to facilitate the development and maintenance of the helping process.

THE HELPING RELATIONSHIP—NECESSARY AND SUFFICIENT?

While it is fair to assume that the helping process involves the application of techniques or procedures, these techniques or procedures are only one part of the helping equation. The second component of this helping equation is the relationship that is developed and maintained between the helper and helpee.

The degree to which the quality of the relationship determines the outcomes of the helping, be it simply a necessary condition, or one which is in and of itself sufficient for helping to occur, is open for debate. For example, the behavioral perspective views the helping relationship as a precondition to helping. The proponents of a behavioral theory, for example, believe that the relationship establishes the setting or the stage within which to do the "helping" work. This perspective presents the helping relationship as primarily a tool, or a vehicle by which the helping goal is achieved (Gelso & Carter, 1985).

An alternative perspective is often presented in a client-centered perspective on helping, where the relationship itself central. Proponents argue that the relationship is not only a necessary condition, but in fact the prime ingredient or sufficient variable in helping (Rogers, 1957; Carkhuff & Berenson, 1977; Truax & Carkhuff, 1965). Thus, from this perspective, helping is not only realized *in* the context of a helping relationship, but occurs *as a direct result* of that relationship. Therefore, the quality of that relationship becomes the keystone to the helping process.

While there is disagreement as to the absolute value of the helping relationship, be it necessary or necessary and sufficient, there is little disagreement that the relationship between the helper and the helpee is one of the primary variables defining potential effectiveness (Highlen & Hill, 1984; Kokotovic & Tracey, 1990; Orlando & Howard, 1986).

THE COMPONENTS AND SEQUENCE OF HELPING

A helping relationship, like all other ongoing relationships, develops and changes over time. From the initial "hello" to the final "goodbye," the helping relationship passes through a number of unique stages. Theorists may differ in their opinions about the specific number of stages, but most will agree that helping proceeds through at least three fundamental stages.

The first stage or focus of a helping relationship involves *coming together, or developing and building a helping alliance.* Once a working relationship is established, the focus the helping encounter turns to identifying the nature of the problem and the goals to be achieved. For the purpose of our discussion, this second stage is termed *exploring together, or reconnaissance.* Finally, with the helper and helpee agreeing upon goals to be achieved and having a shared sense of the resources available, the helping relationship will move toward *acting together, or intervention.*

As presented, the stages appear to be three separate constructs which occur in a somewhat linear form, that is, Stage I leads to Stage II, etc. While such a neat, lock-step presentation is easier for our discussion, in reality these stages are quite interrelated. In the process of helping, movement through these stages is not always linear or lock step. Rather, helping will often move back and forth across the stages. As helping proceeds, the helper, even while in the action stage, may revisit the exploring stage, or return the focus of his or her energies to strengthening the alliance.

While the stages of problem defining (exploration) and intervention (action) will be discussed in detail in Chapter 3, the basic building blocks of a helping encounter (building a working alliance) are discussed in some detail below.

Stage I: Coming Together, or Building a Helping Alliance

As with any encounter, the nature and the character of the helping relationship depends upon the *unique personal characteristics* of those involved, as well as the *focus* of the interaction. No two helping encounters will be exactly alike, nor will the relationships proceed smoothly and predictably. Yet while the content, pace, and steadiness of direction may vary from one helping encounter to another, helping as a process cannot move forward effectively unless the following essentials are present in the helper-helpee relationship.

1. A workable, warm helping relationship
2. An atmosphere of acceptance and understanding
3. A show of confidence by the helper that the helpee can develop or rediscover problem-solving skills if given enough time and support

Coming to someone for help may place the helpee in an unusual social situation. The helpee may encounter a degree of nervousness or anxiety as a result of not knowing what to expect, being unsure about how the helper may perceive him or her, or even simply not knowing how to perform the role of "helpee." If we are truly to help another, we must first attempt to develop a "working," "caring" relationship. We need to assist the helpee to relax and reduce his or her anxieties about the relationship, so that we can begin to focus on the concerns and the resources to address those concerns.

During the first stage of helping, *coming together,* the helper's primary role is to create a warm, caring, working relationship. This is accomplished through the processes of *greeting, structuring,* and *setting the stage.*

Greeting—A Smile and a Hello!

Quite often people needing help feels embarrassed by that very fact. They may feel that they should not be needing help or that they should be able to handle this on their own. They may feel ashamed or foolish for seeking out help. These feelings must be reduced if effective helping is to take place.

Greeting another, or simply smiling and saying "Hello, my name is . . .," may seem like a small thing, but it is one way to reduce the helpee's anxiety about talking with you. In addition to a friendly hello, the helper can place the helpee at ease by taking the initiative in making contact, rather than simply waiting in silence until he or she introduces him- or herself or approaches the helper.

Exercise 2-1 is presented to begin to sensitize you to the discomfort and the anxiety potentially experienced by one seeking help. As with each of the exercises, it is beneficial to discuss your responses either with a colleague or classmate.

It is probably fair to assume that each of the scenarios presented in Exercise 2-1 made you feel uncomfortable. Perhaps you even felt like "forgetting the whole thing" and just getting out of the situation. If that is how you felt, then perhaps you can appreciate that this is a similar experience for many people coming for help. Further, under these conditions most of us would likely appreciate and find some relief from some small sign of greeting, affirmation, or direction from the other in the encounter. The same is true in the helping encounter.

It is important during this initial encounter to convey to helpee that it is okay to be

---

EXERCISE 2-1
The Anxiety of Not Knowing

Directions: For each of the following scenarios identify

1. how you would feel,
2. what you would do; and
3. what the other person could do to help you feel more comfortable, more relaxed, and more like yourself.

Scenario 1: You have just been introduced to a very attractive member of the opposite sex. After having been told your name, he or she simply looks unresponsively at you. This continues without his or her saying or doing anything.

Scenario 2: You are going for a job interview. As you enter the employer's office, you find her sitting behind her desk, which is at least 20 feet from the door through which you entered. She does not get up or say anything to you, but simply stares at you.

Scenario 3: You have done something about which you are very embarrassed. You feel like you need to discuss it with someone, so you ask your best friend if you can talk. Your friend gets a serious look and says, "Shoot, I'm ready for anything!"

here. In fact, it is helpful to convey to the helpee that it is more than okay, and that you believe the relationship will be positive and helpful. This arousal of hope and positive expectations has been suggested by some to be at the core of helping (Frank, Hoehn-Saric, Imber, Liberman, & Stone, 1978; Kirsch, 1990). If this is true, then your initial greeting and warm friendly hello are far from a small thing.

Structuring—What Do You Say after Hello?

Greeting the helpee warmly in a conversational tone and proceeding with social conversation around appropriate non-threatening information (i.e., the weather, recent events, etc.) will help to "break the ice" in this new and perhaps somewhat scary encounter. Following such icebreaking, the helper should provide the helpee with some very clear guidelines about what to expect within the helping relationship. Just as in the encounters described in Exercise 2-1, the more structure and the more feedback a person receives about what is expected and what is going to happen, the less anxiety that person typically feels. The same is true in the helping encounter.

The helpee needs to know his or her role and responsibilities. What can he or she talk about? Is there anything that is off limits? Does he or she have to get right into deep dark secrets or should this develop more slowly? And how about your role as helper? Are you a counselor? To whom do you report? Will you tell people what the helpee tells you? These are just some of the questions the helpee may bring to this initial encounter, questions which need to be addressed.

Since each new helpee will have different concerns, it is hard to state exactly how to structure the encounter. But as a general rule it is useful to

1. introduce who you are, explain your role and your responsibilities, etc.;
2. identify what you are hoping to do in this encounter (e.g., get to know a little about the helpee and the helpee's concern); and,
3. explain the limits of confidentiality, that is, what you can and will keep secret, and what you will not be able to keep confidential. Limits of confidentiality will be discussed in Chapter 15.

In addition to setting the helpee at ease with this procedure, it is also important to begin to structure the nature of the helping process.

It is important for the helper and the helpee to come to agreement on the goals of the relationship and the tasks and the work to be done. This agreement, while not finalized at this point in the relationship, will begin to be formulated during this early structuring phase.

The agreement on goals implies that the helper and helpee share the goals of the work and hold a common view of how these goals may best be attained. This does not mean that the specific steps to problem solving are identified, rather, that both parties will engage in a give-and-take of honest information, with a willingness to risk and become somewhat vulnerable as they mutually share perspectives and resources.

An example of this initial process can be seen in the statements and actions demonstrated by Jessica, a counselor at a high school. Jessica was expecting to meet with a senior student who requested to see the counselor. Having never had the opportunity to meet this student, Jessica was somewhat anxious herself as to what this encounter might bring. The description of the exchange demonstrates some of the verbal and nonverbal techniques Jessica used to begin building a working alliance.

> (knock at the door)
> Jessica (getting up from her desk, opens the door): Hi, Allison?
> Allison (somewhat softly): Yes, I'm Allison.
> Jessica (extending her hand in a handshake): Very glad to meet you. Come on in. Here, this is a comfortable seat. I hope I am not taking up your lunch period?
> Allison: No, it's ok . . . this is study hall.
> Jessica: Study hall? Oh, all right. Well, I know you requested to see the counselor, and as the senior counselor, I was the person that the office directed you to see. If it is all right with you, maybe we could take this period to get to know each other a little bit, and maybe start to look at what it was you wanted to talk about, to see what we can come up with.
>
> Allison, you may already know this, but as a professional counselor in this school, I am ethically bound to keep what we talk about confidential. This means that I really can't tell anyone what we talk about unless you give me permission. The only real limitations to this are if what you are telling me suggests that you are in danger or are going to hurt yourself or someone else. Do you understand that?
> Allison (still softly): Yes, I knew that.
> Jessica: Fine. But I'm doing all the talking, and since we have 30 minutes in the period, I would love to spend that time getting to know a little about you and what it was you wanted to see a counselor about.

Setting the Stage—Establishing Facilitative Conditions

Once the foundation has been laid and the basic nature of the encounter described and structured, as is the case with Jessica and Allison, the helper can now provide the helpee with the sense that a meaningful, working relationship is possible in this particular situation. The helper can foster this expectation by exhibiting those interpersonal traits and characteristics which demonstrate that he or she is a warm, accepting, understanding individual who has both the desire and the competence to assist the helpee in the development or rediscovery of problem-solving skills.

Rogers and others (Berenson & Carkhuff, 1967; Carkhuff & Berenson, 1977; Parsons, 1985; Truax & Carkhuff, 1965) posited that a successful helper must exhibit qualities of *acceptance, warmth,* and *genuineness.* While research (Butler, Crago, & Arizmendi, 1986; Gurman, 1977) would suggest that these conditions are not sufficient for positive outcomes in every case, it does appear that they are key to the helping alliance and contribute in a facilitative way to the positive outcomes of helping (Ivey, Bradford-Ivey, & Simek-Morgan, 1993). As such, these conditions will be discussed in some detail as both a set of attitudes and a set of helper behaviors.

Acceptance.   Accepting another is not always an easy process. If helping is to be effective, the helper must demonstrate acceptance of the helpee. This means that the helper does NOT try to control the helpee, demand that the helpee behave or think in any certain way, or even attempt to impose roles on the helpee, but rather allows the helpee to be him- or herself.

To truly accept this other, this helpee, the helper must put aside any formal status or informal social roles which might interfere with a mutual, open relationship. It does not matter that the helper may have more degrees, more money, more friends, etc. All that matters is that this is an encounter between two less than perfect human beings who are interested in facilitating the solution of one's problem.

Again, this is not always easy to achieve. It requires that the helper interact with the helpee in a real "here and now" frame of reference and ignore roles such as male-female, young-old, black-white, rich-poor, or even helper-helpee.

Acceptance of another does not mean absolute, wholesale approval of everything he or she says or does. If I really care for you, then I will extend myself in hopes of educating, motivating, or encouraging you to grow. However, even when the helper has intentions of changing the helpee, true acceptance demands that the helper must allow the helpee the freedom to choose NOT to change.

Feeling accepting of another is only part of the process. For it to truly affect the helping relationship, the helper's acceptance must be demonstrated and conveyed to the helpee. This is an important point to consider. It may be easy for one to *say* "I accept you as you are," but that acceptance needs to demonstrated and not just spoken. Exercise 2-2 encourages you to discover ways of expressing and demonstrating acceptance.

Non-Possessive Warmth and Respect.   In addition to feeling accepted, the helpee needs to feel valued or prized by the helper. Often, coming for help is a blow to a person's sense of maturity, independence, and personal competence. The helpee may question his or her own personal value. It is therefore important that the helper demonstrate his or her respect for the helpee by appreciating and valuing him or her, simply as a fellow human being.

This characteristic of effective helpers has been termed unconditional, non-possessive regard (Rogers, 1957). This unconditional regard or warmth reflects the helper's deep nonevaluative respect for the thoughts, feelings, wishes, and potential of the helpee. It is the ability to look beyond the conditions of another—for example, appearance, manner of presentation, backgrounds, or even beliefs and actions—to value the fundamental person behind these conditions. The helper exhibiting non-possessive warmth and respect communicates the message that the helpee is a worth-while person, regardless of what he or she is experiencing.

EXERCISE 2-2
Demonstrating Acceptance

You can demonstrate acceptance of the helpee by

1. actively encouraging the helpee to express the ways in which he or she is different from you;
2. showing care and concern for the helpee and the helpee's problem; and
3. allowing the helpee the freedom to choose NOT to change or follow your helping lead.

Directions: For the first two situations, consider the effect of each helper's response. Identify which response appears to be demonstrating acceptance. For the last situation, write a non-accepting response and one which demonstrates acceptance. As with previous exercises, it is useful to discuss your response with your colleagues or classmates.

Situation 1: Helpee: I know I am taking up your time, but I have nobody . . . nobody cares.
Helper A: I care—I really do!
Helper B: Feeling like no one cares is painful, but I'm here now and I am willing to listen.

Situation 2: Helpee: This idea you have is stupid!
Helper A: As we discussed last time, I thought we both believed it was the best we could do. If you have other ideas, or are willing to keep banging away at it, it is okay with me.

Helper B: I don't understand, you agreed to do it. After all, it is the best solution. So what's your problem with it?

Situation 3: Helpee: I'm a mess! You gotta tell me what to do! Should I move out?
Helper A: (write a non-accepting way of responding)
Helper B: (write a response which demonstrates acceptance)

The belief in and communication of such non-possessive prizing is not easy, especially for those in the industrialized climate where status, power, and social prestige have been equated which human worth. Exercise 2-3 invites you to look at some of the conditions surrounding a human being which may bias your valuing or prizing that person.

EXERCISE 2-3
Distracting from Non-Possessive Regard

Directions: While non-possessive regard or unconditional prizing requires us to look beyond the trappings and conditions of another in order to value the person as him- or herself, these conditions or trappings are sometimes hard to ignore and bias (both positively and negatively) our valuing of another. For each of the conditions listed, identify the degree (i.e., not at all, somewhat, strongly) and the direction (positive or negative) to which they would bias your evaluation of the person. As you reflect on your immediate, honest reactions, ask yourself what can you do to look beyond these biasing conditions to be able to value and prize the person.

Description of Helpee	*Direction of Bias*	*Degree of Bias*
1. The president of a Fortune 500 company.	pos	Not at all
2. A high school dropout, currently 46 years old, and working as short order cook.	neg	somewhat
3. A very bright and attractive lawyer.	pos	somewhat
4. A displaced homemaker currently existing as a street person.	neg	not at all
5. A person with very poor personal hygiene habits.	neg	somewhat
6. A very famous person in the field of medicine.	pos	somewhat
7. A renowned researcher.	pos	somewhat
8. A 2-day-old infant.	pos	not at all

As you reflect upon your responses to Exercise 2-3, as well as those of your colleagues and classmates, you may notice something of interest. While many of us may be positively biased toward individuals who are attractive, articulate, educated, achieving, and successful, and conversely negatively biased against those lacking these conditions, most of us will respond warmly—non-possessively—to a 2-day-old infant. This perhaps is the model or prototype to approaching others that we need to highlight. Even though the newborn is often not attractive (using adult standards), articulate, educated, achieving, or successful, we clearly value and prize him or her simply because he or she is a fellow human being. It is this non-possessive warmth, or unconditional regard, that we want to feel and convey to the helpee.

This quality of non-possessive warmth, or unconditional valuing, is an ideal to which all helpers should aspire. At the same time, we need to be aware of the limitations of our own humanity. There may be times and situations in which we find ourselves having difficulty moving beyond conditional valuing of the helpee, unable to see the unconditional worth of the person underneath. Under these circumstances our warmth and respect can be exhibited by referring this helpee to another competent helper who will be unbiased by these conditions.

As an effective, caring helper, you need to monitor the degree to which you are communicating your respect and unconditional warmth for the helpee. This process of monitoring can take place by considering each of the following questions as you reflect on your approach with any one helpee.

1. Was I attending? Was I actively and accurately listening?
2. Did I actively encourage the helpee to contribute?
3. Did I demonstrate the belief that the helpee is competent and capable of caring for him- or herself?
4. Did I enter the relationship assuming goodwill?
5. Did I appear appropriately warm and close in the relationship?
6. Did I give evidence of spending time and energy to truly understand the helpee and his or her problem?
7. Was I judgmental or evaluative in my language?
8. Did the helpee show signs of feeling appreciated? Cared for?

Genuineness.   All of the previous elements to building a working alliance are worthless if they are all done artificially. Being real, being genuine, is essential to effective helping. Yet being genuine is not always easy to achieve.

In my own anxiety as a new helper, I sometimes felt like I had to put on a "game face" every time I met a new helpee. In my eagerness to "do it correctly," I would sometimes try too hard and become somewhat artificial in my care and concern. Often our desire to "do it correctly" or "to be liked by another" forces us to play out a role. We may feel like we are bound to perform or enact certain types of behaviors such as those associated with the roles of a male or female, a parent, or even a helper. When we act a role, we may not be truly genuine. To be genuine, requires us to be role-free. In order to become more aware of threats to your own genuineness, consider Exercise 2-4.

While we may understand how roles can interfere with our being genuine and authentic, it may be more useful to begin to understand what it is to be genuine and how best to maintain our genuineness, especially within the helping encounter.

EXERCISE 2-4
Role-Bound or Role-Free?

Directions: In order to become more genuine in our helping encounters, we must become sensitive to the conditions and the experiences which inhibit our genuineness and encourage our role-playing behaviors. Consider each of the following and discuss with your colleagues and/or classmates the implications your responses may hold for you as a helper.

1. Have you ever responded to someone's question, "How you doing?" by saying "Fine!" even when you were not? Can you think of other examples where an "expected" response may interfere with your genuineness?
2. Can you think of roles that sometimes require those in that role to be non-genuine? What normal and appropriate feelings, thoughts, or actions might be inhibited or prohibited by each of the following roles?
   - Teacher
   - Adult
   - Child
   - Male/Female
   - Helper
   - Student
3. Think of the roles you enact and discuss how they could interfere with your genuineness as a helper.

A helper who is genuine is one who is *open* as opposed to defensive, *real* as opposed to phony. A helper who is genuine is *congruent*. His or her words, actions, tone, thoughts and feelings are all expressing the same message. The genuine person is able to express and admit discomfort, or even disappointment, when he or she is experienced rather than pretend that everything is fine.

Clearly it will be hard to exhibit these characteristics if we are rigidly following a script which we feel accompanies the role we need to play. Being genuine, as implied by Gibb (1961), is being who we are at any one moment. It means being authentic, being real. This doesn't mean that the "genuine" helper has a carte blanche to say or do whatever he or she wishes just because it is truly what he or she is feeling. Being genuine points more to the fact that the helper is open to his or her own experience. The form and depth that the sharing of that awareness may take will be shaped by a sense of care for the helpee. It is important to remember that honest, open disclosure is appropriate only as it facilitates the helping process.

There may be times when you are experiencing some negative feelings in responding to the helpee. As an effective helper, you will need to consider whether or not you should share these feelings. If the feelings can be expressed without being judgmental and with a proper sensitivity to how they will be received by the helpee, then expressing them may prove helpful. This was actually the experience of a residence assistant at a local university.

> Kim was a residence assistant at a local university. Lori sought Kim out because of the difficulty she was having "making friends." All through out the initial meeting, Lori demonstrated a tendency to interrupt Kim every time Kim began to speak. Kim felt very frustrated and annoyed by this. However, she began to hypothesize that perhaps this tendency to interrupt and to try to dominate the conversation might be one of the things contributing to Lori's difficulty making friends. Kim decided to convey her thoughts and feelings on this matter in hopes of helping Lori become more aware of a potentially negative habit.
>
> Kim: You know, Lori, we've been talking for about 30 minutes now . . .
> Lori (interrupting): I know I'm taking up too much of your time. It is always that way . . . I'm turning everybody off.
> Kim: Lori, you may think you are turning me off, but something you are doing is actually tuning me in!
> Lori: What . . . tuning you in? What are you saying? I don't understand.
> Kim: Well, you seem very eager to get me to understand your situation . . .
> Lori (again, interrupting): I am. You don't know how bad it is.
> Kim: As I was saying . . . I know you are eager to get me to understand how it is, but I also noticed that in your enthusiasm and eagerness, you tend to interrupt me as I am speaking.
> Lori: Oh, I'm sorry.
> Kim: I'm not saying this so that you can apologize. Rather, I was wondering if you tend to get enthusiastic and eager when meeting new people.
> Lori: Sure . . . I'm very energetic.
> Kim: Well, is it possible that in being energetic and excited you may interrupt them when they are speaking or maybe dominate the initial conversation?
> Lori: Gosh, I don't know.

Because of her ability to be genuine and sensitive, Kim was able to point out Lori's interrupting in such as way that Lori and Kim were able to investigate the possibility that it was something she may want to learn to reduce. The manner with which Kim was able to confront Kim productively is a skill that will be discussed in detail in Chapter 6. But the point to be highlighted was that being genuine in sharing even negative information is sometimes both necessary and productive if done with skill and sensitivity.

Each situation or encounter we find ourselves in challenges our ability to remain genuine. Exercise 2-5 is presented to help you increase your awareness of what it is like when you are communicating genuinely.

EXERCISE 2-5
Identifying Genuine Communication

Direction: This is a two-stage exercise which will require you to tape record a brief (10-15 minute) conversation. If possible, find a partner willing to do this exercise with you and with whom you are fairly unfamiliar.

Part 1: Tape record a conversation between yourself and your partner. The conversation should last a minimum of 10 minutes with the goal being simply to become better acquainted with one another. Introduce yourself to each other in any way you feel is appropriate, but strive to make the communication a genuine expression of your thoughts and feelings. Try to be congruent in your actions and your statements.

Part 2: Below you will find five characteristics of genuine communication. Review the recording of your conversation. As you listen, ask yourself the following questions, noting places where you were clearly being genuine, as well as places where you were perhaps a little less than genuine. Increasing your awareness of these shifts is the first step in increasing your ability to become more genuine.

1. Role Freeness:
   - Did I "hide" behind titles, labels, degrees?
   - Did I fall into a gender, age, race, or class role?

2. Spontaneity:
   - While being sensitive to the strength of the other person, was I responsive to the moment rather than acting out of a preplanned and rigid script.
   - Although there are instances when it is appropriate not to express feelings or thoughts, did I make these decisions in light of an active awareness of these thoughts and feelings and with an eye for what is best for the other person?

3. Non-Defensiveness:
   - If questioned or criticized, was I able to listen and even demonstrate a willingness to understand the other's point of view?
   - Did I demonstrate defensive communications and even counterattack when challenged?

4. Congruency:
   - Did my words, tones, and bodily actions seem to be expressing the same thing?
   - Did I appear consistent in expressing my thoughts, feelings, and behaviors?
   - Were there any discrepancies between what I was thinking, feeling, and doing?

5. Openness:
   - Did I demonstrate a capability of self-disclosure and mutual sharing appropriate to the relationship?

WHAT NEXT

Whether one argues that the helping relationship IS the essential ingredient to effective helping or is only one of many components may be irrelevant. The fact remains that helping occurs within a social context, within a relationship, and it is clear that this relationship is strengthened and made more positive by the existence of a helper's genuineness, warmth, and acceptance of the helpee.

As you will see, such a helper is able to establish a safe climate that allows the helpee to risk sharing him- or herself and the issues that are causing the difficulty. If the helpee feels deeply and genuinely understood, accepted, and cared about, his or her willingness to explore and express concerns will be enhanced.

These interpersonal conditions of genuineness, acceptance, and warmth can be enhanced through practice. As a serious, caring, and effective helper, you need to

- commit to practice your skills and continue to monitor them and develop them;
- consider using tape recordings of your helping interactions (with the helpees' permission) and evaluate your style of communication in terms of the degree to which you manifested the facilitative conditions;
- seek ongoing supervision and feedback from trained helpers as invaluable ways to increase your use of these facilitative conditions.

REFERENCES AND RECOMMENDED READINGS

Berenson, B.G., & Carkhuff, R.R. (1967). *Source of gain in counseling and psychotherapy.* New York: Holt, Rinehart and Winston.

Butler, L.E., Crago, M., & Arizmendi, T.G. (1986). Research on therapists' variables in psychotherapy. In S. Garfield & A. Bergin (Eds.), *Handbook of psychotherapy and behavior change* (3rd edition). New York: Wiley.

Carkhuff, R. R., & Berenson, B.G. (1977). *Beyond counseling and therapy.* New York: Holt, Rinehart and Winston.

Frank, J.D., Hoehn-Saric, R., Imber, S.D., Liberman, B.L., & Stone, A. R. (1978). *Effective ingredients of successful psychotherapy.* New York: Brunner/Mazel.

Gelso, C. J., & Carter, J.A. (1985). The relationship in counseling and psychotherapy: Components, consequences and theoretical antecedents. *Counseling Psychologists, 13,* 155–243.

Gibb, J. (1961). Categories of defensive and supportive climates. *Journal of Communication, 11,* 141–148.

Gurman, A.S. (1977). The patient's perception of the therapeutic relationship. In A. Gurman & A. Razin (Eds.), *Effective psychotherapy: A handbook of research.* New York: Pergamon.

Highlen, P.S., & Hill, C.E. (1984). Factors affecting client change in individual counseling: Current status and theoretical speculations. In S. D. Brown & R. W. Lent (Eds.), *The clinical handbook of counseling psychology.* New York: Wiley.

Ivey, A.E., Bradford-Ivey, M. & Simek-Morgan, L. (1993). *Counseling and psychotherapy: A multicultural perspective* (3rd edition). Needham Heights, MA: Allyn and Bacon.

Kirsch, I. (1990). *Changing expectations.* Pacific Grove, CA: Brooks/Cole.

Kokotovic, A.M., & Tracey, T.J. (1990). Working alliance in the early phase of counseling. *Journal of Counseling Psychology, 37,* 16–21.

Orlando, D.E., & Howard, K.I. (1986). Process and outcome in psychotherapy. In S.L. Garfield & A.E. Bergan (Eds.), *Handbook of psychotherapy and behavioral change.* New York: John Wiley & Sons.

Parsons, R.D., & Wicks, R. (1994). *Counseling strategies and intervention techniques for the human services.* Needham Heights, MA: Allyn and Bacon.

Parsons, R. (1985). The counseling relationship. In R. Wicks, R. Parsons, & D. Capps (Eds.), *Clinical handbook of pastoral counseling.* Mahwah, NJ: Paulist.

Rogers, C.R. (1951). *Client-centered therapy.* Boston: Houghton Mifflin.

Rogers, C.R. (1957). The necessary and sufficient conditions of therapeutic personality change. *Journal of Consulting Psychology, 21,* 95–103.

Truax, C.B., & Carkhuff, R.R. (1965). The experimental manipulation of therapeutic conditions. *Journal of Consulting Psychology, 29,* 119–224.

▶ 3

From Here to There: Moving through the Helping Process

As noted throughout the initial discussion, helping is *relational*. Helping is also a *process*. It is a dynamic interaction which proceeds from the point of an informal, initial "hello," through the identification and specification of an experienced concern or problem and the subsequent statement of goals and outcomes desired, to the formulation and implementation of an action plan aimed at moving the helpee toward that goal. This movement, this dynamic process, can be seen in the case of Howard F.

Howard F. is a 20-year-old male who has sought out the professional assistance of the college counseling center because, as he states it, "I need to lay out a plan for my future." When Howard entered the counselor's office, he looked quite nervous, yet he attempted to put on a broad friendly smile as if to convey a nonchalant attitude. Below you will find some snippets of Howard's sessions. See if you can identify the change in focus across the sessions.

Session 1
Well, thanks for seeing me. I am not sure where to start. Everything is going great. I am going to be a senior in political science, with a 3.2 average. I just thought it would be a good idea just to come and get acquainted, nothing urgent. So if you don't have time today, no big deal, I can see you another time. You know this is not a crisis or anything like that.

Session 2
You know last week I was a little annoyed at you when you suggested that maybe discussing my career in political science was not exactly what was on

my mind. I thought, how dare you! But the more I thought about it, the more I started realizing you may be right. You know I really don't know why I chose this as a major. I have no idea what I am going to do with this degree. I am stuck. I feel like I wasted all this money and time . . . and for what? This is a mess.

Session 4

I had a great talk with Dr. Ramsey (the Political Science Department chair). You were right. I am not stuck with a degree in Political Science. He and I talked quite a bit about all the things I have learned. I have a lot of skills that I can market. In fact he showed me some of the places that graduates are working and the diversity is amazing. I just need to start focusing on what I enjoy and begin getting information on the type of jobs I might want to follow up on!

Session 6

Well, I have pretty much contacted all the personnel directors that we agreed upon—in fact I am starting to get some of the information I requested back from some of them. That vocational interest test you gave me really helped. Even though I have a good idea about what the plan of action is now and what I am to do next, would it be okay if I stop in, maybe at the end of the semester, just to let you know how it is progressing?

As suggested in the previous chapter, while there are many ways to conceptualize the "relational process" of helping, the model employed here (Parsons, 1985) discusses helping as progressing through the following three separate stages, each with a number of specific focal points.

1. Stage I: Coming together—building a helping alliance
2. Stage II: Exploring together—reconnaissance
3. Stage III: Acting together—intervention

This chapter will help you to understand the skills and orientation needed to facilitate the helpee's movement through this process. Specifically, the chapter will

1. review the unique nature and specific demands of each of these stages of the helping process;
2. highlight the specific outcomes and goals desired at each stage;
3. explicate the helper skills and attitudes required for successful achievement of each these goals.

The opportunity for the development of the specific skills required for effective movement at each stage of the helping process will be provided in later chapters.

STAGE I: COMING TOGETHER—BUILDING A HELPING ALLIANCE

As discussed in the previous chapter, one aspect of the initial stage of helping is preparing the helpee for this special relationship. During this stage, the helper attempts to reduce the helpee's initial anxiety by providing the facilitative conditions essential for helping. In addition to creating a warm and workable relationship and an atmosphere of understanding and acceptance, the first stage of helping is the time when the helper assists the consultee to begin to share his or her story. Through the processes of ventilation, encouragement, and the effective use of silence, the helper will not only assist the helpee to tell his or her story, but will begin to develop initial hypotheses about what is happening and what needs to be done.

The Value of Ventilation

Experiencing the benefits of a helping relationship begins with just encouragement by the helper for the helpee to begin to talk about his or her concerns (i.e., ventilate). In most situations, things have been building up in the helpee prior to coming to the helper—this concern, this problem, is something which has most likely been carried around for some time. The permission or the invitation to simply talk and to get it out is often quite relieving.

Let's look a little more closely at the first session with Howard F.

As Howard F. entered the office, the counselor, Dr. S., got up to meet him at the door.

Dr S.: Hello, Howard, very nice to meet you. Come on in and make yourself comfortable. I enjoyed our brief conversation on the phone yesterday. And I remember that you wanted to discuss your career plans. Perhaps you could tell me a little bit about yourself and your experience here at the University.

As Howard begins to tell his story, Dr. S. not only pays attention but employs some head nodding and brief statements like "hmm, hmm" and "okay" to subtly encourage Howard to share his story.

Because of the need and the value of encouraging the helpee to disclose, it is essential for the helper—especially during this first stage of helping—to talk less and encourage more! The helper needs to assist the helpee to express as much of his or her story, and the feelings tied to that story, as time will permit.

Encouraging

When the helper feels a need to interject or ask a question, he or she should limit these interruptions to those that facilitate the telling of the helpee's story. In fact, the use of what is called *minimal encouragers* (Ivey, 1971) such as "uh-huh," "yes," or "hmmm-hmmm" may be preferred to questions.

For example, as Howard discussed his decision to become a political science major, Dr. S responded in an encouraging way.

> Howard: So I always wanted to get into politics so I thought political science just made sense.
> Dr. S. Uh-huh.
> Howard: Well, it seemed to be the right move. I guess it was. But sometimes, especially lately, I have been wondering . . . well . . .
> Dr. S. Wondering, yes?

Questions can be asked not only to pursue a particular topic but also to encourage the helpee to continue sharing his or her story. One type of question (the *open question*) encourages the helpee to expand and elaborate upon his or her story.

Open questions—those requiring more than a simple yes or no, or one-word answers—invite the helpee to expand and elaborate. "Could you tell me more about that?" is an example of an open question which may facilitate the helpee's explanation. Yes or no or multiple choice questions may simply turn the interaction into a game. The effective use of questions is a very important topic and it will be addressed in detail in Chapter 5.

Silence as Helpful

The helper who wishes to encourage the helpee's disclosure needs to allow the helpee to take plenty of time in revealing his or her story. This means that the helper needs to become more comfortable with *silence*.

There may be times when the helpee just needs to stop and reflect. There may be issues that the helpee is not sure of or doesn't know how to express. It is during periods of silence that much of the decision to risk sharing one's story takes place.

The helper needs to feel comfortable with those moments of silence, and allow the helpee to fill the gaps as he or she needs. Embracing silence as a productive part of the helping encounter is not always easy, especially for the helper who is chomping at the bit to "do something!" Exercise 3-1 will help develop this ability to deal effectively with silence.

With practice, the experience of silence becomes both more comfortable and more productive for the effective helper.

Helper Considerations

As is true of the initial experience of the helpee, the first few moments of the helping encounter are, or can be, anxiety-provoking for the helper. The helper may have many questions about the upcoming encounter:

EXERCISE 3-1
Embracing Silence

Directions: This exercise will require that you work with a partner who will be identified as the helpee in the following role play. The exercise is a three-part exercise and should be tape recorded.

Part 1: Select one of the following themes for the role play and begin an initial interview. Allow the discussion to go on for approximately 5 minutes.
Possible roles/themes:

- a university student who just broke up with his or her steady
- an individual with a career crisis —would like to leave his or her current job but is anxious about giving up the security of having a job
- an individual who feels extremely guilty about cheating on his or her spouse

Part 2: For the next 5 minutes of the interview, the helpee should attempt to provide the information in short, concise sentences. After each sentence (or as often as possible) the helpee should remain silent for periods of time, ranging from 10 seconds to 30 seconds (the helpee controls the length of the silence). As a helper, your task is to allow the silence to go uninterrupted.

Part 3: For the next 5 minutes, the helpee should periodically (not following every sentence) maintain silence (again up to 30 seconds). During these periods of silence, the helper should attempt to concentrate on the nonverbal cues sent by the helpee. For example, observe any shift in body posture, expressions, or gestures that are occurring during the silence. Attempt to hypothesize what these nonverbal cues may be suggesting about the helpee's experience.

After completing the exercise discuss the experience with your partner or classmates. Consider the following questions:

- What was your experience during the periods of silence? What were you thinking, feeling, doing?
- Did the experience of silence become easier with practice?
- Did the experience of silence become easier when your attention focused on the nonverbal messages being sent?
- Did embracing the silence provide you the opportunity to gather information you might have otherwise failed to notice?

- What will I experience?
- What will the helpee be like?
- What might be the nature of their concern?
- Will I really be able to help?

In a lot of ways these are the same type of initial questions which may concern the helpee. The primary difference between the early questions of the helper, as contrasted to those of the helpee, is one of *awareness*.

EXERCISE 3-2
Being an Aware Helper

Directions, Part I: Below you will find a list of Howard's behaviors or responses. Next to each of these descriptors you will find a few examples of Dr. S.'s hypotheses or initial inferences. After reviewing the sample, attempt to develop your own hypotheses about the meaning of the data presented. Later in the chapter, more information will be provided—use this new data to check your original hypotheses.

Howard's Response	*Inference*
Enters with forced smile, sweating palms.	Howard is nervous, as might be expected, but is attempting to mask this anxiety and appear in control.
Well, I'm thrilled to be in my last year—Political Science, you know.	The tone of Howard's voice seems to suggest that he isn't thrilled. He almost sounds frightened.
Yeah, I have a 3.2 gpa, in the honors frat. This should be a great year (forces another smile).	(your inference?)
I really screwed up wasted all this time and money . . . (looks upset, and casts his eyes downward).	(your inference?)

Directions, Part II: Even though the data is inconclusive and there is much more information which must be considered, in one or two sentences describe what you feel is going on with Howard. What is the real issue or concern that is bringing him to counseling?

_____
_____
_____

An effective helper is tuned into his or her own experience, aware of the kinds of questions he or she is asking and the kinds of information and data he or she is receiving. The effective helper will attempt to use his or her questions, concerns, and reactions as part of the data to be understood in this encounter.

With this awareness, the helper begins to generate *initial inferences and hypotheses* about the nature of the helpee's concerns, the potential direction to take, and the role or contribution the helpee brings to both the problem presented and its potential solution.

To some degree, the helping process is a bit like a detective story in which the helpee provides clues to an experience which is not totally clear to him or her or the helper, and which, as it becomes more clearly understood, reveals directions and paths for moving forward. Exercise 3-2 is a two-part exercise, using the case of Howard F. to exemplify this process.

As the interaction proceeds, either in this session or in later sessions, the helper attempts to validate his or her original hypotheses. When the new information conflicts with the original hypotheses, the helper begins to develop new inferences and hypotheses about what it all means and what needs to happen. Exercise 3-3 asks that you incorporate new information into your original hypotheses about Howard. The new information may continue to support your original hypotheses or you may need to make adjustments to your original viewpoint.

Throughout the initial stage of helping, the helper needs to check his or her own accuracy and completeness of understanding of the helpee's story. Questions which can guide the helper during this stage of the interaction are:

- Am I letting the helper tell his or her story? Am I comfortable with silence and his or her pace, or am I rushing it?
- Do I understand what is being presented?

EXERCISE 3-3
Incorporating Additional Data

Directions: Consider each of the following bits of information provided by Howard. After reading each bit of information, discuss how this new information fits into to your original hypotheses. Does it support or fail to support your original hypotheses in Exercise 3-2?

1. Howard: You know, originally I wanted to be a lawyer, like my Dad, but I'm not sure. It just seems less than exciting to me.
2. Howard: I wish I didn't lock into a major so soon. Now what do I do? What can a political science major do if it's not politics or law?
3. Howard: My parents put all this money into my education—you can guess how they are going to feel.

- Do all the parts of the picture as presented seem to fit and make sense?
- What inferences can I make about the helpee and the helpee's experience which are not specifically presented as part of the picture?
- What evidence will I look for to support my inferences?
- Is the pace of the helping process comfortable for the helpee? Am I pushing too fast or not fast enough?

STAGE II: EXPLORING TOGETHER— RECONNAISSANCE

Once the initial anxieties of coming for help have been reduced and the helper has given evidence of his or her genuine acceptance and valuing of the helpee, the process of problem and resource identification needs to begin.

In this second stage of helping, the helper will continue to assist the helpee to ventilate and to share his or her story. However, now the helper should begin to shape or funnel the helpee's disclosures in order to focus specifically on the nature of the problem at hand, as well as identify the various resources available to the helpee for problem solving. This type of funneling or shaping is evident in the brief exchange below, between Tina and her high school counselor.

> Tina: I don't know what I'm going to do. Everything is a mess. Something is wrong.
>
> Counselor: You really sound upset. Could you tell me what you mean when you say everything is a mess?
>
> Tina: Everything is just going wrong. My relationship with my boyfriend is falling apart, my friends think he is a creep and should be dumped . . . I don't know . . . it is just everything.
>
> Counselor: It seems to me that you feel like everything in your life is falling apart, but I get the sense that the real concern is your relationship with your boyfriend?
>
> Tina: Yeah . . . that's what I mean . . . I really care for him, but . . .

As is evident by this brief exchange, quite often the helpee comes with very vague, generalized expressions about what is concerning him or her, so that the primary task for the helper during this second stage of the helping process is to *understand and clarify,* for both him- or herself and the helpee, the actual nature of the issue to be resolved. This task of understanding is far from an easy one.

Understanding

In most of our day-to-day conversations with others—be they around a work or school issue, or simply at a social event—the rule is typically to be polite and listen. But the reality is that quite often we listen only with half an ear.

During our normal conversations, we may find ourselves drifting off into a day-dream (Boy, is she cute!), or focusing on a concern of our own (Gads, I forgot to call home!), or even jumping to conclusions about what is being said (. . . oh, I know where this is leading!).

This tendency to jump to conclusions or become inattentive is one tendency that helpers need to combat. In order to be helpful, a helper must understand what is being presented and demonstrate that understanding to the helpee. This accurate under-standing can be achieved and communicated by the effective use of the skills of *reflection* and *clarification* (see Chapter 4).

As illustrated in our brief example, the counselor not only listened to the words spoken, but also to the tone and manner in which they were spoken. By reflecting her understanding of what Tina was trying to convey, the counselor clarified, for both Tina and herself, the actual nature of the concern.

Mutual understanding and clarification are the goals at this stage in the helping relationship. The helper needs to resist the tendency to rush to a diagnosis and interven-tion plan. Understanding and *not* solving is the goal at this point in the helping process.

In helping we must allow the process to unfold. It is important that we suspend judgment and limit our tendency to come to rapid diagnostic impressions. Developing hypotheses is appropriate; however, it is premature to draw fixed conclusions and provide solid answers.

Helper Considerations

During this stage of helping, the helper's interactions needed to be guided by ques-tions such as:

1. Why is the helpee here?
2. What is the helpee's experience or world like? What is the helpee thinking and feeling?
3. When I reflect my understanding of what the helpee is saying or feeling, am I accurate?
4. Where are the gaps in my understanding of the helpee's situation? Is there infor-mation missing? Is there information which I am having trouble fitting into the picture?
5. Are we—both myself and the helpee—increasing our mutual understanding and clarity of the situation experienced?
6. Are we—both myself and the helpee—increasing our mutual understanding of the desired goal and outcomes the helpee seeks?

STAGE III: ACTING TOGETHER—INTERVENTION

Once the helpee's concerns and goals have been clearly understood and the relation-ship has developed to a supportive, caring exchange, the process of helping can move to the acting stage. It is in this stage that the helper's attention can now turn to

1. the identification of a number of alternatives or solutions to the concerns presented through a process of *planning and strategizing;*
2. the facilitation of the helpee's selection, implementation, and evaluation of one of the strategies for problem solving in a process termed *calling to action;* and finally,
3. assisting the helpee in moving toward increased independence and self-reliance in a process termed *review and termination.*

A number of approaches and skills are employed during this stage of the helping process. Each of these will be presented in depth in Chapters 8 and 9. However, for this brief overview it is sufficient to point out that the strategies or approaches developed need to be feasible given the helpee's style and resources. It is this demand for feasibility that requires that all such strategies develop as a result of a mutual effort, of both the helper and the helpee, Acting Together.

Helper Considerations

As with the previous stages, there are a number of considerations or internal questions which should be used to guide the helper's own interactions during the action stage, such as:

1. Is the helpee actively involved in this process, or merely being directed by me?
2. In addition to strategizing about this problem, am I assisting the helpee in developing his or her own problem-solving skills or merely giving him or her my answer?
3. Is the strategy realistic given the helpee's resources?
4. Is the strategy well planned, well understood, and presented in "do-able" steps?
5. Do I and the helpee approach this plan as a mini-experiment with a let's-see-how-it-goes attitude, or are we making this a do-or-die scenario (an attitude which would be counterproductive)?
6. Am I supportive of the helpee's efforts as well as his or her achievements?
7. Do we have a plan for follow-up and support if such is needed in the future? Does the helpee know and believe I am available?
8. Do we need to consider referral to another support person or service?

WHAT NEXT

The intent of the current chapter was to provide the reader with an introduction to the type of stages or elements which characterize the process of helping. And although the chapter described the helping process in distinct, discrete steps and stages, in reality there is no hard and fast, cookbook approach which can be used in each and every helping encounter.

The theories, the models, the skills, and the techniques need to be understood, practiced, and eventually assimilated into the helper's own style. But regardless of the model or the skills to be learned, it is essential to remember that helping is and needs to remain a fluid, dynamic process—one full of the richness of a genuine, valuing encounter.

Before moving on to the next chapters and a more in-depth, micro analysis of the specific skills and attitudes characteristic of the effective helper, review the following case illustration (Exercise 3-4). This case will assist you in identifying the various stages of the helping process as well as highlighting the richness of a genuine, valuing encounter.

EXERCISE 3-4
The Stages of Helping

Directions: Below you will find an abbreviated view of the helping process in the case of Albert. With a colleague/classmate, review the case noting

- which stage(s) is operative;
- which principle(s) discussed within the chapter is (are) being effectively employed; and,
- where might the helper have improved on her approach.

Further, as you read the presentation, attempt to place yourself in the shoes of the helpee (Albert) sensitizing yourself to the real pain and concern that he may be experiencing.

The Presenting Complaint:

Albert is an 18-year-old first-semester freshman who is having ". . . a lot of problems with his college roommate!" In talking to another person, Albert was told simply to change roommates, or simply "tolerate it—the semester is almost over." Somehow this "help" didn't feel so helpful to Albert, so he decided to come to talk to Linda, his dorm's residence assistant.

The Helping Encounter:

Linda greeted Albert at her door. As they started to talk, Linda was struck by the fact that Albert kept stating that he had ". . . a lot of problems . . .". Her response to him was that it "appears that you are really upset with the situation." She also stated, ". . . even though we may not have an immediate solution, together we may come up with some things to try." These comments and observations seemed to help Albert relax.

Linda told Albert, "We have about 30 minutes before (my) next class, so maybe we could use this time to help me understand a little bit about what is

---

Continued

happening with you and your roommate." She pointed out that they may or may not be able to resolve the problem at this time, but that they could at least begin working on it. Finally, she told Albert that she would keep this discussion confidential as long as the information discussed didn't indicate that Albert or another was doing something which might prove harmful to himself or another.

Albert began to express his frustration and annoyance at the roommate, but his comments also seemed to suggest that he had feelings of isolation and aloneness (". . . he's always going out or having HIS friends into our room, it's like he could give a damn about me . . ."). As Albert talked, Linda faced him, sitting somewhat forward and her chair, keeping eye contact. As he would share his story, Linda would nod her head periodically and utter "hmm, hmm." Often Linda would reflect what Albert said, or the manner in which he said it. For example, she commented, "You sound disappointed that he goes out without you," and on a few occasions she asked questions such as "How do you feel when he hangs with HIS friends?"

It became quite clear that Albert began to relax and show some relief, even though a solution was yet to be found. As they continued talking, they recognized that they needed to determine which of two possible issues was really bothering Albert. Was it that Albert wanted to be included socially and was upset because his roommate did not include him (nor perhaps did anyone else?), or was it that he really would prefer another roommate whose style is more like his own? As they discussed these two possible concerns, it became increasing clear that Albert's real desire and goal was to be included socially.

Linda suggested that perhaps she and Albert could "brainstorm" possible ways toward achieving this goal. As they generated ideas, several seemed particularly practical. For example, it was decided that he could ask his roommate to be included, he could begin developing his own social group, or he could try both.

Since Albert was new to college life and did not completely understand his options, Linda suggested that Albert go visit the counseling office and gather information on the various clubs, fraternities, social groups sponsored by the college; the opportunities for meeting others and interacting (such as upcoming events, dances, etc.), and the possibility of gaining more ongoing support and counseling from the center, to learn how to be more assertive.

Because they were not completely sure how successful these techniques would be, Linda and Albert decided to meet after a week to see how their plan was going, and, if needed, to make some fine-tuning adjustments. At this follow-up meeting Linda also reviewed what they did together, what was learned, and what has changed. She helped Albert consider his options, strategies, and plans for the future (he decided to work with a counselor at the counseling center) while letting him know that she would be available if he wanted to talk.

REFERENCES AND RECOMMENDED READINGS

Avila, D., & Combs, A. (1985). *Perspectives on the helping relationship and the helping professions.* Needham Heights, MA: Allyn and Bacon.

Cormier, L.S., & Hackney, H.L. (1987). *The professional counselor: A process guide to helping.* Englewood Cliffs, NJ: Prentice-Hall.

Egan, G. (1990). *The skilled helper* (4th edition). Belmont, CA: Brooks/Cole.

Ivey, A. (1971). *Microcounseling: Innovation in interviewing training.* Springfield, IL: Charles C. Thomas.

Kanfer, F., & Goldstein, A. (1986). *Helping people change* (3rd edition). New York: Pergamon Press.

Parsons, R. D. (1985). The counseling relationship. Appearing in Wicks, R., Parsons, R. & Capps D., *Clinical handbook of pastoral counseling* (pp. 97–117). Mahwah, NJ: Paulist Press.

Parsons, R. D., & Wicks, R. (1994). *Counseling strategies and intervention techniques for the human services* (4th edition). Needham Heights, MA: Allyn and Bacon.

Prochaska, J.O. (1979). *Systems of psychotherapy: A transtheoretical analysis.* Homewood, IL: Dorsey Press.

▶ 4

Connecting: The Skills of Listening and Understanding

Before we begin this chapter, let me suggest that you do the following brief exercise. Take a moment and make yourself aware of all the visual, auditory, tactile, and olfactory stimuli currently impacting upon you. If you really are attempting to pay attention, you may notice things that are right in front of you that you had not previously noted. You may hear subtle sounds or experience fragrances of which you had been previously unaware.

At any one moment, our senses are impacted by an enormous amount of stimulation, which, when added to all the internal information sent from our muscles and organs, offers our brains a herculean task to decipher. It can become a real overload! Because of this, we have developed techniques—some automatic and some deliberate—aimed at blocking out or ignoring certain stimuli so that we will have the energy to focus on other stimulation. This can be a very useful process when we are in a situation where everyone is talking, and we find that we can block out the other sounds in order to listen to what our friend is saying. But there are times when our techniques and strategies for blocking out signals may in fact work against us, as in the case when we are really not fully attending to concentrating on what another person is saying.

This chapter will discuss a number of these processes which can act as obstacles to our listening to and understanding another person. Specifically, this chapter will

1. discuss the processes of habituation, sensory gating, competing, filtering, and debating as obstacles to accurate understanding;
2. provide suggestions for increasing and maintaining one's attention; and
3. outline various techniques and skills employed to increase one's accurate, empathic understanding of another.

OBSTACLES TO LISTENING

Neurological Obstacles

In addition to those times when we consciously and willingly wish to block out signals or not attend to certain stimuli, there are times or conditions under which we may automatically employ processes which prevent us from attending to a particular signal.

For example, most of us have had the experience of walking into a sandwich shop and being immediately aware of a very strong smell of onions. However, if we stay in the shop very long, we may stop noticing the smell. In fact, after we walk out, others may smell the onions on our clothing even when we don't. The process by which our senses no longer respond to a constant stimulation is called *habituation*. It is a natural process by which we reduce the amount of stimulation fighting for our attention.

There is another process, quite similar to habituation, which takes place in our brains, and is aimed at helping us ignore some stimulation. That is the process of *sensory gating*. If something is stimulating us in a very repetitive, unchanging manner—for example, a very dull, monotonous speaker—we may find ourselves ceasing to pay attention. It is as if our brains say, "Oh, I know what that noise is . . . it isn't changing, so just ignore it," and we do! This process, sensory gating, is controlled at the neurological level, and therefore we may not be conscious that it is occurring. As another example, if you have ever walked into a room with an air conditioner humming, you may have at first noticed the noise, but quickly, and probably imperceptibly, you may sensory gate the sound, and therefore no longer be aware of its presence—until, of course, it comes to halt. Then the silence shocks your brain back into a "what-was-that" state of attention.

These two processes, habituation and sensory gating, can be very useful in restricting stimulus overload. However, these same two processes, as well as a few others to be discussed, can be less than helpful if they block our attending to the important messages communicated to us by another person.

Psychological Obstacles

In addition to the sensory process of habituation and the neurological process of sensory gating, our listening and attending to information may be blocked by a number of psychological processes. Three specifically, *competing, filtering,* and *debating,* are discussed below.

Competing with the Speaker

If you encounter a very attractive person, you may start the interaction by saying, "Hi, how are you?" As the person begins to respond verbally, you may find that in addition to listening to what the person is attempting to say, you may begin to talk to yourself internally. As the speaker is talking you may find yourself thinking, "Boy, is he or she great looking! I hope I don't look weird or come off like a nerd. What can I say to impress him or her?" In fact, you may become so absorbed in your self-conversation that you forget to listen to the other person. Under these conditions, you may be somewhat embarrassed to realize that the speaker has stopped talking and you have no idea what was said. This is one example of how we, as listeners, often compete with the speaker.

Another form of competing with the speaker occurs when we attempt to gain "speak time." Perhaps you can remember a time when you found the presentation by another—a speaker or a teacher—to be boring or irrelevant. Or perhaps you found that one of your own personal issues became more important or more pressing then what was being said by the speaker (e.g., "Gads, did I remember to turn off the stove?"). In these situations, as with the first, we may find that we tune out the speaker in order to tune in our own self-talk. When one is competing with the speaker for talk time, listening to the other and understanding exactly what he or she is attempting to convey are impaired. Clearly it is difficult to fully attend and understand two speakers—myself and the other—simultaneously!

Hearing with Filters

Another psychological block to our effective listening is our tendency to process what is being said through our own psychological filters. Often these are filters of feeling and emotions. This can occur when someone raises a point that has particular emotional value to us. Under these conditions it may be hard not to hear the speaker as we want to hear a message, as opposed to hearing the message as they wish to convey it.

For example, assume that you had a really horrible experience with a particular teacher, and a friend of yours begins to talk about his current experience with that same teacher. As soon as you hear the teacher's name, you may begin to feel negative and remember a lot of the negative experiences you had with that teacher. Under this condition, your feelings may literally color or filter the positive message that your friend is trying to present. You may find also yourself discounting or explaining away what your friend is saying—"Oh, wait until you really get to know Mr. X, you'll change your mind"—or you may actually minimize the positives that are presented and maximize any little negatives that are stated. Rather than hearing the message as: "Mr. X is really creative in class . . . you almost never know what to expect . . . it is so cool," you only hear ". . . in class you NEVER know what to expect . . .!"

Moving to Debate

Finally, we may find it difficult to remain open, attentive, and receptive to another's message because we seem to turn inward mentally or psychologically to evaluate and label what that person is saying and begin to develop and rehearse our response.

This is most often seen when we are in the midst of an argument or a debate. Perhaps you have had the experience of being in the middle of an argument, only to catch the beginning of a person's comment, and then, as they continue to speak, "run" inside of your head with, "Oh, I know where she is going. OK, as soon as she takes a breath, I'll say . . . how about this and that?" If you have ever mentally excused yourself in mid-sentence in order to prepare your rebuttal, you may have also experienced times when you finally speak and what comes out is irrelevant to what the speaker was saying, or even exactly what the speaker was leading to before you bailed out. Clearly moving to debate is a process which will interfere with our listening and accurate understanding of another's message.

If we are to be effective helpers, we must learn how to recognize and overcome all of these obstacles—habituation, sensory gating, competing, filtering, and debating—to our listening and accurate understanding. Exercise 4-1 will help make you more aware of the impact these obstacles have on your own ability to listen. The remainder of the chapter focuses on strategies for overcoming these potential obstacles.

EXERCISE 4-1
Obstacles to Effective Listening

Directions, Part 1: You will need a partner for this exercise. Have your partner select one of the following topics, or anything that he or she wishes to share with you. Your partner should talk to you about the topic for approximately 5 minutes. Your assignment is to be quiet and listen. Don't ask questions, don't speak—simply be quiet and listen!

Possible topics for discussion:

- What I did last weekend
- A book, movie, play, etc. I would recommend
- Something that really bugs me

Directions, Part 2: After approximately 5 minutes, discuss with your partner the following questions:

- What other things in the environment distracted me? (e.g., a noise in the hall)
- Did I experience times when I retreated into my own thoughts? (e.g., concerned if it was 5 minutes yet)
- Did I find myself evaluating or labeling what was being said? (e.g., "That's not correct!")
- Were there internal signals (e.g., muscle cramps, growling stomach, etc.) competing for my attention?
- Were there times when the speaker felt I was not completely listening? If so, can I remember what obstacle may have been operative?

LEARNING TO LISTEN

Given that humans are communicative animals, it may seem strange to suggest that we—especially as adults—need to learn to listen. However, the reality is that while hearing may be naturally perfect, listening is NOT perfect . . . naturally!

The fact is that some of the lessons of communications which we have been taught while growing up may actually interfere with effective listening. For example, many of us as children were instructed to "be quiet and listen!" We may have been told "not to interrupt" or "let the other person finish!" The sad truth is that while hearing may be a passive, quiet activity, effective listening is an active, engaging process requiring energy, motivation, skill, and patience! In fact, we may need to rewrite the rules you previously learned about being a good listener.

To listen effectively:

- one must NOT be still and quiet—one must be ACTIVE!
- one must NOT passively await the reception of the helpee's messages, rather one must reach out and actively involve him- or herself in the gathering of the information provided;
- one must NOT listen with only the ears—one must use all senses to listen effectively.

The skills required to implement these rules of effective listening need to be learned and practiced if one is to become an effective listener and an effective helper. The first step in such skill development is to learn how to truly pay *attention* to the other person.

Attending: First a Physical Response

Attending or "being with" another requires both a physical posture and a psychological orientation. Gerard Egan (1977), for example, pointed out the importance of one's body orientation in the accurate reception of information during a face-to-face encounter, such as that found in helping. He suggests that proper attending behavior may be characterized as being

- **S**traight, face-to-face body orientation, with
- **O**penness in body posture and a slight, forward
- **L**ean, while maintaining
- **E**ye contact, and all done in a
- **R**elaxed manner.

The value of this **SOLER** posture (straight, open, lean, eye contact, relaxed) is supported by numerous authors and researchers (Baker, Daniels, & Greeley, 1990;

EXERCISE 4-2
SOLER as an Invitation

Directions: You will need two people (preferably not in this class or training experience) who are willing to talk with you. Ask one of the people an open question, for example, "What have you been doing today?" As they begin to speak, take up a nonattending, non-SOLER body posture. Start first by leaning back, then cross your arms across your chest, cross your legs, divert your eyes from his or her eyes, and finally slowly start to twist or turn your body away from him or her so that you end up facing off to the right.

With the second person, repeat your question, but this time take and maintain the SOLER posture (i.e., square up with that person, with an open, slightly leaning posture, maintaining eye contact).

Have each person tell you how he or she felt talking with you. Can they identify the things that you may have been doing that contributed to those feelings?

Asbury, 1984; Hermansson, Webster, & McFarland, 1988). A survey of this research suggests that the value of this body position is twofold.

First, the posture places the helper in a body orientation which facilitates reception of the helpee's message. This SOLER position opens the helper to receiving a number of channels of information, while at the same time narrowing the band of potential interference. Just consider the increased number of competing stimuli you would be receiving if, rather than facing your speaker and focusing on his or her eyes, you faced a window with your back turned to speaker.

The second value of the SOLER posture is that it conveys to the helpee (via body language) that the helper is attending and truly open to receive his or her messages. This body language message not only encourages the helpee to disclose information, but has been found to increase the helpee's sense that the helper is warm and caring (Argyle, 1967; Mehrabian, 1967). To demonstrate this point, try Exercise 4-2.

Attending: A Psychological Response

In addition to taking an actively receptive physical stance in the helping interaction, the helper must also be psychologically active in the communication exchange. Too often in our communications we simply hear the words, but fail to truly understand the message. For example, consider conversations you may have had with a friend, parent, or colleague in which you felt and perhaps stated that (he or she) doesn't understand! This sense of frustration, along with the reality that while words may be heard yet the message misunderstood, is evidenced in the following exchange between Carol (age 14) and her mother:

Carol: Mother, I can't go to the picnic! Look at these pimples!
Mom: Now Carol, so you have a few pimples?
Carol: Mother . . . LOOK!
Mom: Carol, I am looking. I see them. There are a few tiny pimples on your
forehead.

It is clear that Carol asked Mom to look, and Mom "understood" her request and did look at Carol's pimples. However, Mom looked with the eyes of an adult woman, secure in her own self-image and relationships with others. She did not LOOK as Carol had requested, that is, with the eyes and experience of a 14-year-old, who is overly concerned about her body image and super-sensitive to the evaluation of others. While the words were heard, the message was missed!

To improve our listening and increase the accuracy of our understanding, it has been suggested (Carkhuff, 1987) that we

- remember our reason for listening. Our attention and our listening will increase if we remember that we are attempting to gather data, or clues, from the helpee's words, tone, and manner, which will help us understand the nature of problem or the goals presented.
- suspend our personal judgment. We need to remember to focus on what the helpee is actually saying and not our personal judgment or evaluation of the comments. Clearly, at some point in the relationship we may want to share our opinions or values, but for now it is important to "hear" the helpee's position, not ours!
- focus on the helpee. It may seem obvious, but the effective helper will resist distractions and keep his or her focus on the helpee's explicit, external messages as well as the implicit, internal experiences. This focusing on the helpee may be the most important thing the effective, active listener can do. And as such is developed in more detail.

BECOMING AN ACTIVE-EMPATHIC LISTENER

In order to increase the accuracy of our listening and our understanding and truly focus on the helpee, we need to become *active-empathic* listeners. Being active and empathic in our listening means that we reach out and psychologically step into the world of the helpee. We need to enter the helpee's frame of reference and communicate to him or her what we hear. With such active, empathic listening we will hear the helpee's message as he or she actually intended and experienced it.

We can begin to develop such active-empathic listening and accurate understanding by developing the skills of *paraphrasing* and *reflection of feelings*.

Paraphrasing (Reflective Responses)

Paraphrasing is the process by which the helper takes the basic message provided by the helpee, and in his or her own words *reflects* the content of that message to the helpee. This can be very helpful in letting the helpee expand or clarify issues, as well as to invite him or her to correct any misunderstanding.

In responding to the content of the helpee's message, the effective helper rephrases that content, and does not simply "parrot" back the exact words. The use of paraphrasing requires the helper to pay attention to what is being said. It also requires that the listener focus on the "who" and the "what," as well as the "what was done."

It is important at this point for the helper to reflect only the *explicit* message the helpee has provided. The goal is not to interpret or add other new ideas. What is needed is for the helper to simply share what was received. Exercise 4-3 will help you become familiar with the process of paraphrasing the content of the helpee's message.

Reflection of Feelings

In addition to hearing the words of the helpee and accurately reflecting those words, the helper must also begin to recognize the feelings and the emotions underlying those

---

EXERCISE 4-3
Paraphrasing

Directions, Part 1: For each of the following, read the paragraph and identify the key experiences—who or what is involved—along with the helpee's expressed feelings and actions. *Part 2:* Write a response summarizing in your own words these explicit experiences, behaviors, and feelings. Start your response with either "In other words . . ." or "I hear you saying . . ." *Part 3:* Share and compare your responses with a colleague or co-learner. Did you stay with the explicit message and NOT interpret? Did you simply parrot the helpee, or place the message in your own words?

Example:
> Frustrated teacher: These darn kids. I've had it. I am so frustrated, I could scream. I tried my best—spent hours—worked hard on developing an exciting lesson and today, nothing. They don't care, they goofed off rather than pay attention. Why bother?

Part 1:
Experiences: kids, teacher, and lesson
Behaviors: teacher prepared lesson; kids unresponsive, inattentive
Feelings: frustrated, had it.

Part 2: Paraphrase:
I hear you saying how frustrated you feel and how you are even beginning to doubt the value of working so hard, because you worked hard on the lesson and the students didn't respond.

EXERCISE 4-3 *Continued*

Case 1:

Worker: "I'm stuck. I hate my job—it is so boring, but I've been here 8 years. I have nowhere to go. I am really unsure if I can make a move.

Part 1:

    Experiences: _____

    Behaviors: _____

    Feelings: _____

Part 2:

    Paraphrase: _____

    _____

    _____

Case 2:

Parent: These kids are getting out of hand. They don't listen any more, they do whatever they darn well please. It's like you have to yell or scream or threaten them before they listen. I don't want to be that kind of parent—it is really upsetting.

Part 1:

    Experiences: _____

    Behaviors: _____

    Feelings: _____

Part 2:

    Paraphrase: _____

    _____

    _____

Case 3:

College student: I think this is the one. I really like him. He is so kind, so respectful, so absolutely gorgeous. I know it sounds goofy, but he is really Mr. Right. I am so excited, I want to tell everybody.

Part 1:

    Experiences: _____

    Behaviors: _____

    Feelings: _____

Part 2:

    Paraphrase: _____

    _____

    _____

words. Like paraphrasing, reflection of feelings requires that the helper provide a brief statement reflecting the essence of the message received. However, where paraphrasing generally reflects the facts of what was said, reflection of feelings reflects the emotions related to those facts. For example:

> Helpee: I don't know what's wrong with us. We used to be so close—now nothing, a big void between us.
>
> Helper: You feel confused and somewhat anxious. *open ended*

In order for a helper to reflect the helpee's feelings accurately, he or she must learn to listen with the eyes as well as the ears. How does the helpee look as he or she shares his or her story? What might his or her posture, facial expression, or gestures be expressing? Such expressions, along with tone of voice, may give the helper clues as to how the helpee is feeling.

Further, Carkhuff (1987) suggests that in order to identify what the helpee may be experiencing, we ask ourselves the *empathy question.* According to Carkhuff, we need to ask ourselves "How would I feel if I were doing or experiencing these things?" Answering this question can help us identify both the helpee's feeling and even the intensity of that feeling. This information is what we wish to reflect to the helpee, as our *reflection of feelings.* Exercise 4-4 will help you begin to develop the ability to reflect feelings accurately.

As the helper begins to attend to both the content and the feeling expressed in the helpee's message, he or she may notice that at times the words of the helpee convey one thing, and the expression or tone of voice suggests something else. One of the values of reflecting both content and feelings is that it may help expose and clarify these mixed messages. If the helper discerns more than one message ("No, I really like my roommate" said very curtly and with a frown), the helper needs to reflect both the content (I like my roommate) and the feelings suggested (annoyed?).

Under these conditions it is important to not evaluate the message, simply describe it and ask the helpee to confirm your accuracy of understanding. A response such as "I hear you saying that you like your roommate, but I detect in your tone and facial expression that there is something bothering you about the roommate?" will invite the helpee to clarify the message.

Moving from the Explicit to the Implied

Theodore Reik (1948) describes a process in which the therapist uses his or her own internal experiencing to "hear" meanings that go beyond the words the helpee uses. The concept is that when we are truly present to another, when we are fully attentive to another's messages, we will begin to record not just the words but the tone, not just the verbal message but the feelings beneath the message, and not just the intended message but often the issues well beneath.

EXERCISE 4-4
Reflection of Feelings

Directions: After reading each of the following statements and attending to the behavioral expressions, ask yourself, "How would I feel saying these things?" and "How do I usually feel when I act or sound that way?" Then write a response using the formula "It seems that you are feeling . . ." or "You're feeling . . .".

It is helpful to share and compare your responses with those of a colleague or co-learner. Did you agree on the feelings expressed? If not, which cues were you using? Did you agree with the level of intensity? If not, again what cues were you each picking up and responding to?

Example:

> Helpee: (sighing) I just don't know what to do. (looks down at the ground, with a frown on her brow and sighs a second time)
> Helper: It seems that you are feeling confused and somewhat hopeless about what to do.

1. Helpee: (sitting up on the edge of the seat, turning red in the face, and raising his voice) If you only knew what I have to put up with! (smacks his hand down on the chair)

   Helper: You seem to be feeling _____

   _____

   _____

2. Helpee: But you have got to help . . . (voice is high-pitched, facial expression appears pleading, actually reaches toward you)
   Helper: You're feeling _____

   _____

3. Helpee: Oh, it is hard to contain myself (sitting up, gesturing with hands and smiling as she speaks)! The class is just so (dragging out "soooooo") GREAT! (with emphasis)
   Helper: You feel _____

   _____

   _____

For example, consider the following:

Tom (smiling, somewhat nervously): What a week . . . car broke down, lost my report, and my doctor found a spot on my Xray. How's your week been?

At one level you could respond, "It seems that you have had three things happen to you" (paraphrase). You may even reflect the feelings expressed and respond "Your tone of voice and smile suggests to me that you feel nervous." However, if you look at Tom's expression, listen to his tone and nervous laugh, and truly put yourself in his shoes, you may find that you hear something a little differently and respond: "You're really upset and concerned—it seems like nothing is going right, so I guess you're expecting the worse possible news on that spot?" If your reflection is greeted by "Oh, yes . . . that's it . . ." from Tom, it can be assumed you heard the message implied as well as that explicitly stated.

As Reik suggested, it is like listening with *the third ear*. It is that "ear" which leads you to draw conclusions or inferences that accurately reflect another level of the helpee's words.

This is neither an automatic response nor an easy process to develop. It will take time and experience, but it can be developed. Understanding what is implied in another's message requires that we listen intently, experience the entire story as if we were living it, and then put our understanding into words that the helpee can affirm or correct.

It must be noted that this is not an open invitation to guess and interpret underlying issues. Such "mind reading" and "playing psychologist" can end open communications. Premature interpreting may cause the helpee to feel extremely vulnerable, and as a result he or she will close down to protect him- or herself, rather than continue with the open self-disclosure.

What is suggested is that as you develop your attending skills, learning to hear the explicit messages—both content and feeling—you will find yourself moving to reflect that which is implied. You need to let reflection flow from the deep and accurate understanding of the relationship, and not try to force it like a technique!

WHAT NEXT

There is no doubt that listening is hard work. It requires intense concentration. But if listening is hard, understanding, truly understanding, can seem insurmountable.

Listening and understanding are essential core ingredients to connecting with the helpee. They are a must. And while both are difficult processes to do correctly, both are learnable. They are skills that can, through practice and corrective feedback, be established and developed. The answer to the question "What next?" is practice, practice, practice!

Our closing exercise is designed to start you on your practice trail. At first paraphrasing content or reflecting feelings may feel "unnatural" or "awkward." These processes may even appear to interrupt the natural flow of a conversation. But as you practice, you will notice that they become a meaningful part of your natural conversational style, a part which increases your accurate understanding of the helpee.

EXERCISE 4-5
Putting It All Together

Directions: This exercise will require the participation of three individuals: one will be the helpee, one the helper, and the third a referee. Videotaping this exercise would be useful, so that in addition to focusing on your verbal style, you can monitor your use of SOLER positioning, and identify any distracting mannerisms you may exhibit.

Phase 1: Select either a real issue that the helpee would like to discuss or role play one of the following situations.

• The helpee is unsure about making a job change
• The helpee wants to end a relationship, but is concerned about hurting the other person
• The helpee is tired of being taken for granted in a particular relationship

The discussion should last approximately 5 minutes. During this phase, the helper's task is to listen. The helper is restricted in what he or she can say. The helper can only use minimal encouragers or paraphrases of content. He or she is not allow to share his or her opinion or ask questions.

The referee's job is to monitor the length of time for Phase 1, stopping at 5 minutes, and insuring that the helper follows the rules. If the helper goes beyond the regulations of what he or she can do, the referee should interrupt the conversation and remind the helper of the rules.

Phase 2: For the next 5 minutes, continue the conversation, or the helpee and the referee can change roles. The helper can now use minimal encouragers, paraphrases of content, and reflections of feelings. He or she is still not allowed to ask questions or share his or her opinion. The role of the referee is again to keep the 5-minute time limit and interrupt the conversation if the helpee exceeds the rules.

Phase 3: In the final 5 minutes of the conversation, the helper is now allowed to ask questions and share his or her feelings on the issue. HOWEVER, prior to sharing his or her feelings, or prior to asking a question, the helper is required to *actively reflect* the content and feelings of what the helpee just presented. The referee should stop the helper from asking questions or sharing information, if he or she did not first actively reflect the helpee's message.

REFERENCES AND RECOMMENDED READINGS

Asbury, F.R. (1984). The empathy treatment. *Elementary School Guidance and Counseling, 18,* 181–187.

Argyle, M. (1967). *The psychology of interpersonal behavior.* Baltimore: Penguin.

Baker, S., Daniels, T., & Greeley, A. (1990). Systematic training of graduate-level counselors. Narrative and meta-analytic reviews of three programs. *Counseling Psychologist, 26,* 81–84.

Carkhuff, R.R. (1987). *The art of helping VI.* Amherst, MA: Human Resource Development Press.

Carkhuff, R.R. (1986). *The art of helping video series,* Tapes 2 and 3. Amherst, MA: Human Resources Development Press.

Egan, G. (1977). *You and me: The skills of communicating and relating to others.* Pacific Grove, CA: Brooks/Cole.

Hermansson, G.L., Webster, A.C., & McFarland, K. (1988). Counselor deliberate postural lean and communication of facilitative conditions. *Journal of Counseling Psychology, 35,* 149–153.

Mehrabian, A. (1967). Orientation behaviors and nonverbal attitude communication. *Journal of Communications, 17,* 324–332.

Reik, T. (1948). *Listening with the third ear.* New York: Grove Press.

▶ 5

Exploration

You may have heard the phrase "What you see is what you get". This is not always the case in a helping relationship. Quite often the concern or problem that a helpee initially presents to a helper is not at all the problem or concern which needs to be addressed. And even when what is presented IS the concern to be addressed, this first presentation of the problem is often quite sketchy and not fully developed.

Because of these realities, the effective helper needs to learn how to assist the helpee to explore not only the depth and breadth of the concern, but also to begin to examine the personal and extrapersonal resources he or she may have available for resolving the concern.

This chapter will

1. present a systematic approach to this process of exploration;
2. provide a review of the skills required for facilitating such an exploration; and
3. highlight the art and usefulness of appropriate questioning.

A SYSTEMATIC VIEW OF EXPLORATION

Prior to assisting the helpee with the resolution of his or her problem, the helper needs to clearly understand the nature and complexity of the problem being presented. As suggested in the previous chapters, the early stages of helping are devoted to the development of a facilitative relationship. Once this is established, the helper will already have begun to understand the reason the helpee is seeking help.

As the helper attends and listens to the helpee's story, what might first be presented as the issue may peel away, like the outer layers of an onion, to reveal a story or a concern which is at the core of the helpee's problem. Consider the following dialogue between a psychologist and a man seeking assistance because of marital conflict.

Gino: Well, Dr. S., I'm not sure if you can help, but something has to be done. My wife is driving me crazy. She is always nagging about stupid stuff. Maybe it's just normal husband and wife nonsense.

Dr. S.: Always nagging?

Gino: Well, obviously not always, but too much for my liking. She gets her teeth into something and never lets go.

Dr. S: What types of things does she confront you with? *Clarification*

Gino: Well, the usual stuff, I guess. But the real hassle is her thing about my drinking.

Dr. S: Your drinking?

Gino: So I have a few beers every night and go out with the guys on Friday night before I come home from work. Big deal.

Dr. S: So you have a few beers every night.

Gino: It's not like I need it or anything—you know just a six-pack or so to relax.

Dr. S: Your wife feels that a six-pack of beer each night is too much? *Sum. Clarif.*

Gino: Well it's not just that, but sometimes I get a little out of hand.

Dr. S: Out of hand?

Gino: Well (silent), . . . Well, lately I've been yelling at her and throwing things. I've never acted like this before—maybe I can't hold it like I used to. It scares me to think I may have a drinking problem.

Clearly, what was presented as "normal husband and wife nonsense" is much more serious. Gino's problem may in fact have little to do with husband and wife bickering and be more an issue of his use and abuse of alcohol.

Before jumping in to help solve a problem, the effective helper will *explore* the depth and breadth of the concern being discussed, as well as begin to identify the resources available to the helpee for resolving the problem. It must be emphasized that while the helpee can begin to explore particular areas for more in-depth information, a real focusing occurs in the next stage of the helping process (see Chapter 6). The task at this stage of helping is to allow the helpee to become comfortable with sharing his or her story, and for the helper to become increasingly clear as to the depth and degree of complexity of the problem presented.

This process of exploration entails a real reconnaissance or exploration of the helpee's total experience, so that all of the relevant data can be gathered and processed. The quantity and diversity of the information a helper gathers during this exploration stage can become overwhelming. The more systematic the process is (while the helper remains natural), the easier it is to begin to organize the data into some meaningful whole, and there will be less chance of missing information of importance or being overwhelmed by the quantity of material shared.

Hutchins and Cole (1992) discuss a process they term *chunking* as a way of organizing key words in order to explore content systematically. For example, they suggest that the term "behavior", when considered by the helper, can represent concepts of the helpee's thinking, feeling, and acting. Or, the term "situation" may lead to an exploration of people, things, and places of significance to the helpee. Another simple model for organizing the gathering of information may be to use the 5Ws of a journalist; that is, learn to identify the who, what, when, where, and why of the situation.

- Who and what was involved?
- What was done?
- Why and how was it done?
- When and where was it done?

In the exploration stage, the helper assists the helpee to move from a there-and-then discussion to more of a here-and-now. The helper assists the helpee to turn inward in order to identify feelings and experiences as reflective of the problem, while at the same time turning outward to identify the conditions, events, and people connected to the problem.

The goal of the exploration stage is simply to assist the helpee in telling his or her story, with all of its relevant detail.

Consider the previous dialogue between Gino and Dr. S. Using essential relationship skills along with artful reflection and questioning, Dr. S. was able to assist Gino to move from talking about his wife and what she did, to focusing on himself and what is currently concerning him.

EXPLORING THROUGH THE USE OF OBSERVATIONAL SKILLS

Quite often it is not the words of a song that move us, but rather the tune and tone underneath. Such is true also for the helping relationship. There are times when it is not the explicit message provided by the helpee, describing the specifics of his or her concerns and/or *presenting complaint,* that needs to be the focus of the helping process, but rather the more subtle, underlying tones and implied messages of concern. Observing and attending to the helpee's nonverbal messages can be a valuable source of data for understanding this more subtle component of the problem.

Observing skills, according to Carkhuff (1987), are the most basic helping skills. Observation of the helpee's style, nonverbal behavior, and use of silence can provide valuable data from which to begin to develop inferences about the helpee.

It needs to be highlighted, however, that interpreting the helpee's style, nonverbals, or periods of silence must be tempered by knowledge of the helpee's culture and racial standards for behavior (Ivey, Gluckstern, Ivey, 1992). For example, Highlen and Hill (1984) cited research suggesting that Caucasian Americans and African Americans have different norms for eye contact. According to these authors, Caucasian Americans tend more often to look while listening, whereas African

Americans are more likely not to look while listening. Similarly, Sue and Sue (1977,1990) noted that some cultural groups avoid eye contact as a sign of respect and deference. Research also supports the notion that culture strongly impacts the use of space (proxemics) in the encounter (Hall, 1968). As with all interpretations, the helper needs to be careful and tentative in the conclusions he or she draws about the helpee from observational data. Further, it is important that the helper provide the helpee with feedback about these observations, so that the helpee may correct any incorrect interpretations drawn by the helper.

Exploring the Helpee's Style

During this stage of exploration, the helper makes a preliminary reconnaissance or survey of the helpee's style of interaction, personal assets and liabilities, and how these can be brought to bear on the presenting concern. Often the type of responses given by the helpee will provide clues to the helpee's general style in dealing with his or her world.

For example, as noted previously, a person coming for help may feel a bit insecure or anxious. Under this type of stress the helpee may retreat to a style of false bravado. He or she may try to put these feelings of concern out of consciousness and exhibit the opposite to what is, in fact, felt. The helpee may attempt to deny the need for assistance or eagerly attempt to take all the responsibility for solving this problem.

Bravado that conceals fear can be dangerous. Consider an individual who quietly suffers mild chest pain, "biting the bullet," only to find that these were the early warning signs of an impending heart attack. Or, the student who is experiencing tremendous stress adjusting to college but keeps up a good act so as to not look like a wimp, only to develop a bleeding ulcer. Individuals who exhibit such bravado need to be helped to feel more secure in the helping relationship so that they may be willing to risk sharing these concerns.

Another style often encountered in helping is that of the overly sensitive, defensive helpee. Hitting a sore spot often makes the helpee withdraw. Learning to attend to areas of psychological soreness may help the helper more fully appreciate the helpee's style and presenting concern.

When under stress or feeling anxious, a helpee may resort to a defensive style of interaction. He or she may defend him- or herself in a variety of ways, such as denying that what is being discussed in really important, trying to justify or "excuse" away what is being presented, or simply withdrawing and refusing to speak about it. In later chapters we will discuss how to address and confront such defensiveness, but for the time being it is simply valuable, during the exploration stage, to make a mental note of both the areas of sensitivity and the style with which the helpee responds to these areas. This knowledge may assist the helper to more fully understand the issues confronting the helpee as well as the degree to which the helpee's style may be contributing to both the problem and the potential solution.

Exploring the Helpee's Nonverbals

In the previous chapter we pointed out the importance of the helper taking up an attending body position (SOLER) in order to facilitate his or her own attending, and to convey the message of "being with" the helpee. Nonverbal messages can often provide clues to the underlying feelings the helpee is experiencing at the moment, and thus can prove invaluable sources of data for the sensitive and perceptive helper.

For example, a helpee shifting his or her body positioning away from the straight, open, forward-leaning style of an open receiver, or averting eye contact during a discussion of a particular topic may suggest that this is a topic which is a bit too uncomfortable for him or her to discuss. Understanding that our message or discussion is being blocked is important if we are to be effective communicators. We need to register this awareness, while at the same time, pull back from the discussion at that point.

Similarly, when we experience our helpee's adjusting his or her body posture to a more receptive stance (open, straight, leaning forward with increased eye contact), it is a clear clue that he or she is interested in what we are doing or saying at the moment. It is evidence that the helpee is receptive to the message being conveyed and that perhaps we are on target.

By paying attention to the subtle (and sometimes not so subtle) messages conveyed by the helpee's body language and nonverbal communications (inappropriate smiling, shifting, gesturing) and the tone, pitch, and general pattern of the verbal style, the helper may begin to understand more fully the helpee's style of reaction as well as some of the underlying "tone" to the song being presented.

While there are numerous materials written on the topic of nonverbal communication and the business of interpreting body talk, I generally think that a more common-sense approach to interpreting nonverbals can be as useful. The effective helper takes note of the helpee's bodily behavior, such as posture, body movement, and gestures. The effective helper learns to listen to both what is being said and how it is being said; that is, the tone of voice, pitch, intensity, inflection, etc. The effective helper will look at the helpee's facial expression for signs of emotional reaction. Exercise 5-1 highlights some of the nonverbal cues a helper should note.

While any one theory may place more or less emphasis on the meaning of the helpee's nonverbal messages, it can be safely said that regardless of theory, a helper should, at a minimum, note and/or point out this nonverbal presentation and the messages it is sending to the helpee. The effective helper can and will reflect nonverbal messages the same as verbal messages. Specifically, the effective helper will

1. attend to the degree to which the helpee's verbal message is congruent with his or her nonverbal behavior. Is the helpee stating he or she is angry, and does his or her nonverbal behavior (voice rising in pitch, body stiffening, jaw tightening) support that message? When the messages are not congruent, the effective helper can either make a special mental note or reflect the messages received so that the helpee can clarify the meanings.

EXERCISE 5-1
Interpreting the Nonverbal

Directions: For each of the following nonverbal cues, generate at least two possible interpretations. Share your interpretations with a colleague or classmate and note points of agreement and places of disagreement.

Nonverbal Cue   *Interpretation*

 1. Moisture or tears   _____   _____
 2. Eye shift   _____   _____
 3. Smile   _____   _____
 4. Lips tight or pursed together   _____   _____
 5. Biting lower lip/lip quivering _____   _____
 6. Furrow on brow   _____   _____
 7. Nodding head up and down   _____   _____
 8. Hanging head down/jaw on chest _____   _____
 9. Fist clenching   _____   _____
10. Foot tapping   _____   _____
11. Turning (looking) away from the helper   _____   _____
12. Whispering   _____   _____
13. Voice becoming high-pitched _____   _____
14. Moves back from helper   _____   _____
15. (Others that you can think of) _____   _____

2. attend to nonverbal cues when the client is silent (these can be reflected just as verbal messages). A caution for the helper is to remember not to rush in too quickly to fill the silence.

Exploring Periods of Silence

We live in a very fast-paced stimulating world; we are accustomed to a lot of stimulating, constant interaction and the absence of social voids. Thus, when we encounter a period of silence, we may be tempted to fill the gap. I can remember one student, concerned that she was wasting time by letting the client be quiet. "I should do something!" she stated. I replied that she should do something, and that what she should do . . . is listen! Listen to the silence. Attend to the messages being sent by the client during periods of silence.

As noted in the previous chapter, it is important for effective helpers to develop a level of comfort with silence. The helper must learn to be an active, reflective listener when the helpee is talking, but similarly must remain active, attentive, and reflective when the helpee falls silent. In addition to becoming comfortable with silence, the effective helper needs to know how to interpret or understand silence in the helping encounter.

Periods of silence happen as a natural part of the interactive process. However, there are times when the helpee becomes silent for reasons other than simply as a point of a natural break or transition in the communication. For example, the helpee may be embarrassed, angry, or confused, or may be "editing" what he or she wishes to convey. As a result, the helper may experience a pause, an interruption, a silence in the interaction. Often, the helpee becomes silent as a resistive act—unsure of the trust level of the relationship, or concerned about the helper's reaction.

Attending to the helpee's expression, manner, and nonverbal style during these periods of silence may give the helper a clue as to what it is the helpee is feeling during these particular moments of silence. Consider the possible meanings of each of the following examples of helpee silence (Exercise 5-2).

EXERCISE 5-2
Interpreting Silence

Directions: Supply an interpretation for each of the following examples of helpee silence. Share your interpretation with a colleague or classmate and note points of agreement and places of disagreement. What specific cues did you use to draw your interpretation?

1. "This is not the easiest thing in the world to say, but, oh, well, . . . I" (helpee becomes silent)
   Interpretation: _____
   _____

2. "He's been gone now for 4 months. He was so young, so young" (looks down, becomes silent)
   Interpretation: _____
   _____

3. "I got no problem drinking, and that's that!" (sits back, and becomes silent)
   Interpretation: _____
   _____

4. (Helper) "Well, Jamie, I know your mom and dad brought you here to talk with me. Perhaps you could tell me what has been going on."
   (Jamie sits expressionless, looking straight at the helper, silent)
   Interpretation: _____
   _____

EXPLORING THROUGH THE ART OF QUESTIONING

In addition to gathering data by way of observation, the effective helper also wants to engage the helpee and invite him or her to "tell your story." Facilitating such storytelling and gathering the data needed to be of assistance is greatly aided by the artful use of questioning.

The art of questioning is a keystone to the exploration process. The helper who has mastered the use of questions can elicit very helpful information from the helpee, and do so in a way that is non-threatening and even comforting.

There are times when the use of a question can assist the helpee to *probe* more deeply into the issue. For example:

> Helpee: I just don't understand, he says he likes me, but he treats me so, so, strangely!
> Helper: How does he treat you?

Questions can also be used simply to *highlight* a certain piece of information that is provided by the helpee. Often such highlighting, or emphasizing, will enable the helpee to be a bit more specific, or will invite the helpee to focus more intensely on one specific aspect of his or her experience. For example:

> Helpee: My boss just makes me so mad, so furious, I could just explode!
> Helper: Explode?

And finally, one of the primary values of questioning is that it can be used to *clarify* what it is the helpee is truly seeking to convey. For example:

> Helpee: Okay, so I drink a little bit, but everybody is on my case—my friends, my mom and dad, gads, even my advisor at school is on me about my drinking.
> Helper: You say you drink *a little bit,* but it seems that a lot of people are concerned about your drinking. Can you help me understand why so many people may be concerned about what you call *a little bit?*

Guidelines for Effective Questioning

Questioning can be a very useful tool for a helper to begin to gain a real understanding of the issues confronting the helpee. However, questioning, if done inappropriately, can do much to block a helping, facilitative relationship. There are a number of guidelines which, when used, can increase the therapeutic effectiveness of our questioning.

Be Purposeful

It may be said that one of the most basic rules governing the exploration stage is that questioning and data collection should be purposeful. We can ask questions for a variety of reasons—as a form of "small talk", or as a way of backing another into a corner, almost like a prosecuting attorney.

We must remember that, unlike other times when we are engaged in social interchanges, we are there to assist or to help another. We are not simply asking questions for our own benefit or as a way of "peeping" into another person's life. We are attending and questioning because we wish to understand another person's situation so that we can assist him or her in moving in the desired direction. The asking of questions within a helping context is purposeful. Questions are aimed at gathering information needed for the helper to clearly understand the nature of the helpee's concerns, his or her resources for solving the problem, and the solutions available. When we keep our purpose in mind, our questions will reflect that intent. When our questions are aimed at helping us complete the story, or the puzzle, then the questions we ask will be helpful.

Be Clear, Concrete, and Simple

A second guideline for asking questions in the helping context is to keep the questions clear and simple. Questions should be asked in a manner and with language that the helpee can understand. Asking compound questions, or using slang or jargon, will not only be confusing to the helpee, but may make the helpee increasingly nervous and thus block communications.

For example, consider the following scenario:

Helpee: Gads, I'm nervous. I don't know why . . . just kind of seems strange having to talk to someone.

Helper: Is it strange that you have to talk with someone, or are you saying it is strange for you to be talking with someone? You know, is it a commentary on your social style, or the fact that your ego defenses block you from seeing yourself as a person who would need help . . . any thoughts?

With a helpee who has already expressed some anxiety and nervousness about talking to a helper, it is clear that the multiple questions and the introduction of terms like "social style" and "ego defenses" may be somewhat unnerving, and actually block the exploration of the issue at hand.

Be Conservative—Ask as Few Questions as Possible

The third guideline is that we should only ask the minimum number of questions needed to gather all the relevant data required to help another. The helpee comes to the interaction with an agenda, a desire to express a concern. Our first goal, as helpers, is to interact in such a way as to facilitate this expression of that concern, to allow the helpee to ventilate and not block it. Thus, while we need to gather information, we need to be careful not to turn our questioning into a extensive barrage of rapid fire interrogations.

Helpee: I don't know where to begin . . .

Helper: Tell me about yourself.

Helpee: Like what? My name is Sean, I'm a sophomore.

Helper: Do you have a girlfriend? Do you live on campus? Are you originally from around here?

Helpee: Well . . .

Helper: Who recommended that you see me? What is it that I can do for you?

Asking a set of rapid-fire questions does little to place the helpee at ease, and may in fact force the helpee into a shut-down, protective mode.

Questions which can be answered with a simple yes or no response, or which can be answered with a few words, multiple choice style, are generally considered *closed questions.* This type of questions not only sets the stage for the helpee's feeling as if he or she is on the witness stand, but will also create a pattern of communication that places all of the responsibility for structure and direction on the helper, as opposed to allowing the helpee give the needed direction. Examples of closed questions would be: How many days have you missed class? Do you take medication? Well, do you think she is angry or just playing hard to get?

In contrast to this style of closed questioning, the effective helper will develop the ability to employ questions which *invite* the client to *expand, elaborate,* and *expound* on a point, rather than simply answer yes or no. Questions such as this are considered *open questions.*

Open questions are particularly useful in the early stages of the helping process in that they invite the helpee to structure the direction of the interaction. They act as invitations for the helpee to tell his or her story.

Open questions can be framed in ways which express interest (Could you tell me more?), the desire for clarification (How did you think it happened?), or even direction (Could you tell me a bit more about that?). They allow the helper to retain some control over the direction of the helping process open questions, but do not restrict the types of information provided by the helpee, as might happen in a very structured, question/answer format of closed questioning. Open questions often begin with words such as who, what, when, where, how, and why. For example: Who is impacted by your decision? What motivated you to seek help at this time? Where do these feelings typically occur? When did you first begin have these feelings of anxiety? How long have you been experiencing these feelings? Why do you think she may have asked to leave?

Even though a "why" question invites the helpee to talk, it may also make some helpees feel defensive, as if they need to justify what happened. It is usually more effective to ask what and how questions to get at the same information. For example, rather than ask a helpee, "Why do you feel anxious?" it may be less threatening to ask, "What happened to make you feel so anxious?"

Now even though the emphasis here has been on the value of open questions as invitations for the helpee to speak, in reality the purposeful, systematic inquiry of a helper will use both open and closed questions. During the early stage of the helping interaction, when a helper is attempting to explore the depth and breadth of the helpee's problem, open questions appear to be most useful. But in the later stages of helping, as the helping process begins to focus in on specific information, without the helpee's elaboration, then there may be an increased use of closed questions. Exercise 5-3 provides an illustration of the differential effect of closed- and open-ended questions.

While closed questions may be useful in narrowing down the information or focus of the conversation and can even be used to obtain clearly defined factual input, they often restrict the helpee's opportunity to reveal his or her feelings, unique personality, or distinctive style and orientation. Under these conditions, open questions appear much more useful. As evidenced in Exercise 5-3, narrowing the focus too quickly may lead the helpee to miss some of the significant elements of the problem. I am not sure the helper in Scenario I understood the role the helpee's male friends are playing in problem.

EXERCISE 5-3
Styles of Questioning

Directions: Review the following two dialogues between a helper and a helpee. In both situations the helper is attempting to *explore* the nature of the problem. The first helper employs a number of closed-ended questions, whereas the second helper relies on a open questioning style. Answer and discuss the questions following each of the dialogues.

Scenario I: Closed Questioning

> Helpee: Boy, am I having a problem with my girlfriend!
> Helper: What, is she treating you like dirt?
> Helpee: No, not exactly.
> Helper: Oh, well, just having a little spat?
> Helpee: Well . . . it's a bit more than that!
> Helper: So it's like it's just a rough spot . . . not too bad, but not the way you want it to be?
> Helpee: Yeah, I guess you could say it like that.

For consideration and discussion:

1. How do you think the helpee feels at this moment?
2. What is the helpee expecting from this helping relationship?
3. What have you learned about the helpee?
4. What have you learned about the helpee's situation?

Continued

EXERCISE 5-3   *Continued*

Scenario II: Open Questioning

> Helpee: Boy, am I having a problem with my girlfriend!
>
> Helper: When you say "problem," what is it you mean?
>
> Helpee: Well, we've been going together now for 13 months. She's really the first girl I've dated that long. But anyway, the last couple of weeks she has really been bugging me about spending more time with her. You know, like I go out with my friends to play basketball, or get a beer . . . or whatever . . . and she gets all upset. It's like she's trying to own me.
>
> Helper: What is it about her reaction that bothers you?
>
> Helpee: Well, I mean, hey, I really like her . . . but I'm not getting married yet! It's getting to the point where the guys are getting on my case . . . you know asking me "if I am allowed out to play . . .". It is really getting embarrassing!

For consideration and discussion:

1. How do you think the helpee feels at this moment?
2. What is the helpee expecting from this helping relationship?
3. What have you learned about the helpee?
4. What have you learned about the helpee's situation?
5. Contrast the data you received using open questions as opposed to that in Scenario I.

EXPLORATION AS AN INITIAL ASSESSMENT

One final aspect of the exploration stage which needs to be highlighted is that it is the time for the helper to perform a preliminary assessment. The helper needs to have a feeling for both the severity of the problem and the resources available to support the helpee as he or she works through his or her problem.

Mehrabian and Reed (1969) suggest that a problem's severity can be conceptualized by using the following formula:

$$\text{Severity} = \text{Distress} \times \text{Uncontrollability} \times \text{Frequency}.$$

As Egan (1990) noted, and as suggested by the formula, even small levels of distress, if experienced as uncontrollable or extremely persistent, can result in the experience of a severe problem. However, reducing any or all of the factors on the right side of the equation can effectively reduce the severity of the problem. Thus, if the frequency of occurrence can be reduced, the helpee can gain some control, or even if the impact of the problem can be reduced, then clearly the situation or issue becomes less severe and less problematic.

There may be times when the helpee is experiencing such severity and is in such crisis that a helper must take a more concentrated and directed form of assisting. During these times, the helper may need to refer to other professionals for assistance. The conditions under which such crisis intervention and/or referral may need to take place will be discussed in detail in Chapters 12 and 14. The point to be made here is that the decisions regarding severity and the ability of this helper to assist this helpee need to be made during this early exploratory helping phase.

WHAT NEXT

While there are a number of specific directions and focal points the helper may want to pursue, the directive at this stage of the relationship is *to go slow*. The purpose of the exploration stage is for the helper to develop a fuller understanding of the how the helpee sees him- or herself and his or her world. It is truly a time to *explore*. Explore all the possible elements of the helpee's concerns, as well as the personal and extrapersonal resources which may be available for use in developing a solution to this problem.

The techniques employed during this stage are all intended to assist the helpee in telling his or her story with increasing breadth and depth, and to begin to identify the resources available to the helpee for resolving the problem. Going slow and exploring takes practice; attending to and interpreting nonverbals takes practice, as does the art of questioning. One way of developing your own helper skills is to get in the habit of observing effective and ineffective interviewers on television. Do they employ the SOLER posture? Do they ask open or closed questions? What cues are sent by their interviewees' nonverbals? Observing others and modeling are useful ways to increase your own knowledge and skills.

We close the chapter with one additional practice exercise (Exercise 5-4). It will not only reveal the value of exploration, but will provide you with the opportunity to begin processing the helpee's story—looking for all of the issues and possible resources.

Exercise 5-4 is a brief case presentation which will demonstrate the use of questioning, as well as the interpretation of nonverbals, as the helper moves from the presenting complaint to the presentation of the real concern. Further, attending to all of the parts of the story will allow the helper to begin to develop a sense of the resources available to the helpee.

EXERCISE 5-4
Practice in Exploration

Directions: Below is a dialogue between a 32-year-old single mother and a counselor in the personnel office of her company. She came to see the counselor because she was a brand new employee and wanted to get some "information about daycare facilities for (her) 18-month-old child."

Part 1: As you read the description of the exchange, list any additional issues (other than simply seeking information about daycare) that may be revealed by the exploration process. Also, note what you believe to be personal resources, assets, etc. which the helpee seems to possess as well as extrapersonal (resources or sources outside the helpee) resources available to the helpee.

Part 2: With a colleague or classmate review each line of the exchange and discuss the following:

- How did you interpret the information provided?
- Did you draw similar conclusions? If you derived different interpretations, discuss why.
- What do you feel is the real problem for which the helpee needs assistance? Is it finding daycare?
- What special resources (personal or extrapersonal) can be used to help resolve the problem?

Exchange	*Additional Issues Revealed by the Exploration*	*Resources*
1. Helpee: Hi, I was sent to see you about some information.	_____ _____	_____ _____
2. Helper: Have a seat and perhaps you could tell me what it is you are looking for.	_____ _____	_____ _____
3. Helpee: I need information on daycare facilities.	_____ _____	_____ _____
4. Helper: Daycare?	_____ _____	_____ _____
5. Helpee: Yes, you see I'm a single parent (starts to move a bit in her seat) and (pause) I just came back to work. (silent)	_____ _____	_____ _____

6. Helper allows silence of _____   _____
approximately 40 seconds. _____   _____

7. Helpee: It's tough, you know _____   _____
(eyes watering). I've got a _____   _____
beautiful little girl and she's
ONLY 18 months old. But I've
got to work! You understand,
don't you?

8. Helper: You feel sad about _____   _____
leaving your daughter. _____   _____

9. Helpee: Sad, yeah, but (she _____   _____
looks away from the helper) . . . _____   _____
yeah, sad . . . (helpee becomes
silent, looks down to the ground,
with a frown on her brow)

10. Helper: You look concerned. _____   _____
_____   _____

11. Helpee: I am concerned! _____   _____
_____   _____

12. Helper: Concerned? _____   _____
_____   _____

13. Helpee: As a single parent I _____   _____
need to work to provide for my _____   _____
child. I love her . . . I do!
But . . . a parent should . . .
(pause) a good parent should
stay home with her child! I know
my mom will help out, and my
sister already said we could take
turns helping each other, you
know like a co-op. (becomes
silent, begins to cry)

14. Helpee: I feel so rotten, like I _____   _____
am abandoning my baby. _____   _____

REFERENCES AND RECOMMENDED READINGS

Carkhuff, R.R. (1987). *The art of helping VI.* Amherst, MA: Human Resources Resource Development Press.

Cormier, W.H., & Cormier, L.S. (1991). *Interviewing strategies for helpers.* Belmont, CA: Brooks/Cole.

Egan, G. (1990) *The skilled helper.* Belmont, CA: Brooks/Cole.

Hall, E.T. (1968). Proxemics. *Current Anthropology, 9,* 83–108.

Highlen, P.S, & Hill, C.E. (1984). Factors affecting client change in individual counseling: Current status and theoretical speculations. In S. Brown, & R. Lent (eds.), *Handbooks of counseling psychology* (pp 334–396). New York: Wiley.

Hutchins, D.E., & Cole, C.G. (1992). *Helping relationships and strategies.* Belmont, CA: Brooks/Cole.

Ivey, A.E. (1988). *Intentional interviewing and counseling,* (2nd edition). Pacific Grove, CA: Brooks/Cole.

Ivey, A.E. Gluckstern, N., & Ivey, M. (1992). *Basic attending skills* (3rd edition). Amherst, MA: Microtraining Associates.

Mehrabian, A., & Reed, H. (1969). Factors influencing judgments of psychopathology. *Psychological Reports, 24,* 323–330.

Parsons, R., & Wicks, R. (1994). *Counseling strategies and intervention techniques for the human services.* Needham Heights, MA: Allyn and Bacon.

Sue, D.W., & Sue, D. (1977). Barriers to effective cross-cultural counseling. *Journal of Counseling Psychology, 24,* 420–429.

Sue, D.W., & Sue, D. (1990). *Counseling the culturally different* (2nd edition). New York: Wiley.

▶ 6

Focusing: Moving the Helpee toward Clarification

I just feel so horrible. Nothing is going right. I just can't seem to get it together and I don't know what else to try or were else to turn. (spoken by Annie, age 38)

The primary goal for any helper hearing Annie's lament would be to assist her to take constructive action on her own behalf. For many helpees, like Annie their attempts at taking such constructive action is inhibited because of their own lack understanding about the true nature of their problems. Thus, an important step in helping is the process of *focusing*.

Focusing assists the helpee in moving from storytelling toward story understanding. Following the initial exploration stage and the facilitation of helpee's ventilation, the helper needs to assist the helpee to begin to identify and define—in clear, specific, concrete terms—the nature of his or her concern, the nature of his or her problem.

This chapter will discuss the process of focusing. Specifically, the chapter will

1. define and describe the skills of focusing: *clarification, summarization, confrontation,* and *interpretation,* and;
2. provide the reader with guidelines for the effective use of focusing skills.

CLARIFICATION

As the helpee shares his or her story and explores its various dimensions, he or she may employ terms or phrases which lack clear meaning (e.g., "it's like", "they", "them"), or words which have a number of meanings (e.g., "stoned", "trip", "ripped"). Such lack of clarity needs to be addressed by the helper. The use of inclusive (e.g., "they", "them"), ambiguous (e.g., "you know"), or mixed presentations (e.g., "semi-okay") makes it nearly impossible to understand or resolve the helpee's concern. When the helpee presents vague, generalized, or ambiguous descriptions, the helper, through the use of clarification, will invite him or her to elaborate or expand on the topic. Clarification not only assists the helper in developing a fuller understanding of the issue under discussion, but serves as a tool to assist the helper to focus the conversation.

Typically, the helper's request for clarification is posed as an open question and simply asks the helpee to elaborate on something that is vague or ambiguous to the helper. For example, assume that a helpee stated the following:

Helpee: Boy, it make me furious when creeps like him get away with stuff like that!

Obviously, it will be hard to assist the helpee in this situation unless the helper clearly understands what is meant by terms such as "creeps" and "stuff". Through the use of an open question, the helper will attempt to gain a better understanding (i.e., clarification) of what the helpee intends. The helper might say:

Helper: What exactly do you mean when you say "stuff like that"?

A request for clarification from the helper will not only provide a more accurate picture of what it is the helpee is experiencing, but, depending on what it is the helper selects to have clarified, may act to focus the discussion. If you consider the above example, the fact that the helper asked for clarification on the term "stuff", as opposed to the term "creep", will focus the helpee away from a barrage of negative descriptors and criticism of this other person, and invite him or her to speak more about what has actually happened.

Clarification may also prove to be what the helpee is actually seeking, or at least one of the first major steps to problem resolution, since it is often the helpee's lack of clarity about the nature of the problem that adds to his or her feelings of helplessness. As the helpee gains increased clarity about the specific behaviors, attitudes, and factors involved in his or her problem, the feelings of confusion and helplessness diminish.

The use of clarification is thus a key element in the process of helping. To be an effective helper, one needs to resist assuming understanding when the helpee employs generalized, vague, or ambiguous terms. The effective helper develops skills in focusing discussion with a goal of clarification. Exercise 6-1 provides an opportunity to identify vague, generalized, and ambiguous terms and to develop a request for clarification.

EXERCISE 6-1
Clarification

Directions: For each of the following helpee messages, develop a sample clarification response. Before responding, ask yourself:

- What has the helpee told me?
- What parts of the message are either unclear, vague, or possibly missing?
- How can I request information, focusing the helpee on the part I want clarified?

Discuss your response with a colleague or classmate. If you have selected different points for clarification, why? What might be the effect of such different focusing?

1. Helpee: Gads, my grades suck. I don't know what's happening to me.
   Helper: _____

2. Helpee: Okay, so she dumped me. Big deal. I got things under control!
   Helper: _____

3. Helpee: They are always on my back, hassling me. I can't take it anymore, I've had it.
   Helper: _____

SUMMARIZATION

A second way in which a helper can both explore with the helpee and assist the helpee to focus is through the use of summarization. In summarizing, the helper pulls together several ideas or feelings, provided by the helpee, into a succinct, concrete statement which is then reflected to the helpee. Such a summarizing process has been found useful in bringing a discussion around a particular theme to a close, or even to explore a particular theme more thoroughly (Brammer, 1988).

For example, consider the situation of the following helper attempting to respond to a helpee who has a tendency to ramble off in many directions.

Helpee: Wow, what a week. You gotta hear this and then I'll tell you what happened at the job interview—you know the one we prepared for last week.

Well, anyway, it's Monday, and I'm going for this job interview, just like we planned. But you ain't going to believe what happened!

First, I go to get in my car and the battery is dead. So I call road
service and have to wait 45 minutes until they get there. I get a jump and
now I'm off (late, of course) for the meeting. Well, traffic is bumper to
bumper on the expressway. So I'm now a good hour and a half late for
the interview. Oh, but it doesn't end there. Sitting in traffic the car starts
to overheat. Do you believe this? This car is the absolute worst. I've had
nothing but bad luck since I got it last year. The damn thing cost me
$16,000 . . .

Helper (interrupting): It appears that you have had a number of problems
with the car, but in spite of that you seem to suggest you did have the
interview.

The helper's brief summary of the ongoing discussion of the car invites the
helpee to end the discussion of that particular topic and focus on a more thorough
presentation of the experience of the interview.

In addition to closing a discussion or focusing on an aspect to develop, summarization can be used to focus the helpee's scattered thoughts and feelings. As the helpee's
story unfolds, the helper needs to attend to certain consistencies or patterns—of feelings
(e.g., anger, sadness, etc.), behaviors (e.g., avoidance, procrastination, etc.), and experiences (e.g., abandonment, rejection, etc.) shared by the helpee. These consistent patterns, or *themes,* will be repeated or referred to over and over as the helpee shares his or
her story. For example, imagine that in talking with a helpee, you become aware that he
or she has provided four separate instances in his or her life where something negative
has occurred (e.g., lost a job, broke up with a love one, got seriously ill, and was
involved in an accident). Further, each time the helpee discussed one of these events, he
or she referred to him- or herself as an innocent victim. You could use a summarization
to "pull together" these various experiences around this single theme of victimization.
You may suggest, "As you have been talking, I have become aware that you have
spoken consistently about being an innocent victim. Perhaps this issue of being an
innocent victim is one which you might want to focus on?"

Inviting the helpee to consider the possible existence of a pattern or theme in his
or her experiences may begin to move him or her to fuller understanding of him- or
herself, as opposed to simply attending to a discussion of what at first appears to be a
set of separate, unconnected events.

As evident in the examples provided, summarization requires the helper to

1. attend to and recall varying verbal and nonverbal messages presented by the
   helpee;
2. identify specific themes, issues, and feelings conveyed by the helpee; and
3. extract the key or core ideas and feelings expressed and integrate them into a
   concrete statement.

As with many of the skills of helping, summarization is not an easy skill to
employ. It is one, however, that becomes easier and more effective with practice.
Exercise 6-2 is provided to assist you in that practice.

EXERCISE 6-2
Developing Summarizations

Directions: For each of the following helpee presentations consider the follow-ing questions and develop a simple, concrete summarizing statement. Share your summaries with a colleague or classmate and discuss points of similarity and difference. In your discussion identify the possible impact each summari-zation may have on the direction of the helping encounter. Questions to con-sider in preparing your summaries are:

1. What is the message the helpee is sending? What are the key elements? (feelings? content?)
2. Is there a recurrent message? (i.e., patterns, themes?)
3. Which of the helpee's words can I incorporate into a summary statement?

Helpee 1: I've tried to speak with him but he just won't listen. It is so frustrat-ing. It's like he has his mind made up and what I feel just isn't important. Maybe I'm not important. It's been like that since we've been married.
Summarization: _____

_____

_____

Helpee 2: (this is the third time you have met, and each time you come up with a plan of action the helpee comes up with an excuse as to why he or she can't do it) Boy, I bet you are going to be pissed off! I know we decided last week that I would contact the career center and begin to schedule for that vocational test, but I had so many projects to do this week that I just couldn't get down there. It wasn't my fault that the frat had rush scheduled for the first week—you know I have to be available for that. And okay, so maybe last week I could have gotten down there, but I was hurting with my allergies. But this is different. I really had a lot to do.
Summarization: _____

_____

_____

Helpee 3: I really feel like such a wimp. I can't seem to assert myself. I am at work and I am using the copier and George comes over and simply takes over. He says, "You don't mind do you? I only need a couple of copies", and before I can say anything, he pulls my stuff out and sticks his in. I don't understand why a company our size only has one machine. I mean, we have to do a lot of copying. Don't you thinks it makes sense to invest in more than one copier? In fact, the one we use is even too small to handle all the load—it is always breaking down. Boy, it can be frustrating.
Summarization: _____

_____

_____

CONFRONTATION

In addition to clarification and summarization, a third skill to be employed by the effective helper in focusing the helpee is the skill of confrontation. When attempting to understand the value and use of confrontation in helping, the helper must overcome the general tendency to equate the word "confrontation" with that of a destructive, aggressive, hostile act. Confrontation when used within a helping context does not take the form of lecturing, judging, or punishing. These are examples of the abuse of confrontation, rather than the appropriate use of confrontation. Within the context of a helping relationship, confrontation represents an *invitation* by one participant to have the other participant look at, discuss, clarify, or reconsider some event occurring within the helping exchange. It is truly an invitation to explore all the facets of what is being presented. When done by a helper who is empathic, genuine, and respectful of the helpee, such confrontation can actually facilitate the helpee's own self-exploration.

For example, we have all had occasion, while talking with a friend, to question a point he or she made where we had contradictory information. Imagine the following dialogue between two students:

> John: Gads, how will we ever get through this assignment, especially when we have to go on that training seminar this weekend!
>
> Mary: Gee, I may be wrong, but I thought the memo said that the training seminar was next weekend!

The interaction, while not a hostile, attacking, or destructive exchange, is nonetheless confrontational. In fact it reflects a particular type of confrontation called a *didactic* (informational) confrontation—a confrontation in which one member of the dialogue invited the other member to reconsider his or her position in light of this more accurate information.

Typically, confrontations are useful when the helper experiences

1. an inconsistency between what the helpee says and how he or she behaves. For example, perhaps the helpee states that he or she finds it difficult to talk, and yet is disclosing freely and with apparent ease and comfort to the helper.
2. a discrepancy between what the helpee "knows" to be true, and the evidence or facts as the helper knows them. This was the case with the previous example regarding the training weekend.
3. a contradiction between the verbal and nonverbal expressions of helpee's emotions. This may be the case when the helpee states that "nothing is bothering" him or her, and yet at the same time he or she is grinding his or her teeth, clenching his or her fist, and hitting the table with his or her hand.
4. an inconsistency between two pieces of information the helpee presents verbally. An example of this is in the situation where a helpee says he or she wants to be a good student and then states he or she never does homework or studies.

These four situations illustrate when a helper should seek clarification of the inconsistencies, contradictions, or discrepancies; however, in reality confrontation occurs any time we call to question another's behavior, attitude, or feelings. Since confrontations are inevitable, the effective helper will need to understand the elements which make a confrontation productive, facilitative, and relationship-building, rather than destructive and attacking.

In attempting to confront a helpee, the effective helper will consider each of the following guidelines:

1. Present the apparent discrepancy or inconsistency in a tentative manner. Since it is our perception versus another's, and not necessarily absolute facts that we are discussing, we need to present our confrontation as our tentative feelings or opinion about the event. What appears to us to be an inconsistency may in fact be totally consistent from the helpee's point of view.

    This need to be tentative in our conclusions is especially important when confronting a helpee in the early stages of the helping relationship. During the early stages, we as helpers may not have a full grasp of the helpee's world and thus misread experiences they share.

2. Keep a clear sense of the motive for our confrontation. Pointing out a discrepancy or an inconsistency in hopes of embarrassing or humiliating another will certainly be confrontational, but not helpful. The confrontation, to be helpful, needs to be presented from a helping, caring, and supportive intention or motive. It should reflect our desire to clarify and understand rather than exhibit power or oneupmanship.

3. Use descriptive, non-judgmental language and tone in your presentation, rather than a judgmental and labeling style. The helper is not trying to evaluate the helpee. Rather, the helper's goal is to describe his or her own experience and points of confusion with hopes that the helpee provide clarification.

4. Consider how the confrontation will be received. The confrontation should be presented in a way that maximizes the other's ability to receive it. While the above characteristics will assist, it is also important to provide the confrontation from a perspective of empathy for the other. The helper needs to consider how his or her confrontation will appear to the helpee.

    The helper needs to ask him- or herself how receptive or open he or she would be to this confrontation if he or she were in the helpee's shoes at this time.

    Keeping this perspective of the helpee as a guideline, the helper may find that it is more helpful to present the confrontation in small specific steps, rather than to dump one large, general blast of issues on the helpee.

    The focus here is to "pace" the confrontation so that it can be received and "absorbed" by the helpee. (see Chapter 9)

The helper who, from a perspective of empathy with the helpee, can *descriptively* and *tentatively* point out areas of helpee misinformation or mixed and confusing messages can constructively move the helping relationship to a greater level of accuracy and clarity. This is the essence of a helping confrontation. For example, the confrontation presented in the training seminar example moved the interaction to a clearer, and more accurate communication. However, that confrontation would have been less productive and much more destructive to the relationship if Mary had stated, "You are really a nerd! You never read anything. The training memo said . . . the training seminar is NEXT weekend. . . . WAKE UP!"

Even when we attempt to follow the guidelines to appropriate confrontation, our confrontation still may be less than productive or effective. The real proof of effectiveness is not in the degree to which all the "correct" elements were present, but rather the degree to which the desired effect was achieved.

If the helpee attempts to discredit the statement, or argue the point, or devalue the importance of the confrontation, he or she may be giving evidence that the confrontation was too much for him or her to accept, and thus is unsuccessful. Remember that the purpose of the confrontation is to move the helpee to a clearer and more accurate understanding of what he or she is experiencing. When this happens, the helpee is likely to openly accept and consider the confrontation, rather than deny or defend against it. So the proof of the effectiveness of the confrontation is in the response of the helpee! Exercise 6-3 will assist you in employing the previous guidelines to formulate your confrontation. As you formulate the confrontations, consider the possible impact your comment may have on the helpee.

INTERPRETATION

The final skill to be discussed in this chapter is that of interpreting. As the helper continues to attend to the helpee's story, he or she may begin to gain an insight into some underlying meaning, connections, or themes which are being described by the helpee. Interpreting is a process employed by a helper to provide feedback to a helpee, so that he or she is able to see his or her story in a different light—a light that shines on these meanings, connections, and themes.

According to Brammer, Shostrom, and Abrego (1989, p. 175), interpretation involves "presenting the client with a *hypothesis* about *relationships* or *meanings* among his or her behaviors." It is a process by which the helper provides the helpee with a fresh look at him- or herself, or with another explanation for his or her attitudes and behaviors (Ivey, Gluckstern, & Ivey, 1992).

Unlike reflective listening, where the helper was attempting to provide the helpee with feedback about his or her own frame of reference—the helpee's *explicit message*—the process of *interpreting* is one of offering the helpee a new frame of reference from which to view the problem or his or her life situation, highlighting the *implied messages and themes.*

The concept of interpretation as part of the helping process is most often discussed in the context of more formal and enduring counseling or therapy relation-

EXERCISE 6-3
Helpful Confrontations

Directions: Complete an appropriate confrontation for each of the following. Be sure to

- consider the perspective of the helpee;
- use descriptive language;
- provide small steps of confrontation; and
- have your tone reflect your helping intentions.

1. Helpee: I'd like to ask her out (smiling), but she's probably too busy (looking anxious).
   Helper: _____

   _____

2. Helpee: My dad really bugs me—he will never let me grow up.
   Helper: _____

   _____

3. Helpee: I'm really going to do well this semester—but I really need to sleep in today. Missing one class won't hurt.
   Helper: _____

   _____

4. Helpee: NO! There's NOTHING wrong! Get off my back!
   Helper: _____

   _____

ships. In that context, the helper's interpretation usually reflects his or her particular theory or model of helping. This frame of reference or theory (e.g., client-centered, gestalt, behavioral, cognitive, etc.) will clearly "flavor" the interpretation, and a brief discussion of these theoretical models will be presented in Chapter 13. However, even in less formal helping encounters, the helper may at times derive some assumptions or hypotheses about the real issue or theme underlying the helpee's story. For example, consider the helpee who complains about a series of "bad luck" in relationships. She has been seriously involved with a man who is abusive, previously involved with one who was an alcoholic, another who was a gambler, and is now developing a relationship with one who is a womanizer. A helper might hypothesize (interpret) that it is not so much bad luck that is causing her problems, but her own attraction to destructive relationships. Interpreting the connection between separate events, experiences, or behaviors as they may reflect a pattern or theme for the helpee can be a potentially useful tool for the helper to employ.

Consider the exchange between two friends:

Tina: You know I really care for Julio. He is probably the first person I have ever felt so close to. It is really different than when I was engaged to Roy, or even Jim. But I don't know, maybe it's getting too serious . . . too fast.

Maria: Tina, you and Julio have been dating now for over two years. And you are starting to back off from this relationship like you have with others. Is it possible that you're feeling anxious about this relationship with Julio because you are afraid of making a commitment?

Interpretations can also be used when the helper wishes to point out what he or she believes to be the connection among the various helpee behaviors, ideas, or events. Consider the situation where a helper notes that the helpee "becomes extremely anxious about succeeding at a variety of tests and tasks. While the tests and tasks differ, they all seem to be tied to gaining the approval of another person. It is as if, without the approval and acceptance of the other, the helpee feels that he or she is unacceptable and valueless as a human being. Therefore, the helpee approaches each task, seeing it as not simply a test, but as a test of his or her ultimate worthwhileness." As a second example, consider the following exchange between a helper and helpee in a college setting.

Helpee: I'm failing everything! Gads, are my parents furious! (relaxed, smiling)

Helper: When you state your parents are furious, you seem to smile. It appears that you want to make them angry and are enjoying making them furious?

When such connections or interpretations are offered with *appropriate timing and style,* they can prove quite useful—even in these less-than-formal helping relationships.

Presenting an Interpretation

Your style of interpretation should be molded by the same principles and guidelines used for creating an appropriate confrontation. Interpretations should be done with the proper intention and motivation: exhibiting an empathic "eye" to the helpee, employing descriptive language, and provided tentatively and in small steps. The timing of an interpretation should dictated by the helpee's readiness to explore or examine him- or herself.

Since interpretations are by definition conclusions drawn from the helper's perspective, a helpee's openness to such interpretation comes only after

1. a working relationship between the helper and helpee has been developed;
2. the helpee feels safe and not vulnerable with the helper; and,

3. the helpee has experienced the helper's accurate understanding of his or her situation.

Such readiness usually only occurs in the later stages of the helping relationship, after the helper has established the supportive environment and generally demonstrated non-judgmental understanding of the helpee.

In preparing to make an interpretation, the effective helper will consider the following guidelines:

1. Extract the central message or theme running through the various pieces of information the helpee has provided.
2. Provide the helpee with a summary of the points shared in the relationship.
3. Share his or her understanding of what the helpee is saying, as a HYPOTHESIS to be considered. The helper should formulate his or her feedback or interpretation with *a slightly different* view or frame of reference from that of the helpee.
4. Try to present the interpretation in a way that highlights the positive and the opportunities for growth or change.
5. Finally, look to the helpee's reaction as a measure of the effectiveness of the helper's interpretation. Is the helpee open and receptive or resistant and defensive?

As suggested in the above guidelines, it is important to base your interpretation on the actual data provided by the helpee, and not on your own bias, personal agenda, or issues. For example, if you had a bad experience with a relationship and generally believe that people should stay out of intimate, exclusive relationships until they are out of college, it may be hard for you to support the implied interest and valuing of a particular relationship that a helpee is discussing. Thus, rather than understanding that the helpee's message is really "Our relationship is going through a tough period, but I guess I should stick it out . . . it's important to me", you may interpret the message as "The relationship is in trouble, as are all exclusive relationships at this young an age. It's sad, but give it up. Wait until later in life."

Interpretation, as is the case with confrontation, is effective when it facilitates the understanding and focusing of the problem. An interpretation is ineffective if it blocks the free and open exchange of information. If our interpretation is met with a resistant, defensive stance by the helpee, then it is ineffective. Under these conditions, the interpretation may simply be inaccurate. However, it may also be, that while the interpretation was correct, the manner or timing of presentation was such that it created a defensiveness on the part of the helpee. As Brammer, Shostrom and Abrego (1989) suggest, even a useful and valid interpretation may be met with resistance. When resisted, it is useful to back off and repeat the interpretation at a more appropriate time, with additional supporting material and perhaps in a slightly different form.

It is essential to remember that the goal of interpretation is *not to prove I (the helper) am right,* but rather for the helpee to gain *new personal insights and self-interpretation!* To paraphrase one theorist, Karl Menninger (1958), it is more useful to time the interpretation and present it in such a way that helpee, not the helper, takes credit for the discovery.

Exercise 6-4 will enable you to practice making effective, helpful interpretations.

EXERCISE 6-4
The Art of Interpreting

Directions: For each of the following presentations develop an interpretation, highlighting either the underlying issues or themes present or the possible connections between the various elements. In preparing your interpretation, remember to follow the guidelines:

1. Extract the central message or theme (implied)
2. Provide the helpee with a summary (explicit)
3. Share your HYPOTHESES
4. Highlight the positive

Share your interpretations with a colleague or classmate, noting your points of similarity and differences and speculating on the differential effect on the helpee or the helping relationship of these different interpretations.

Scenario 1

Helpee: The helpee is a 22-year-old college senior who has come to you expressing feelings of depression. The helpee notes that he has been actively involved in college (joining professional organization, fraternity, playing intramural sports, and chairing senior homecoming), has always had energy, and felt joy in school—and really doesn't understand why he feels so down, so crappy! He states: "I don't understand it . . . I hate ending my college career feeling so crappy, especially when it has been the best four years of my life!"

Step 1: Identify the *implied* portion of his message.

_____

Step 2: Reframe his *explicit* observations in such a way as to reflect what he said, but adding a slightly different focus or view on the issue.

_____

Step 3: Write out an *interpretation* which will be empathic, descriptive, tentative, positive, and in a tone which provides the helpee a positive expectation of an opportunity for growth.

_____

EXERCISE 6-4 *Continued*

Scenario 2

Helpee: A woman who has been married to a man for 30 years, states: "He is such a sweet guy. A good provider, never abusive. Everybody loves him. I should be happy but I'm not. No one will understand why I am unhappy. I don't know what's wrong with me. How could I ever think about leaving him? But I don't know if I could stay—I really don't love him."

Step 1: Identify the *implied* portion of her message.

_____

_____

Step 2: Reframe her *explicit* observations in such a way as to reflect what she said, but adding a slightly different focus or view on the issue.

_____

_____

Step 3: Write out an *interpretation* which will be empathic, descriptive, tentative, positive, and in a tone which provides the helpee a positive expectation of an opportunity for growth.

_____

_____

WHAT NEXT

The process of focusing and moving the helpee toward clarifying the problem is an essential step in the helping dynamic, but it is not always actively embraced by the helpee.

While the helpee may come to the helping relationship with a sense of exploration, we may find that as we begin to focus on the specifics, the themes, and the underlying issues, the helpee may show some resistance and even defensiveness.

Quite often a person who has been experiencing difficulty comes to the helping encounter having developed techniques and strategies which help him or her avoid emotional pain. However, during this phase of the helping process—through our use of the skills of clarifying, summarizing, confronting, and interpreting—we invite the helpee to lower those defenses in order to develop a new style and awareness. Such an invitation to lower defenses may be met with resistance.

At these times when we encounter defensiveness and resistance, it is essential that we remind ourselves of our purpose and goal. We must remember that our purpose is not to be right, to find the answer, or to solve the problem. Our purpose is to assist the helpee.

If our interpretations or confrontations are met with resistance, we need to back off.

We need to see our helpee's resistance as a request for more time, more space, and more evidence that this is (can be) a supportive, non-judgmental, genuine relationship.

Even though we are presenting the helping relationship as a stepwise activity of problem identification and problem solving, it is important to remember that the essence of helping is the context of the relationship. The skills we discussed in the previous chapters, aimed at building a helping alliance, need to be present consistently in our encounter.

So as we ask the question "what next?", we must be mindful not only to look ahead to the skills involved in developing and implementing problem-solving strategies, but also to look back and recommit to the relationship skills so essential to helping.

REFERENCES AND RECOMMENDED READINGS

Brammer, L.M. (1988). *The helping relationship.* Englewood Cliffs, NJ: Prentice-Hall.

Brammer, L.M., Shostrom, E.L., & Abrego, P.J. (1989). *Therapeutic psychology: Fundamentals of counseling and problem-solving skills.* New York: Haworth Press.

Claiborn, C.D. (1982). Interpretation and change in counseling. *Journal of Counseling Psychology, 29,* 439–453.

Hein, E.C. (1980). *Communications in nursing practice* (2nd edition). Boston: Little, Brown.

Gelso, C.J., & Fretz, B.R. (1992). *Counseling psychology.* New York: Harcourt Brace Jovanovich.

Ivey, A.E., & Gluckstern, N. (1976). *Basic attending skills: Participants' manual.* Amherst, MA: Microtraining Associates.

Ivey, A.E., Gluckstern, N., & Ivey, M. (1992). *Basic attending skills* (3rd edition). Amherst, MA: Microtraining Associates.

Menninger, K. (1958). *Theory of psychoanalytic technique.* New York: Harper & Row.

Mehrabian, A. (1970). *Tactics of social influence.* Englewood Cliffs, NJ: Prentice-Hall.

Pierce, R. M., & Dragow, J. (1969). Nondirective reflection vs. conflict attention: An empirical evaluation. *Journal of Clinical Psychology, 25,* 341–342.

▶ 7

From Problems to Goals

Up to this point, we have focused on the reasons for establishing a helping relationship, as well as the skills needed to formulate and maintain such a relationship. A supportive, genuine, trusting, and non-evaluative relationship is important if the helpee is going to risk sharing his or her story and exploring his or her concerns.

However, the intent of helping goes beyond simply "relating" or being a "helping listener". In most cases the helpee seeks out a helping relationship because he or she experiences something as wrong or bothersome in his or her life. It is clear that the helpee wants things to be different than they are.

This chapter will discuss the helper skills and processes used in assisting the helpee to move from feelings of concern to the clear formulation of achievable and helpful goals. Specifically, the chapter will

1. present a multi-dimensional model for defining a helpee's problem and articulating helping goals;
2. discuss a decision model for establishing priorities in goal setting; and
3. provide guidelines for establishing clear, achievable helping goals.

HELPING AS A GOAL-ORIENTED PROCESS

The focus taken within this text is that helping IS a goal-oriented process. Assisting the helpee to share and elaborate upon his or her problem is only one of the many important steps in the helping process.

Following such a ventilation and disclosure of the helpee's concerns, the helper needs to assist the helpee to

1. define the nature and scope of that problem concretely;
2. set priorities among the various problems, and translate these problems into attainable, observable goals.

Consider the case of Lori, to which we will refer throughout this chapter.

Lori

Lori is a 27-year-old single female who recently came for counseling because of feeling "very sad about breaking up with her boyfriend". As the story unfolded the helper discovered that Lori had even contemplated killing herself over the breakup. She noted, "Look, if he doesn't love me, no one will! I can't stand living my life all alone. I am worthless, just taking up space and time, waiting to die anyway."

Lori told the helper that she has always felt insecure and sees herself as needing to rely on others to make important decisions for her or take care of her. "I know I shouldn't, but I am constantly calling my one and only friend, Sherri, and crying on her shoulder. But I need her to tell me what to do!" Further, since the breakup, Lori has basically withdrawn from the friends she has met through her ex-boyfriend. She reports having difficulty sleeping and has not been eating. Lori told the helper that she is losing weight, has headaches almost everyday, and feels sick to her stomach most of the time.

In Lori's situation, simply helping her to identify her sad feelings would not be enough. While the identification of such feelings and even the events associated with them are necessary and of value to the helping process, they are not sufficient. Helping is a process, an action, aimed at achieving some type of goal or outcome.

While we, as helpers, may assume we know the outcomes or goals desired by the helpee, it is not for us to assume. It is for us, along with the helpee, to know! Often, what appears to be the "obvious" goal or outcome is not in fact the one sought by the helpee. For example, let's reconsider Lori's situation. For purposes of our discussion, we will assume that Lori's sadness could be the result of one of the two different situations. While on the surface, both situations involve the loss of a boyfriend, the actual goals or outcomes desired differ greatly from one situation to the next.

In the first situation, Lori's sadness, while clearly associated with the breakup with her boyfriend is, in fact, a manifestation of her feeling alone now that she has less opportunity to be socially active, since "all of her current friends are dating and go out as couples". In the second situation, however, Lori's sadness is a function of her belief that losing this one boyfriend is evidence that she is not an attractive or desirable person, and therefore will spend the rest of her life alone and unloved. Under these conditions, Lori feels that she would rather die than live such a life.

In listening to Lori's story, the effective helper will identify the goals desired. In each situation, whether the goal is finding ways to connect socially (as in scenario 1), or developing self-esteem and positive self-concept (as suggested in scenario 2), these goals will: 1) provide the helper and helpee with a direction to pursue in the process of helping; 2) direct the helper and the helpee in their selection and use of the various strategies available, and even 3) enable a helper to determine whether or not he or she has the skills, abilities, or desire to help this particular person. As is evident in this one case illustration, the clear, concrete establishment of goals is an essential step in the helping process.

DEFINING THE NATURE AND SCOPE OF THE PROBLEM

Frequently, by the time a person seeks help, his or her problem has been distorted, his or her direction clouded, and his or her problem-solving abilities paralyzed. More often than not, what is presented is a somewhat loose set of concerns or problems. This was certainly true of Lori's initial encounter with the helper.

> Lori: I feel so absolutely yucky, nothing is going right. I hate my job. I have no money. I am wasting my life, I'm stuck at home still living with my parents and now my boyfriend dumps me!
> Helper: Nothing is going right?
> Lori: Well, that's how it seems. I am 27 years old, a college graduate, and I am still living at home. With this dumb job I have I can't even get an apartment. It didn't seem so bad when at least I had the distraction of a boyfriend . . . now even that is over. I just can't stand it any more! I have absolutely no future, why bother?

As noted in the previous chapter, often the initial description of the problem by the helpee can be vague and disjointed. Even the helper's initial attempts at clarifying the specific scope of the problem may result in a continued listing of loosely connected issues.

Before alternative strategies, approaches, or solutions to the problem can be found (Chapter 8), the helpee needs to have an accurate picture of the nature and scope of the problem. The helpee needs to define the relevant issues, behaviors, and elements which are supporting (if not creating) this problem. Once these vague feelings of concern are translated into concrete, specific definitions of how things are, then the helper can assist the helpee in articulating how would like things to be (goals).

BASIC ID ~Essay ?~

While there are many interesting and varied approaches to problem definition, one which I have found to be comprehensive, and which I feel leads to concrete conceptualization about solutions, is that presented by Arnold Lazarus (1981, 1986, 1989).

Lazarus presents a model he terms *multimodal.* The essence of his multimodal approach is that a person's functioning or dysfunctioning can be defined as manifesting within seven areas, or modalities: **behavior, affect, sensations, images, cognition, interpersonal relationships and drugs** (or biological functions). Using the acronym **BASIC**

ID to represent these various modalities, Lazarus argues that a complete identification of a helpee's problem must take into account each modality of this BASIC ID. Therefore, the first step in our process of problem definition starts with the comprehensive assessment of each of these modalities of human functioning, as they relate to the helpee's presenting complaint. Because of the value of this model, each modality is described below, along with the type of questions to be posed and considered by the helper (Lazarus, 1989) in attempting to define the helpee's problem.

B: Behavior

For Lazarus, it is important to be mindful of areas of behavioral excess (e.g., helpee drinks too much? interrupts too often?) and deficit (e.g., doesn't initiate conversation, fails to do homework, etc.). Thus, it is important to begin to identify how it is that the helpee "acts". What does he or she DO and what are the conditions under which he or she acts or behaves differently?

In regards to the helpee's presenting concern, what behaviors do he or she exhibit, or fail to exhibit, and which appear part of the problem experienced? Asking the helpee questions such as "What would you like to do, or stop doing?" or "What specific behaviors keep you from getting what you want?" will help to identify habits or behaviors which need to be targeted for change.

Consider Lori's situation. Lori suggested that she is saddened by the fact that she and her boyfriend have ended the relationship. As a result of this, Lori reports that she cries a lot, calls her only girlfriend "to cry on her shoulder" and finds herself "withdrawing" from friends and social interaction. Thus, in defining Lori's "sadness", you would want to include these behaviors as possible areas for change.

In looking at the helpee's behavior, we must also consider what events (antecedents) lead up to his or her acting a certain way, and similarly, what are the results (consequences) of his or her actions? Oftentimes, a person's behavior is heavily influenced (if not caused) by these antecedents and consequences. For example, if every time Lori cried, her friends immediately rushed to her side and showed her extra special concern, it might be hypothesized that Lori's crying behavior was being "rewarded" by the special attention she received. Such an understanding not only clarifies the nature of the problem, but also may help Lori and the helper identify other ways of gaining the support and the attention she would like to have.

Those interested in more fully understanding the relationships between behavior and antecedent and consequential events are referred to the work of behavioral theorists such as Watson and Tharp (1989) or Wilson, Franks, Kendall, and Foreyt (1987).

A: Affect

When most people think of helping, they generally envision someone asking the helpee, "How do you feel about that?" Feelings are important aspects of the human experience and thus need to be identified, especially as they are tied to presenting complaint. However, identifying feelings, in and of itself, is not sufficient. The helper needs to be attentive to those feelings which are reported and those which are never or rarely noted. The helpee needs to consider the degree to which the feelings appear appropriate to the situation, as well as the degree or intensity with which the feelings are experienced. Questions such as "Are these emotions overdone and the helpee too sensitive?" or "Are the helpee's feelings being blunted, somewhat insensitive, or underdone?" need to be considered by the helper. Also, the helper needs to consider the degree of control (too much, too little) the helpee exhibits in the expression of his or her feelings.

Perhaps the sadness Lori is experiencing is appropriate following a loss, but is it proportional to the actual loss? Does Lori experience the loss in other ways, other than sadness? Does she feel depressed, hopeless? Does she find any pleasure in the activities she liked prior to the breakup? Finding the answers to this type of questions not only clarifies the depth and breadth of the problem, but begins to identify goals and outcomes desired.

S: Sensation

When considering the helpee's sensations, we are obviously concerned about the five major senses, and the degree to which the helpee is accurately receiving the signals around him or her, but we also need to listen to the degree to which their problem is presented in the form of body sensations (e.g., nausea, dizziness, headaches, etc.) For example, when Lori speaks of being upset, does she also mean that she feels sick to her stomach, or has headaches or muscle tension?

The sensations the helpee reports may be valuable for two reasons. First, as with the other modalities, identifying sensations associated with the concern more clearly defines the nature of the problem and how it is experienced. Secondly, the identification of such sensations may even provide us with an earlier diagnostic-warning system, as when a person experiences a muscular tension (in neck) before becoming very angry. Such an early warning system could be useful in developing strategies for reducing the problem.

I: Imagery

For Lazarus, imagery involves the various mental pictures that seem to influence our life. For example, the student who "sees" himself as being laughed at may tend to withdraw from volunteering an answer in class, or the person who may "see" him- or herself as fat, even after losing weight, may still act and feel fat. Having a better understanding of the way the client "sees" him- or herself and his or her world is useful information. It not only reflects a part of the helpee's concern, but it can also suggest a helpful goal to be achieved. Questions such as "What bothersome dreams or memories do you have?" "How do you view yourself? " "How do you view your future?" may begin to reveal such imagery. Again, consider Lori.

As noted, she has withdrawn from social interaction (behavior), and in fact feels faint and sick to her stomach when approached with the idea of going out (sensation). As Lori continues disclosing in the helping encounter, she reports actually "seeing him (her ex-boyfriend) standing there in front of (her) and saying, 'Lori, I am seeing somebody else and I want to end this relationship'." Lori states, "I can't get that image out of my mind". Clearly this image plays an important role in the overall problem Lori is experiencing. Further, helping Lori remove or reshape that image would be a very valuable goal for the helping encounter.

C: Cognitions

The "C" in Lazarus' BASIC ID stands for cognitions. Cognitions are our thoughts, beliefs, or ways of making meaning out of our experience. Often, the way we interpret our experience is inaccurate. We need to learn to identify when our thinking is distorted, and thus learn to correct it.

The effective helper needs to unearth the helpee's cognitive patterns as a part of his or her overall experience of the problem. Seeking the answers to questions, such as "What does this mean to the helpee?" "What assumptions about him- or herself, his or her world, is he or she making?" will provide a clearer picture of the helpee's cognitive orientation.

For example, while the experience of loss which Lori has had is one which is both undesirable and disappointing, it is not unbearable, nor does it provide evidence of her unlovability. As Lori noted, "Look, if he doesn't love me, no one will!" This interpretation of this one experience as evidence of her unlovability is certainly a distortion of reality. Such a distortion exaggerates both the importance of this event and leads to an exaggerated sense of pain over the situation. Further, correcting such a distorted interpretation would prove to be a very useful and helpful goal.

I: Interpersonal Relationships

As "social animals", how we behave, or not behave, with others is an essential element of our human experience. We need to begin to assess how the helpee approaches others, responds to others, and communicates with others.

In assessing the interpersonal modality, the helper may come to understand how this component both reflects the problem experienced and contributes to it. Again, in the case of Lori, we come to understand that she becomes overly dependent on her friends. This tendency to be overly dependent in relationships can certainly increase the experience of anxiety and concern when Lori has no relationship to depend upon. Further, Lori's style of being overly dependent and demanding in a relationship may have actually contributed to eventual breakup with her boyfriend. Perhaps she was coming on "more strongly" or "more intensely" than her boyfriend wanted or was willing to give back. Thus, a useful goal for this helping relationship would be to assist Lori not only learn to be independent and self-reliant, but also to assist her to approach relationships from a position of interdependence, rather than of dependence.

D: Drugs (Biology)

While the "D" certainly does complete the acronym it may be a bit misleading. Lazarus is not focusing only on drugs. He is suggesting that we consider the nonpsychological aspects of a person's experience. We need to consider the helpee's diet, general health and well being, and general physiology (hormones, nervous system, etc.).

As a helper, we may not be trained to intervene with organic conditions, but we need to increase our awareness of the affect of substances (such as chemicals, food additives, or even natural substances such as caffeine) and physiology (e.g., hormones) in creating problems in our lives. In Lori's case, the helper needs to consider whether Lori's reaction may be associated with her menstrual cycle, or her recent dieting. Does Lori's emotional response pattern, her apparent depression, have any possible connection with any medicine she may be taking, or has stopped taking? Again, seeking the answers to such questions not only gives the helper a more complete picture of the depth and breadth of the problem but also begins to provide clarity about the goals to be achieved.

While the purist may wish to define a helpee's problem in terms of each of these seven modalities, what is being suggested here is that the BASIC ID model is a useful template, or guide, for systematically assessing the helpee's situation. Whether the helpee employs seven or fewer modalities, such a model enables the helper to define the nature and scope of the clients concern more specifically and concretely, as the first step to formulating useful and achievable goals and outcomes. What follows is an illustration demonstrating the use and value of problem defining using the model of the BASIC ID.

An Example of Problem Definition—Todd

Presenting Concern: Todd came to counseling because he was ". . . not very happy with (his) life".

Exploring and Clarifying the Concern: Todd is a 32-year-old male, who states that he is approximately 40 lbs overweight and is somewhat "concerned about this weight thing". Todd noted that he leads a relatively sedentary life, somewhat of a "couch potato". Overall he feels he is in good health (with the exception of the weight), but does have some muscle tension in his chest and mild stomach upset ("gas") periodically.

He came to the counselor because he is ". . . not very happy with his life."

Through the initial interviews, Todd disclosed that he had been previously in a marriage that lasted five years, but has been divorced from his wife for the last three years. Todd expressed feeling ashamed talking about this marriage, since, as he stated, "I am such a sap". "I was married for five years, and from day one, she was having affairs with other guys". "I feel like such a fool!"

Todd also admitted that this is not the first time he felt abused or victimized in a relationship . "Everybody seems to take advantage of me. I am such a nice guy, I guess it is easy to put one over on me!" "I just don't know how to say NO! I never could . . . After all, who wants somebody to get angry with you?" He often has dreams of magically becoming famous and powerful so that people respect him and never abuse him. Since the end of the marriage, Todd reports being more withdrawn, more non-social and is now recognizing that he is very lonely.

Modality Profile:

B: (behavior)	• overeating
	• withdrawal from social contact
A: (affect)	• alone/lonely
	• anxious about weight
S: (sensation)	• muscle tension in chest
	• stomach—gas?
I: (image)	• sees self as victim
	• sees self as "sap"
	• fantasizes about power and fame (magically derived)
C: (cognition)	• believes he can't say NO
	• believes others' disapproval is totally unacceptable
I: (interpersonal relationships)	• exploited by others at work
	• exploited by ex-wife
	• withdrawing from social contact
d: (drugs/biology)	• overweight (40 lbs)
	• stomach upset
	• headaches
	• good health, yet sedentary life style

Moving from the original presentation of "not being very happy with (his) life", the helper, using the BASIC ID model, was able to redefine in more concrete, manageable terms, the various components or facets of this "unhappiness". Such redefinition of the nature and scope of the problem will better enable the helper and helpee to begin to conceptualize both goals they would like to achieve and strategies for achieving them.

In order to develop the skills of problem definition, follow the case of Todd as a model and redefine the presenting concern as offered in the case of Kathy (Exercise 7-1).

SETTING PRIORITIES AND FINDING A PLACE TO START

With such a broad framework with which to identify and define a helpee's problem, we may become overwhelmed by the number of concerns or issues which need to be addressed. But if we approach it as if it were a large jigsaw puzzle, one piece at a time, the connection and relationship between the various pieces become clearer as the larger picture takes shape.

EXERCISE 7-1
Problem Defining with BASIC ID

The Case of Kathy

Directions: Using the case of Todd as a model, review the data provided below, and translate the presenting concerns into the specific modalities involved.

Presenting Concern: Kathy is a 19-year-old college sophomore, majoring in elementary education. She has come to the college counseling center because lately she has "been feeling weird".

Exploring and Clarifying the Concern: Using relationship skills and skills which facilitated exploration and focusing, the counselor helped Kathy define what she meant by "feeling weird".

Kathy noted that for the last two months she has been having trouble staying asleep. She wakes up in the middle of the night and can't seem to get back to sleep. She stated that sometimes she is awakened by a recurring nightmare in which she sees herself as a teacher, who for some reason "all the parents hate and are trying to hurt." This really frightens her, since she "really loves kids" and "needs to be liked by them". She worries that these dreams may come true, and that she "will never become a successful teacher".

Kathy also reported that she will be sitting in class sometimes, and for no apparent reason, she begins to feel her heart race and she feels dizzy. Then she begins to worry that she is going to pass out or something else which would be a "total embarrassment".

As the counselor probed, Kathy reported that within the last few months several other things have changed in her life. She had recently gone on a dieting program, hoping to go from her current 130 lbs to about 110 lbs. Her diet is one that all her sorority sisters use—it involves calorie reduction to 1000 calories a day and the elimination of all red meats. Also as part of her weight reduction program, she has begun a relatively rigorous exercise program which includes running 3 miles a day, and lifting weights every other day.

Modality Profile:
B: (behavior) _____

_____

_____

A: (affect) _____

_____

S: (sensation) _____

_____

_____

Continued

EXERCISE 7-1 *Continued*

I: (imagery) _____

_____

_____

C: (cognition) _____

_____

I: (interpersonal relationships) _____

_____

D: (drugs/biology) _____

_____

_____

Exercise 7-2 will assist you in beginning to recognize and identify the complexity and multifaceted nature of a presenting complaint, as well as in seeing how the various pieces begin to fit together.

EXERCISE 7-2
Identifying the Many Sides of a Problem

Directions: Below you will find the listing of presenting complaints for each of the major cases referred to in this chapter. Identify three aspects, dimensions, or facets which could serve as separate problems or targets for intervention for each of these cases. You may want to remember the BASIC ID as you search for the facets of the problems. Discuss your observations with a colleague or classmate. Did you focus on different facets of the problem? If so, were you aware of the other facets?

Lori: "very sad about breaking up with (her) boyfriend"
        Dimensions/facets of this problem: _____

_____

Todd: "not very happy with his life"
        Dimensions/facets of this problem: _____

_____

Kathy: "been feeling weird"
        Dimensions/facets of this problem: _____

_____

In working with a helpee, it should be obvious that we cannot address all of the issues simultaneously. In fact, it may have been the helpee's inability to prioritize the various issues which may be making that person so ineffective in resolving his or her own problem. The effective helper needs to assist the helpee to find some order and priority to the issues being confronted.

The helper can use the following guidelines to assist the helpee in identifying priorities and the place to start.

1. **Address the immediate pain.** When the helpee is experiencing a crisis, the first target is to help him or her to manage that crisis. Crisis intervention is a somewhat special form of helping and is addressed in detail in Chapter 12. But beyond working with the helpee in crises, the effective helper should focus on those issues which are causing the helpee the most pain or discomfort. These are most likely the issues that the helpee would be most motivated to do something about, and thus less resistant to the process of helping.
2. **Take the helpee where he or she is.** Focus on the issues which the helpee feels are important, or are the ones that the helpee explicitly states an interest in addressing. Having the helpee demonstrate a willingness to work is the first step in

---

EXERCISE 7-3
Establishing Priorities

Directions: Using the list of dimensions or facets of the problem which you generated in Exercise 7-2, identify one priority issue to be focused upon for each of these cases. To assist you in your decision consider the following questions:

-   Which issue is the most painful? Around which issue is the helpee in most crisis or most concerned?
-   Which issue does the helpee appear most interested in and willing to work on?
-   Which issue appears to provide a high probability of success in resolving?

Discuss your priority listing with a colleague/classmate noting where and why your priorities may differ.

1. Lori: Priority focus? _____

   _____

2. Todd: Priority focus? _____

   _____

3. Kathy: Priority focus? _____

   _____

maintaining a good working alliance. His or her cooperation will not only assist in the helping alliance, but can then be built upon in order to begin to address some of the more difficult or more sensitive areas.

3. **Create success.** The helpee is entering a relationship, willing to disclose personal information and be confronted by the helper. This can be a somewhat "costly" experience. It is important, therefore, that the helpee experience a "payoff" in the relationship as soon as possible.

Granted that your attending, caring, and warm style is a payoff in the relationship, but it is also important to assist the helpee to experience success in goal achievement as evidence of both the "hopefulness" of the situation and the "helpfulness" of the helping relationship.

It is useful, therefore, to begin with a problem or issue which is manageable. Thus, it might be important to attempt to break the larger problem down into more manageable subparts which can be addressed one at a time. Once this is accomplished, start with the task that appears to have the most likelihood of success.

MOVING FROM PROBLEM IDENTIFICATION TO GOAL SPECIFICATION

Clearly, the purpose of helping is NOT simply to define the helpee's problem more clearly, although this process can, in and of itself, bring relief to the helpee. Generally, the intent of our helping is to assist the helpee to move away from the conditions or situations he or she is currently experiencing toward some more desirable situation. Thus, once the "what is" has been concretely defined, the helper and the helpee need to identify "what will be". This process of identifying the "what will be" is achieved by establishing realistic, achievable goals.

While it often easy for the helpee to present us with a list of problems or concerns, it may be quite another story for him or her to identify the desired outcomes or goals.

⚡ Goal Identification

One way to assist the helpee in identifying a more adaptable future scenario is to ask future-oriented questions (Egan, 1990). These questions, which have been integrated with the BASIC ID model of problem defining (Lazarus, 1981), are presented below.

- How would life be if the problem did not exist?
- How would he or she behave, feel, think, or see him- or herself if he or she were handling this situation differently?
- If he or she left this helping session and everything was better, how would his or her relationships look, or what would he or she be experiencing?

EXERCISE 7-4
Goal Identifying

Directions: Using yourself as a helpee, identify one area of concern in your life.

1. Pick something which you would feel free to discuss with your colleagues or classmates (e.g., concern about your smoking, your finances, your weight, etc.).
2. Consider each of the above future-oriented questions in response to that concern, writing out your response.
3. Discuss your responses to the questions with a classmate/colleague, identifying the goals implied in your responses.

- If he or she were "better", how would he or she act? What decisions would he or she make? What would he or she be doing or accomplishing?

This is not intended to be an exhaustive list of future questions, but it is provided to give you an idea of the type of questions you would want to be considering as a way of conceptualizing goals and directions. Exercise 7-4 will help you experience the effect of such questioning.

Goal Specification

The outcome of the helping encounter should be directly related to the helpee's needs (problem definition) as well as his or her resources and the direction he or she wishes to go. Since the nature of the need—resources—and direction is "helpee specific", the helper needs to be flexible and approach the goal-setting process as one which is subject to adjustment and modification. Goal specification is a collaborative effort.

There are, however, a few guidelines which seem to facilitate both the goal setting and the eventual achievement of these goals:

1. Goals should be personal and positive:
   What does the helpee wish to achieve as a result of the helping relationship? Refer to the helpee's response to the future oriented questions. Goals should be stated in positive terms that define what the helpee will be doing (e.g., I will write one sentence versus I will not procrastinate; I will exercise versus I will not eat between meals).
2. Goals should be clear and concrete:
   Is the goal clearly and concretely defined in observable, measurable terms? For

---

EXERCISE 7-5
Goal Specification

Directions: Using a partner (a colleague or classmate) first complete Exercise 7-4. In discussion with your partner, identify your desired goal. Next, review each of the six guides to goal specification and modify your goal specification so that it concurs with each of these guidelines.

---

example, rather than say, I will watch my weight, state, I will restrict my daily fat intake to 20%.

3. Goals should expand across modalities of experience:
   Has the goal been defined using many modalities? Rather than say, I will feel better, answer How will feeling better translate into behavior? affect? imaging? sensations? cognitions? interpersonal relationships? drugs (health)?
4. Goals should specify direction:
   Is the direction of change specified? Will we increase some aspects, reduce some, stabilize some? For example, say I will exercise more, reduce the amount of time watching TV, and continue to maintain my current calorie intake.
5. Goals should be attainable:
   Is the goal reasonable and realistic, given the helpee's abilities and resources?
6. Goal setting should consider impact of goal attainment:
   Has the effect (both positive and negative) of goal attainment—on the helpee, the helpee's environment, and those significant to the helpee—been considered and accepted?

The use of these guidelines can lead to the specification of reasonable, achievable goals. Exercise 7-5 will assist you to experience the benefit of goal specification.

As you most likely experienced in completing Exercise 7-5, goal specification not only focuses the helpee's and helper's energies, but even begins to stimulate the identification of strategies aimed at goal attainment. The creation of these strategies becomes the focus of the next step in the helping process, our next chapter.

WHAT NEXT

The process of moving a helpee from his or her vague and disconnected presentation of his or her problem to a clear, concrete statement of concern, with all of its facets and dimensions, and then translating that problem into a set of achievable goals is not easy. Like many of the other skills discussed, it does become easier with practice. Thus, practice is essential. The more you practice these techniques and skills, the easier they become. Therefore, before moving on to the next chapter, complete Exercise 7-6.

EXERCISE 7-6
From Problem to Goal

Directions: This exercise requires three people. Each person involved will take turns playing the role of helpee, helper, and observer.

Part I: You as Helpee
In Part I, you are to take the role of a helpee with one of the other two colleagues/classmates becoming the helper, and the other an observer. Your task is to simply present the helper with an initial concern or issue which you are willing to discuss and which you would like some help in resolving. The helper's role is to employ the processes and skills noted in this chapter to move you from problem presentation to goal specification. Following the exercise, discuss your experience as a helpee. The helper should also share his or her experiences. And finally, what did the observer note?

Part II: You as Helper
Repeat the above exercise and discussion, but with you in the role of helper, one of the other two colleagues as helpee, and the other as observer.

Part III: You as Observer
Finally, repeat the process with each of the other two participants taking the roles of helper and helpee. Your task is simply to observe the process. Pay attention to the content of what is being said, also how the process seems to unfold. Share your observations during the discussion period.

REFERENCES AND RECOMMENDED READINGS

Carkhuff, R.R., & Anthony, W.A. (1979). *The skills of helping.* Amherst, MA: Human Resource Development Press.

Childers, J.H. Jr. (1987). Goal setting in counseling: Steps, strategies and roadblock. *The School Counselor, 34,* 362–368.

Cormier, W.H., & Cormier, L.S. (1991). *Interviewing strategies for helpers* (3rd edition). Monterey, CA: Brooks/Cole.

Egan, G. (1986). *The skilled helper: A systematic approach to effective helping* (3rd edition). Monterey, CA: Brooks/Cole.

Egan, G. (1990). *The skilled helper: A systematic approach to effective helping* (4th edition). Monterey, CA: Brooks/Cole.

Frey, D.H., & Raming, H.E. (1979). A taxonomy of counseling goals and methods. *Personnel and Guidance Journal, 58,* 26–33.

Krumboltz, J.D. (1966). Behavioral goals for counseling. *Journal of Counseling Psychology, 13,* 153.

Lazarus, A. (1971). *Behavior therapy and beyond.* New York: McGraw-Hill.

Lazarus, A. (1981). *The practice of multimodal therapy.* New York: McGraw-Hill.

Lazarus, A. (1986). Multimodal therapy. In J. Norcross (Ed.), *Handbook of eclectic psychotherapy* (pp 63–93). New York: Brunner/Mazel.

Lazarus, A. (1989). *The practice of multimodal therapy.* Baltimore: John Hopkins University Press.

Mahoney, M.J., & Thoresen C.E. (1974). *Self-control: Power to the person.* Pacific Grove, CA: Brooks/Cole.

Watson, D.L., & Tharp, R.G. (1989). *Self-directed behavior: Self-modification for personal adjustment* (5th edition). Pacific Grove, CA: Brooks/Cole.

Wilson, G.T., Franks, C.M., Kendall, P.C., & Foreyt, J.P. (Eds.) (1987). *Review of behavior therapy: Theory and practice, Vol 11.* New York: Guilford Press.

▶ 8

Pathfinding: A Process of Strategy Development

Imagine that you are in need of a vacation, a trip to some place for relaxation. While the need for a break may be very real to you and the idea of a vacation quite exciting, it is only when you translate the idea into a specific plan that you will begin to move toward satisfying your need.

As is probably obvious, there could be any number of vacation locales which would satisfy your need. Therefore in planning your vacation, you need to not only identify all these possibilities, but begin to evaluate each possibility in terms of your need(s), the resources required to get there and those which are available to you, and finally, your chances of actually taking that vacation. This process of identifying paths for goal satisfaction, which is employed in our day-to-day activities such as planning a vacation, is also essential in the helping process.

Knowing what you want to accomplish (i.e., goal), is only the precursor to knowing how to accomplish it. Moving from goal statement to the identification of the best way to attain that goal (i.e., *pathfinding*) is the next step in our helping process, and the skills necessary for this step are the focus of the current chapter. Specifically, the chapter will:

1. discuss a practical, problem-solving approach to pathfinding; and
2. demonstrate the use of several techniques for generating and selecting intervention strategies.

A PRACTICAL, PROBLEM-SOLVING APPROACH TO PATHFINDING

As previously noted, helping is more than chatting or simply talking, it is an action-oriented process. As the helping relationship progresses, the helper and helpee explore and focus on the helpee's story; they define the problem in its various dimensions and eventually identify realistic, concrete goals.

Once these phases of the helping process are completed, the helper and helpee will engage in the process of developing an action strategy, a plan, a path, which will lead toward the attainment of these concrete goals.

A helpee's goal(s) can, in most instances, be attained via a variety of strategies or paths. The selection of a strategy or path for goal attainment is influenced by

- the nature and focus of the helpee's goal;
- the choices of paths available;
- the resources required by each path, and those available to the helpee; and finally,
- the decision criteria, established by the helper and the helpee.

In the previous chapter, we discussed the skills and processes required to accomplish the first of these requirements, that is, defining the nature and the focus of the helpee's goal. What remains is for the helper and the helpee to identify or develop a variety of possible paths, and evaluate each path as to its value for the helpee.

TECHNIQUES USED IN PATHFINDING

Step I: Developing a Variety of Possible Paths

Helping centers on opening up alternatives which the helpee can accept as realistic for him- or herself, and which to this point, the helpee failed to notice or embrace. Thus, the goal is not simply to solve the helpee's problem, but rather to introduce the helpee to new perspectives and new approaches.

All too often in our rush to help, we may target only one approach and cut off the possibility of identifying a more effective path to follow. It can be argued that the quality of the strategy finally chosen is augmented by the ability to choose from among a number of possibilities. Thus, in the process of pathfinding, we need to avoid this danger of closing off options prematurely, or blindly and rigidly locking into one, and only one, approach. We need to employ skills which will encourage and support the helpee in his or her development of as large an array of paths as possible that will lead toward achieving his or her goals.

Two classic techniques which facilitate such a creative venture, and result in the identification of a large pool of various paths to goal attainment are *brainstorming* (Osborn, 1957; Maier, 1970) and *divergent delphi*.

Brainstorming

Brainstorming is a technique which facilitates the generation of creative ideas. It is a process which encourages divergent thinking, and thus often leads to the identification of ideas, strategies, and approaches which initially were not evident to either the helper or helpee. In order to gain the maximum benefit from this process of brainstorming, the helper and helpee should observe the following simple rules (Osborn, 1957; Maier, 1970; Corey, 1990).

1. **Suspend judgment:** The purpose of brainstorming is to be creative. As a result, some of the ideas may seem a bit off the main track. It is important that the participants suspend judgment; it is important not to evaluate or find fault with any of the suggestions. This may inhibit both the flow of contributions and a participant's willingness to risk a creative response. Evaluation of the usefulness of the ideas will take place in the second stage of our pathfinding.
2. **Target quantity not quality:** As suggested in the first rule, the goal is to develop as many ideas as possible. Ideas are to be expressed without regard for quality. The quality of each will be assessed at a later time. Often an idea which might appear to have minimal value serves as a stimulus to the creation of another idea which proves quite productive.
3. **Build on previous ideas:** It is useful to combine ideas previously offered, or attempt to expand on ideas previously noted. Elaboration of one person's ideas by another is not only permitted but encouraged. Such building or combining often produces creative strategies and paths.

Exercise 8-1 will help you experience the value of brainstorming, while at the same time practicing the implementation of these guiding principles.

Divergent Delphi

A possible limitation of the brainstorming process is that often the most creative or most assertive member (helper or helpee) may dominate the process and thus inhibit the productivity of the other member, limiting the other member's potential contribution and thus reducing the effectiveness of the technique. In such a situation, the use of a divergent delphi technique may be preferred.

As with brainstorming, the divergent delphi process begins by clarifying the target—the goal desired. Then each participant offers his or her ideas, taking turns. The process becomes more creative after the initial rounds, as the helper and helpee deplete their standard responses and now struggle to produce responses during their turns. The one operating rule (in addition to those suggested for brainstorming) is that a participant must respond. That is, the helpee or helper can't pass or repeat what was previously said. They can, however, build on a previous idea, modify it, or even move to the absurd.

Step II: Assessing and Selecting a Path

After the helpee and helper have generated a list of possible paths to goal attainment, they need to engage in a process of evaluation of the various paths and the selection of the approach which will then be implemented in the ACTION phase of helping.

The evaluation and selection of the path to be followed can be facilitated by a number of techniques. Two such techniques, a *pragmatic approach* and a *cost/benefit analysis,* are presented below.

EXERCISE 8-1
Brainstorming

Directions: The following exercise requires you to work with a colleague or classmate. Below you will find a statement of a helpee's goal.

Helpee's goal: My roommate often invites people into our dorm room to talk, play Nintendo, or just goof around. I need a quiet place to study—when she does this, my room is too noisy. How can I get quiet?

Step 1: Take 5 minutes and create a list of paths the helpee could take to reach her goal.

Possible Paths/Strategies: My list _____

_____

_____

_____

_____

_____

Step 2: Again using a 5-minute time limit, work with your colleague and create a new list. You are not allowed to read from your first list, but you are allowed to repeat those strategies, should you remember them. In Step 2, remember the rules of brainstorming—don't evaluate, go for quantity, and build on previous ideas.

Possible Paths/Strategies: Brainstormed list _____

_____

_____

_____

_____

_____

_____

Step 3: Compare the lists created in each of these previous steps. Which list had more ideas? On which list did you find the most creative solutions?

A Pragmatic Approach

A straightforward, practical approach to path evaluation and selection requires that the helper and helpee assess each of the paths generated against each of the following practical criteria. The path most clearly satisfying each criterion is selected for implementation.

Criterion 1: Path is goal-related. Be sure that the path logically leads to the original goal(s) desired. On review, does this particular path seem to have a high degree of likelihood of leading to that desired goal?

Criterion 2: Resources required match those available. Review the match between the skills and resources needed for implementation of this strategy to those available to the helpee. Does the helpee have the required resources? Will the helpee have to develop additional skills or acquire resources before employing this strategy? The less the helpee needs to develop before taking action on the selected path, the more effective it will be.

Criterion 3: Path is owned by the helpee. Check to see that the helpee "owns" the strategy. Does the helpee embrace this as a path he or she wishes to follow? Of the paths identified, is the helpee excited about this path? Does he or she express a sense of ownership of this strategy and exhibit a positive expectation about its outcome?

In order to experience the value of this process, complete Exercise 8-2, keeping each of these principles in mind.

EXERCISE 8-2
Path Selection

Direction: This exercise will require that you work with another person. Using the list below, or an item of your own choosing, identify a goal for personal betterment which you would like to achieve.

Step 1: After identifying your goal, have your partner suggest five possible strategies/paths for accomplishing that goal. Write these strategies down.

Step 2: Review each of the suggested strategies and evaluate each path against the three criteria listed above. Which strategy

- appears most logically related to the goal?
- requires resources you already possess or could possess with little effort?
- do you personally feel as if you could own?

If none of the five paths offered meet all of the above guidelines, generate a path that would fulfill all of the criteria.

Possible targets for self-growth:

- increase exercise
- modify diet
- improve time management
- improve stress management
- other

A Cost/Benefits Approach

Another somewhat more extensive approach to the evaluation and selection of problem-solving paths or strategies is through the use of a costs/benefits analysis. The technique described below is a slight modification of the balance sheet approach offered by others (Corey, 1990; Mann, Harmoni, & Power, 1990; Ivey, Bradford-Ivey, & Simek-Morgan, 1993; Wheeler & Janis, 1980).

This approach assumes that each path which has been generated brings with it a number of benefits (in addition to leading to the desired goal) and a number of costs (physical, psychological, social, etc.). In using this approach, the helper and helpee attempt to identify which path or strategy has the highest potential benefit or payoff-to-cost ratio. It is important to realize that while each strategy may offer benefits for those involved, in most cases it will also incur a cost of some sort. For example, an individual who seeks to stop smoking will clearly gain a number of payoffs or benefits: better health, money savings, and possibly even new taste sensitivity, etc. However, even such a positive act may have personal costs. The individual may find that he or she gains weight, finds it uncomfortable taking a work break with the same "old smoking crowd", or even may find that he or she becomes a little bit jittery or on edge.

Thus, in selecting a path toward goal attainment, it is important to identify the real costs and payoffs for each path, and identify the path which provides the best benefit-to-cost ratio.

In using this cost/benefits approach, the helper and helpee need to consider each of the following questions.

1. Benefits to helpee:
What are the benefits to be gained by the helpee?

In answering this question we must consider all the possible benefits (physical, social, psychological, etc.), both big and small. Taking our smoker as an example, it is clear that he or she will

- save money,
- begin to have better stamina, and
- feel good about him- or herself.

Can you identify other possible personal benefits?

2. Benefits to significant others:
What are the benefits which may accrue to others that are significant to the helpee?

For example, for our smoker, significant others may

- not have to put up with dirty ashtrays,
- not worry about the person's health,

- not have to experience someone's smoker's breath,
- not experience the effects of secondary smoke, etc.

Can you identify other possible benefits for significant others?

3. Costs to the helpee:
What are the physical, psychological, and social costs which will be experienced by the helpee?

For example, our smoker may

- experience stress and tension,
- experience a loss of social contact (not going out for a smoke at break),
- experience a "craving," or
- begin to gain unwanted weight.

Can you think of other possible personal costs?

4. Costs to significant others:
What are the physical, psychological, and social costs to those significant in the helpee's life?

In our example, perhaps the significant others in the smoker's life will experience

- his initial irritability;
- restriction of their own social life, avoiding being with friends who smoke; or
- an indirect or direct confrontation about their own smoking.

Could you identify other possible costs to the significant others in our helpee's life?

In order to help develop your cost/benefits analysis skills, complete Exercise 8-3.

WHAT NEXT

In terms of the helping relationship, what's next is for the helping process to move forward toward implementation of the selected path. Such an ACTION phase is often accompanied by some uncertainty and anxiety. It must be remembered that what we have done is only the selection of one *possible* path to goal attainment. It is neither the definitive path nor the only path. We need to move ahead, and assist our helpees to move ahead with a positive, yet somewhat tentative anticipation of "let's see what happens", knowing that we can modify and adjust our goals or our plans as needed.

EXERCISE 8-3
Cost/Benefits Analysis

Directions: In Exercise 8-2 you were asked to identify a goal for personal growth and betterment. You also generated a number of paths for attaining that goal. In this exercise you will be asked to select two of the strategies you listed in Exercise 8-2 and apply the process of cost/benefits analysis to them.

Fill in the following grid using the paths supplied in Exercise 8-2.

Goal: _____

	BENEFITS		COSTS	
Path/Strategy	To Me	To Others	To Me	To Others
1. _____	_____	_____	_____	_____
_____	_____	_____	_____	_____
_____	_____	_____	_____	_____
2. _____	_____	_____	_____	_____
_____	_____	_____	_____	_____
_____	_____	_____	_____	_____

In terms of what's next for you, the reader—developing your pathfinding abilities is essential. Techniques and strategies abound within the helping profession. The choices are broad. Each of the theories to be discussed in Chapter 13 will provide a variety of techniques aimed at moving a helpee toward his or her goal. Needless to say, as you continue in your training as a helper, it will become important that you become more familiar with these theories and the strategies they offer. But in addition to becoming more versed in these formal theories, you need to

1. become aware of the professional literature and research suggesting valuable and effective approaches to the resolution of various presenting concerns;
2. learn about how others have approached helping a person with the type of problem(s) our helpee may be encountering;
3. dialogue with others who are developing and employing helping skills; and
4. PRACTICE, as always, the skills required for this phase of helping (pathfinding).

In line with this last point, the chapter will close with one final exercise, the case of Ms. Sinderela (see Exercise 8-4).

EXERCISE 8-4
The Case of the Frustrated Partygoer

Directions: Read the presenting complaint and factors involved in the following case of Ms. Sinderela.

Presenting Complaint: Ms. Sinderela is the youngest stepdaughter in a single-parent family. She lives with her stepmother and her two stepsisters. There is a major party scheduled in three weeks and Ms. Sinderela would like to go. However,

- she doesn't have the proper attire,
- she doesn't have transportation,
- her mother and sisters seem non-supportive of her interest in going, and
- she has a lot of household chores for which she is responsible.

With a colleague or classmate:

1. Develop a goal statement _____

   _____

   _____

   _____

2. Employ brainstorming or divergent delphi techniques to generate as many paths as possible for goal attainment

   _____

   _____

   _____

3. Utilize the criteria of a pragmatic selection process to identify two useful paths

   _____

   _____

4. Utilize the cost/benefit analysis procedure to identify the best path for goal attainment

	To Me	*To Others*
Benefits:	_____	_____
	_____	_____
	_____	_____
Costs:	_____	_____
	_____	_____
	_____	_____

REFERENCES AND RECOMMENDED READINGS

Burke, J.P., Haworth, C.E., & Brantley, J.C. (1980). Scientific problem-solver model: A resolution for professional controversies in school psychology. *Professional Psychology, 11,* 823–832.

Carkhuff, R.R. (1987). *The art of helping* (6th edition). Amherst, MA: Human Resource Development Press.

Corey, G. (1990). *The skilled helper.* Belmont, CA: Brooks/Cole.

Dixon, D., & Glover, J (1984). *Counseling: A problem-solving approach.* New York: Wiley.

Egan, G. (1990). *The skilled helper* (4th edition). Belmont, CA: Brooks/Cole.

Heppner, P.P. (1978). A review of the problem-solving literature and its relationship to counseling process. *Journal of Counseling Psychology, 25,* 366–375.

Ivey, A.E., Bradford-Ivey, M., & Simek-Morgan, L. (1993). *Counseling and psychotherapy: A multicultural perspective* (3rd edition). Needham Heights, MA: Allyn and Bacon.

Kanfer, F.H., & Schefft, B.K. (1988). *Guiding therapeutic change.* Champaign, IL: Research Press.

Mann, L., Harmoni, R., & Power, C. (1990). The gofer course in decision making. In J. Baron & R. Brown (Eds.), *Teaching decision making to adolescents.* New York: Erlbaum.

Maier, N.R.F. (1970). *Problem solving and creativity in individuals and groups.* Pacific Grove, CA: Brooks/Cole.

Osborn, A.F. (1957). *Applied imagination.* New York: Scribner.

Watson D.L., & Tharp, R.G. (1989). *Self-directed behavior* (5th edition). Pacific Grove, CA: Brooks/Cole.

Wicks, R. (1982). *Helping others.* New York: Gardner Press.

Wheeler, D.D., & Janis, I.L. (1980). *A practical guide for making decisions.* New York: Free Press.

▶ 9

Call to Action

Karen: Well, Diane, how did it go?

Diane: You know when we worked it out on paper, it seemed to be so easy. But I had so much trouble trying to do it! To be honest, I really wanted to do it . . . really. But I just didn't get around to it. I don't know what went wrong.

Often a helper, like Karen, envisions that the hard work of the helping process is complete once the problem-solving path or strategy has been identified. As is evident in the brief exchange between Karen and Diane, this is not the case!

Calling the helpee to action, once the path has been identified, takes time and skill. Knowing what to do and why one would wish to do it is only the beginning. Knowing how to do it and doing it are the next essential steps in the helping process.

Taking action is not always a simple task. Often there are forces—coming from within the helpee, from the helper or even from the environment—which inhibit the helpee's successful implementation of an action plan (Cormier & Cormier, 1991).

The current chapter:

1. highlights possible roadblocks to successful ACTING, including those originating from the helpee, the helper, and the environment;
2. describes strategies that can be used to reduce or circumvent such roadblocks to action.

ROADBLOCKS

Originating with the Helpee

The helpee's attempt to implement an action strategy may sometimes be blocked by his or her lack of understanding about the strategy or skills needed to implement the plan; his or her fear or anxiety about attempting the strategy, or even his or her overall sense of hopelessness about the situation or the strategy. Each of these blocks need to be understood, recognized, and removed if the action plan is to be successful.

Lack of Understanding and Skill

It is important that the helpee understand the reason for the procedure and also the components of its implementation. Consider the exchange between Maria and Bob.

> Maria: Now, Bob, if I understand you correctly, each time you have a test, you find that you get so nervous that you almost feel like you are going to pass out.
>
> Bob: That's right! It's horrible—my heart starts pounding, I feel like I can't get enough oxygen, and then my head starts to spin.
>
> Maria: And if I heard you correctly, you really would like to be able to study in order to get better grades.
>
> Bob: Yes, that's my goal.
>
> Maria: Ok, Bob, I am going to give you this tape which will teach you a breathing exercise. I want you to practice this for a week and come back next week. Okay?

While perhaps Maria's recommendation of having Bob listen to the tape and practice this exercise is somehow logically connected to the overall plan of reducing his anxiety and increasing his ability to study, this connection may not be all that clear to Bob. If Bob's compliance and cooperation are desired, his lack of understanding about the reason or value of this recommendation needs to be removed.

Research (Wilson & Evans, 1977; Cormier & Cormier, 1991) suggests that providing a rationale for the strategy fosters realistic expectations about a particular treatment, and further, such realistic expectations facilitate action implementation.

In assisting the helpee to develop this sense of understanding, it is essential that the helpee "owns" the strategy rather than feel coerced into accepting it. This need for helpee ownership may be sometimes overlooked by the helper, who in his or her enthusiasm for the plan, may push it down the helpee's throat. A helper must remember that any plan is only as good as its implementation, and good implementation requires helpee understanding and ownership.

In addition to understanding the rationale for the action plan, the helpee also needs to understand and be able to employ the steps required to implement this action plan.

Knowing how to "do" the strategy includes knowing all the dos and don'ts of the strategy. The helpee may need assistance in developing the specific behaviors required of the action plan. For example, in the case of Bob, it would be better if Maria

1. explained that this breathing exercise will not only provide relief from the anxiety by relaxing Bob, but will also be used later as part of a two-step process that will eventually lead to Bob's "calling up" this feeling of relaxation anytime he feels anxious.
2. explained the specific steps of the procedure.

For example:

> Maria: Bob, first I want you to find a comfortable chair, sit, close your eyes, and take a deep breath. Hold that breath as long as you can. Concentrate on that feeling in your chest, your stomach . . . Is this the feeling you have when you are anxious? Next, release the breath. Breathe as normally as you can. You will probably notice you are breathing rapidly, and probably in a non-rhythmic, jagged manner. What we are going to do is learn to breathe in a slow, smooth, rhythmic pattern. A pattern people use when they are relaxed.
>
> Try to imagine your breathing as occurring in a rhythmic fashion, almost like a swing. A swing goes forward, pauses slightly as it reverses directions, then comes back, pauses slightly as it goes forward, etc. Now, inhale smoothly, with a slight pause, as you reverse directions to exhale. Again, pause, just a slight pause, don't hold it, as you reverse directions and inhale. Try to make your breathing as smooth and rhythmic as possible, allowing for those very slight pauses as you reverse directions. Let's practice this step.

In addition to explaining the rationale for the strategy and developing the specific steps to be taken, the helpee may also need the steps demonstrated by the helper. In this situation it would be helpful for Maria to demonstrate the steps for Bob, and have Bob practice them with her, so that they can identify questions, concerns, or problems that may occur and address them immediately.

Helpee Fear

A second source of helpee resistance to action may be his or her sense of fear over trying something new. Beckhard and Harris (1977) have identified the process of moving from strategy development to implementation as a transition state. Ferguson (1980) suggests that helpees feel at risk during this time of transition.

Moving from an old pattern or way of responding to a new way of responding can be unsettling. This is true even if the old pattern wasn't working very well. After all, at least with the old pattern, the helpee knows what to expect.

This risk, this sense of unsettling, has been very vividly portrayed by Gerard Egan (1990). Egan suggests that what the helpee experiences in moving from the old to a new way of coping is much like that experienced by the trapeze artist as he or she prepares to move from one trapeze to another. The helpee may find him- or herself stuck in the old pattern, not progressing, as if swinging back and forth holding tightly to one trapeze. If progress is to occur for the helpee, or in the case of our metaphor, if the trapeze artist is to move to the other side, he or she must risk letting go of the old (and safe) bar (or in the case of the helpee, an old style) in order to grab hold of the new. It is in the experience of anticipating letting go, prior to grabbing onto the new bar, that the helper experiences fear.

This fear can be so strong that it actually blocks the process of letting go, and thus blocks the movement toward the helpee's goal. Consider the case of Linda, presented in Exercise 9-1.

Helpless and Hopeless Feelings

A third block to the helpee's movement or action taking, may be his or her own sense of helplessness and hopelessness about his or her situation. Consider the following dialogue between Richard (a depressed, middle-aged man) and Charles (a psychologist).

> Richard: You are the sixth therapist I've come to over the last 18 years. Why should I bother?
>
> Charles: Why should you bother?

EXERCISE 9-1
When Fear Blocks Activity

Directions: Read the brief case presentation, then complete the activities which follow.

Case Presentation

Linda is a 49-year-old mother of two. She has been married for 26 years, and has essentially served as mother and wife for those 26 years. As she stated to her counselor, "For 26 years I took care of the house, my husband, and my children. I hate it. For 26 years, I have been verbally abused, and more than once physically abused by that drunk I call my husband. He's not drinking any more, but we don't have anything in common. We are not even friends, much less lovers. I'm only 49 and I feel my life is over. I really want to leave. Go out on my own. I want to establish my own life. But I can't. Well, I know I can—I have a place where I can live, and I know I can get a job, but it just seems like I am unable to leave. I've been trying to do this for 5 years now. It just seems so scary."

1. Identify Linda's desired goal. _____
   _____

2. List Linda's strategy or plan of action. _____
   _____

3. Hypothesize about the possible sources of fear/anxiety which block Linda's taking action. _____
   _____

4. Discuss your observations with a classmate or colleague, noting other possible sources of fear which you may have missed.

Richard: Here, look . . . this is a list of the medications I've tried. NONE of them have helped. I'm still depressed. Things have gotten worse. I'm losing more weight, I will probably lose my job if I don't snap out of this. My family has had it with me, I mean who wants to be around somebody like me? I know you care and you think you can help, but I'm just not sure anyone can help me.

Clearly, a helpee like Richard who has had a number of unsuccessful attempts at finding help can very quickly "learn" to assume that all is hopeless and that he is helpless. Such an attitude needs to be removed for Richard, or any other helpee, to begin to implement an action plan.

Helpees have often approached the helping encounter after exhausting all of their own coping and adjusting strategies. As they implement their own strategies, only to experience recurring failure, they may begin to develop an expectation that nothing has or will ever work. This expectation leads to the feeling of hopelessness and helplessness, as exemplified in the case of Richard. But such hopeless, helpless feelings occur under less dramatic conditions. Consider the following dialogue.

Shelley: This is getting out of hand. I studied using all the techniques you suggested and I still got a D.
Rose: Perhaps next time, we could try starting to study earlier.
Shelley: Why? Just so I can waste more time and energy and still get a D?

Promoting positive expectations and overcoming this sense of helplessness and hopelessness is essential if the helpee is to implement the action plan. As Bandura (1977) noted, it is a person's expectations of him- or herself that will determine to a great degree, his or her willingness to persist at a new task. Following Bandura's observations, it appears reasonable to suggest that in order to overcome the helpee's sense of helplessness and hopelessness, and to encourage his or her positive expectations about the action plan, the helper must

1. assist the helpee to believe that this action plan will most likely lead to a desired result. This reinforces our previous observation about the need to have the helpee understand and own the action plan.
2. assist the helpee to believe that he or she can successfully engage in this activity. The helpee needs to be assisted in developing a positive expectation of self-efficacy. That is, in addition to believing in the plan, he or she must believe he or she can implement the plan successfully.

One procedure useful in assisting the helpee in maintaining these positive expectations and hopeful attitudes is for the helper to design the implementation process, or action plan, in such a way that it can be implemented in small successful steps. For example, consider the following case illustrations.

Case 1: Kris, the Couch Potato

Kris: This time I mean it! I've got to get in shape. No more messing around. I
   know I've said this before, and I also know I've been Mr. Couch Potato
   for the past two years. But this time it's different. What should I do?

Fred: Okay, look. First, we will put you on a 3/3 regimen. That is, every
   other day you do weight training (approximately two hours a day) and
   the off days, you do aerobics. Let's do five miles a day.

Case 2: Drew, Slow but Sure!

Drew: This time I mean it! I've got to get in shape. No more messing around.
   I know I've said this before, and I also know I've been Mr. Couch Potato
   for the past two years. But this time it's different. What should I do?

Bob: Okay, this is super that you are now ready to do something, but let's be
   realistic. After two years of doing nothing, we may need to start out with
   some small steps, but we'll get up and running soon. Is that okay?

Drew: I guess. What do you mean?

Bob: For the next three weeks, let's develop the following step plan, with the
   goal that by the end of three weeks you will be running/walking 1½
   miles each day.

Week 1: • Establish a time for exercise
         • Get a track or path to follow and mark it off
         • Get proper clothes and shoes
         • Practice warm up and stretching exercises
Week 2: • Warm up
         • Run ¼ mile
         • Walk ¼ mile
         • Run ¼ mile
         • Walk ¼ mile
         • Cool down, and give yourself a pat on the back
Week 3: • Warm up
         • Run ½ mile
         • Walk ¼ mile
         • Run ½ mile
         • Walk ¼ mile
         • Cool down
         • Treat yourself to that new tie you wanted when you
           reached your goal.

Which person, Kris or Drew, do you feel will be most positive and most hopeful
about beginning his action plan?

Introducing the plan in small steps increases the helpee's probability of success,
which in turn serves as the encouragement needed for the continued implementation
process. Exercise 9-2 provides you the opportunity to take an action strategy and
break it down in smaller, more easily attainable substeps.

EXERCISE 9-2
Setting Realistic Steps to Action Plan

Directions: For each of the following goals and action plans, rewrite the action in terms of smaller, more easily accomplished steps. Write as many substeps as you feel are needed.

Case 1

Goal: I really don't know anybody, and I am really alone. I want to get married.
Action: You need to get more social.
Substeps:

_____

_____

_____

_____

_____

_____

Case 2

Goal: I have to do a big oral presentation in class in three weeks. It makes me a wreck. I want to be able to do it and be relaxed.
Action: You need to practice it.
Substeps:

_____

_____

_____

_____

_____

_____

Case 3

Goal: When I am at a meeting at work, I really want to assert myself and speak up. But I find it very hard to do. I get very nervous.
Action: You have to learn to say what's on your mind.
Substeps:

_____

_____

_____

_____

_____

_____

Originating with the Helper

In addition to the helpee's action being blocked by his or her own lack of knowledge or skill, fear, or sense of hopelessness, action can be thwarted or blocked by the helper. Often the helper has unrealistic expectations, and may become disappointed with the helpee's failure to achieve immediate success. Further, a helper, intent on resolving the issue at hand, may be so focused on the outcome that he or she fails to support the helpee's efforts as well as his or her achievement. Both of these tendencies can act to undermine the action implementation.

Unrealistic Expectations

The path toward goal attainment is strewn with possible pitfalls and roadblocks. Often, the inexperienced helper approaches this implementation phase as the "do-or-die" stage of helping. It is as if this is the ultimate test of his or her competence as a helper. Such a do-or-die or "this-is-it" attitude or approach must be avoided.

Granted, the helper and helpee have worked hard to define the problem, and have been creative in identifying possible paths toward goal attainment, but both the helper and helpee must be mindful that the action selected is *only one* of many possible helping strategies. They must approach the implementation with a sense of positive expectation, of cautious optimism, but one which is soften by the realization that this is really a "try-and-see" experience.

Typically, helpers and helpees alike are eager to try the action strategy and may rush in expecting that they have found "the answer". While this eagerness and optimistic approach need not be squelched, it may need to be tempered. Rarely do the helpee's initial efforts result in all that he or she envisioned. There will be setbacks and disappointments for both the helper and the helpee. The helper must be prepared to assist the helpee to work through the needed "fine tuning" of the action plan. He or she can do this if he or she has a realistic expectation about the amount of time and energy still needed for resolving the problem.

Failure to Encourage

A second roadblock to the helpee's successful movement may be the helper's own failure to encourage the helpee. Helpees should be encouraged to try and test new waters tentatively, knowing that they are capable of responding to roadblocks and problems they may encounter while implementing the action plan.

It is important that the helper be supportive of the helpee's efforts—not just his or her achievements. The action phase needs to be viewed as both a resolution of a problem, and also an opportunity for additional information gathering from which more clarity about goal definition and goal attainment can be made. Using this as a framework, even efforts which are unsuccessful are not failures. They provide essential data for the adjustment of the intervention strategy.

The value of each of the helpee's attempts, whether or not his or her efforts achieves the final goal, is highlighted in Exercise 9-3.

EXERCISE 9-3
Good Effort, Good Information

Directions: Read the following case information. With a colleague or classmate answer the questions following.

Case Illustration

Jonathan: Well, Den, how did it go? I know you were a little nervous, but you were going to give your mom and dad a call and tell them that it was going to take you 5 years to complete college.

Dennis: Not so good. It took me three days since last time we met just to get the courage up to call them. I finally called them yesterday. Gads, I thought I would die. My heart was in my throat, but I kept reminding myself, like you told me, that they did love me and at worse they would just be temporarily disappointed for me and not at me. Well, anyway, we got to talking about everything in the world, my sister, the game last Saturday, yo u name it we talked about it. And then my mom said "How're your classes?" I thought, this is it, here is my chance . . . and I blew it! I couldn't say it. I wimped out. All I got out of my mouth was that classes were really difficult and it is hard carrying all these credits.

1. While Dennis did not accomplish the task, what did he achieve? _____

2. What productive, valuable outcome(s) resulted from Dennis' actions?
   _____
   _____

Environmental Roadblocks

Quite often the helpee's ability to move toward his or her goal, or to successfully implement the decided upon action plan, is blocked by forces or conditions operating within the helpee's environment. There may be situations where the various elements (e.g., rules, payoffs, people, etc.) found in the situation may actually enable or encourage the helpee NOT to change, or NOT to resolve his or her problem.

For example, consider the case of Howard. Howard is a problem drinker. Howard has been drinking more frequently and has lately begun to miss work because he has a hangover from the night before. Howard is really a nice guy, however, and most of his family and friends know that he has been under a lot of pressure since his girlfriend broke up with him. Therefore, his friends and family "excuse" Howard's excessive drinking. They have even made up excuses to his employer so that he would not get fired for missing work. For example, on one occasion, his mother phoned his boss to explain that the family had experienced a personal tragedy and that's why Howard would not be able to be at work that day. His best friend, Tom, has even taken Howard out to the bar after work, just so he won't be alone or have to drive home drunk.

Actions like these by the people in Howard's environment actually encourage or enable him to continue to be an excessive drinker, and thus interfere with any action plan designed to help Howard face his responsibilities in a more mature manner.

In other circumstances, the people within the helpee's environment may not actively encourage the dysfunctional behavior, but they may actively block the specific alternative. Consider the situation where a person is in an unhappy relationship and wishes to leave it, but each time he or she think about breaking up, the other person pleads, begs or in some way coerces him or her to stay.

For example, Maura tells Bruce, "I am really unhappy in this relationship. I am going to move out!" Bruce responds by stating, "Please stay just until after Christmas", or "Please, not now, you know I am in the middle of comprehensive exams. I can't take any more pressure—it will only be another month." Such action on the partner's part may interfere with the person's plan to leave.

RECOGNIZING FACILITATING AND INHIBITING FORCES

It is clear, therefore, that in calling the helpee to action, the effective helper must be alert and sensitive to the various forces (coming from within the helpee, from him- or herself or from the helpee's environment) that not only promote his or her movement toward goal attainment, but which also attempt to block or thwart such movement. One technique which a helper and helpee can use to identify these facilitating and inhibiting forces is the process of force-field analysis (Lewin, 1969).

Lewin noted that movement from one point toward another is often assisted or inhibited by a variety of physical and psychological forces. He termed these forces facilitating and restraining forces, respectively. Facilitating forces help, encourage, and support the movement toward the goal. Restraining or inhibiting forces act as obstacles to goal attainment.

As noted, these forces can be external to the helpee or within the helpee, and can be of a physical, social, or psychological nature. For example, if we revisit the case of Howard, we may come to identify the various facilitating forces:

1. Howard wanted to stop drinking;
2. Howard became friends with a recovering alcoholic who introduced him to non-drinking social activities;
3. Howard's boss encouraged him to sign into a rehabilitation treatment program.

Clearly, Howard's motivation and social supports (i.e., his new friend and his boss) would act as forces which facilitated his movement toward his goal of sobriety.

However, Howard may also encounter forces (again coming from himself or outside of himself) which actually interfere with his movement toward his goal. For example:

1. Howard's mother makes excuses for Howard any time he gets drunk, so that "he won't be embarrassed";
2. Howard's old classmates have a ritual of going out to the bar every Friday to play darts and "get ripped" (i.e., drunk); and
3. Howard has developed the tendency to justify what he does when he drinks, since, as he puts it "I am under a lot of pressure."

These are all forces which are inhibiting or restraining Howard from reaching his goal.

The helpee who is "frozen" and unable to move toward his or her goal is clearly exhibiting the power of the inhibiting forces. If implementation of the helpee's action plan is to take place, the helpee and the helper need to: 1)increase facilitating forces, 2) reduce restraining forces, or 3) employ a combination of both processes.

WHAT NEXT

As may be apparent from the discussion, the force-field analysis is a nice, simple model for identifying all of the potential roadblocks to taking action. The most productive and useful "next step" is for you to

1. personally experience how difficult change can be; and
2. experience the value of the force-field analysis as a tool for conceptualizing roadblocks to change and identifying ways to overcome them.

This chapter closes with the following exercise.

EXERCISE 9-4
Personal Application

Directions: 1. Identify a personal goal you have been trying to accomplish (for example, saving money, losing weight, improving grades, or asking someone out). List your goal on the line labeled goal.

2. Under each of the appropriate columns, list forces which appear to be restraining you from goal achievement, as well as any which are facilitating your movement. Be sure to consider psychological, physical, social, and environmental forces.

Continued

EXERCISE 9-4 *Continued*

3. Estimate strength of each force. Use a subjective ranking scale, perhaps from 1–10.

4. Develop methods for increasing or weakening the appropriate forces.

5. After you have reduced or weakened the restraining forces or increased the facilitating forces by the procedures listed in step 4, do you find movement toward your goal more easily achieved? If not repeat this exercise using a colleague or classmate as a consultant.

Goal: _____

_____

Restraining Force(s) (psychological, physical, social, environmental, etc.)	Strength 1 . . . 10	Strategy(ies) to reduce strength or remove

_____

_____

_____

_____

Facilitating Force(s) (psychological, physical, social, environmental, etc.)	Strength 1 . . . 10	Strategy(ies) to increase strength or add additional facilitating forces

_____

_____

_____

_____

REFERENCES AND RECOMMENDED READINGS

Anderson, C.M., & Stewart, S. (1983). *Mastering resistance: A practical guide to family therapy.* New York: Guilford Press.

Bandura, A. (1977). Self-efficacy: Toward a unifying theory of behavioral change. *Psychological Review, 84,* 191–215.

Beckhard, R., & Harris, R.T. (1977). *Organizational transitions: Managing complex change* (1st edition). Reading, MA: Addison-Wesley.

Burns, D. (1981). *Feeling good.* New York: Signet Books.

Chamberlain, P., Patterson, G., Reid, J., Kavanagh, K., & Forgatch, M. (1984). Observation of client resistance. *Behavior Therapy, 15,* 144–155.

Cormier, W.H., & Cormier, L.S. (1991). *Interviewing strategies for helpers* (3rd edition). Pacific Grove, CA: Brooks/Cole.

Ellis, A. (1974). *Disputing irrational beliefs (DIBS)*. New York: Institute for Rational Living.

Egan, G. (1990). *The skilled helper*. Belmont, CA: Brooks/Cole.

Ferguson, M. (1980). *The aquarian conspiracy: Personal and social transformation in the 1980s*. Los Angeles: J.P. Tarcher.

Grieger, R., & Boyd, J. (1980). *Rational-emotive therapy: A skills-based approach*. New York: Van Nostrand Reinhold.

Lewin, K. (1969). Quasi-stationary social equilibria and the problem of permanent change. In W.G. Bennis, K.D. Benne, & R. Chin (eds.), *The planning of change*. New York: Holt, Rinehart & Winston.

Seligman, M. (1975). *Helplessness: On depression, development, and death*. San Francisco, CA: W. H. Freeman.

Simons, A.D., Lustman, P.J., Wetzel, R.D., & Murphy, G.E. (1985). Predicting response to cognitive therapy of depression: The role of learned resourcefulness. *Cognitive Therapy and Research, 9(10)*, 79–89.

Wachtel, P. (ed.) (1982). *Resistance: Psychodynamic and behavioral approaches*. New York: Plenum.

Wilson, G.T., & Evans, I.M. (1977). The therapist-client relationship in behavior therapy. In A.S. Gurman & A.M. Razin (eds.), *Effective psychotherapy: A handbook of research*. New York: Pergamon Press.

▶ 10

Evaluation and Termination

Since no one is perfect, and therefore each helpee could continue to find areas in his or her life where continued helping could prove productive, it may be suggested that helping could continue indefinitely. As Kanfer and Schefft (1988) noted, however,

> . . . the (helper) must accept the inevitability of termination, even with a client who has made good progress but who remains short of perfection (p. 275).

Attempting to identify the "right" time to close or terminate the helping relationship is not always an easy task. Typically termination occurs when at least one of the following conditions is present:

1. The goals of the helping process have been achieved
2. There has been a change in the helpee's motivation or reason for being in a helping relationship
3. Progress has been stymied, and referral needs to be made to a professional who has the skills and competencies to work more effectively with the client and the situation (see Chapter 14)

Not only is finding the right time to terminate a difficult task, but sometimes, because of the nature of the helping relationship, termination may meet with resistance from either the helpee or helper. This chapter will

1. describe methods of formative and summative evaluation and demonstrate the value of each in the process of preparing for termination;
2. discuss the "why" and "how" of preparing the helpee for termination;

3. discuss the process of termination and look at ways of overcoming the resistance to termination which is sometimes encountered.

EVALUATION

Evaluation of the helping relationship and its impact is very often viewed by helpers as superfluous, or as only tangential to the primary function of helping. While many in the human service arena give little credence to the importance of evaluation to the helping process, it has been demonstrated to be an extremely valuable and useful tool for the effective helper. Hackney and Cormier (1991) suggest that one of the primary abuses in helping is the failure to monitor and evaluate the effects of the intervention strategies. Knowing how to monitor and evaluate one's helping activities is essential to effective helping.

Having a system of evaluation in place can

1. serve as an ongoing reminder that the helping relationship is not one upon which the helpee can remain dependent;

2. be used as a useful and helpful tool to foster an anticipation that the helping relationship is coming close to a termination;

3. provide the decision criteria needed for knowing when termination is appropriate. Assessing the impact of the helper's and helpee's actions may provide a checkpoint against which to measure whether progress is occurring, and to determine if the helping session can start to tone down.

Forms of Evaluation

Evaluation, as an ongoing part of the helping relationship, takes two forms: formative and summative.

Formative evaluation is used at strategic points throughout the helping interaction to assist in the ongoing decisions to continue or modify the action plan. Its purpose is to gather data to expedite decision making about the upcoming steps and procedures in the helping relationship. Such evaluation provides the basis on which to better "form" the process for attaining desired outcomes.

Formative evaluation can often be achieved by simply setting aside time for the helpee and helper to "process" or discuss the relationship and the procedures employed up to that point. Often an informal procedure, such as asking the helpee for his or her feelings about the plan or the progress he or she has made to date, will serve the purpose of formative evaluation. Informally, the helper can assess progress by the oral responses of the helpee. Having the helpee discuss his or her feelings about the strategy, the problems he or she experienced, and any ideas about future use are ways to gather soft information about the intervention.

Such a formative evaluation can begin as early as the first session. Consider the following exchange between a helper and helpee, which occurred at the end of their first session.

> Dr. K: Well, Anthony, I certainly appreciate your willingness to come in and share your concerns with me. I can see how your current dissatisfaction with your job and your confusion about your career choices can certainly be upsetting. I feel that we have made a good first step, especially in agreeing that next time we meet, you will take the Vocational Interest Test. It may give us something to focus on in terms of a career search. Before we end this session, I would be very interested in receiving your feedback about our interaction. How did you feel about our session today?
>
> Anthony: When I first came, I was a bit nervous. I never went to a psychologist before. But I was surprised how comfortable I felt with you. You made it very easy to talk to you. In fact, I am surprised how much I did talk—usually I am pretty private.
>
> Dr. K: Well, I appreciate your willingness to trust me and risk opening up. Thank you. How did you feel about the direction the session took?
>
> Anthony: Well, I wish I had an immediate answer as to what I should do, but I know that's not very realistic. I do feel good about taking the interest test. I think that may give us some place to begin to focus. So I guess to answer your question, I feel like it was a real productive session—you seem to understand my concern and we seem to know where to go next, so that feels pretty good to me.
>
> Dr. K: Me, too. Anthony, before we stop, is there anything that you would like me to clarify, or anything you would like to ask me?
>
> Anthony: Oh, I'm sure there is, but I can't think of anything right at this point . . . maybe next time.

Even though this was only the first session, Dr. K. employed formative evaluative questions to assess Anthony's comfort with the process and understanding of the strategies (taking an interest test) to be employed. Such a formative evaluation also provides the helpee with a sense of being an active contributor, a collaborator, in this helping process.

Summative evaluation addresses the issue of goal attainment. The specific intent of summative evaluation is to show that the action plan has reached its original objectives. A summative evaluation may attempt to answer the following questions:

1. Were the objectives/goals attained?
2. What factors in the action plan contributed to goal attainment or inhibited it?
3. What is the value of this action plan in contrast to alternative plans?

On a more structured or formal level, the helpee can be assisted to actually collect data which would be used to assess the degree to which progress has been made toward his or her goal. The establishment of such a formal, or structured, form of evaluation is greatly assisted if during the problem identification stage and goal setting stage, the goal was specified in concrete, quantifiable terms. It is easier to know when the helpee has achieved his or her goals when those goals have been clearly and concretely articulated. A goal stated vaguely, such as "I will study more", is much more difficult to assess than one which is placed in observable, quantifiable terms, such as "For each day of the remainder of this month, I will spend 2 hours reading and outlining my chemistry notes."

Learning to quantify the helpee's goals is an essential step in the evaluation process. Exercise 10-1 is designed to provide you with practice in this phase of the evaluation.

In addition to defining the helpee's desired goal concretely, it may be a useful procedure, even during the problem identification phase, to have the helpee take a

---

EXERCISE 10-1
Quantifying Goals

Directions: For each of the following presenting complaints identify two concrete, quantifiable forms of the implied, desired goal.

Presenting Complaint	Goal 1	Goal 2
1. (sample) "I eat too much!"	Eat 1200 calories a day for one month	Eat 3 meals a day— no more—for one month
2. "I lose my cool"	_____ _____ _____	_____ _____ _____
3. " I have no social life"	_____ _____ _____	_____ _____ _____
4. "People walk all over me"	_____ _____ _____	_____ _____ _____
5. "When it comes to school I'm lazy"	_____ _____ _____	_____ _____ _____

count of the frequency of occurrence of the undesirable behavior, or even a count of the degree to which the desired goal was present, prior to treatment. Such baseline data will serve as a reference point against which to estimate the effectiveness of the treatment strategy.

For example, in one case, the helpee, Tom, was asked to keep a daily record of the number of cigarettes he smoked as well as how far down he smoked each cigarette. This data was collected and it was discovered that he smoked, on the average, 40 cigarettes a day, and 100% of them were smoked down to the filter. As a preliminary goal, he decided to cut the number in half, and stop smoking each cigarette at the midway point. Such baseline data not only helped in establishing a workable goal, but it also proved to be a reference point from which to judge the progress that was being made, even when the progress was slight, as with the case when the helpee noted that he smoked 35 cigarettes a day over the past week.

Such monitoring will not only assist the helper and helpee in identifying when the goal had been reached, but it will also provide them the opportunity to fine tune the action plan (i.e., formative evaluation). Thus, the data can serve a diagnostic function, while at the same time providing encouragement to the helpee. This was the situation with the case described above.

Tom had tried on a number of occasions to quit smoking "cold turkey". He was never successful, and therefore had approached the task with very little optimism. After establishing the baseline, Tom and the helper set the following goals: 1) For the next week, Tom would smoke NO MORE than his usual 40 cigarettes a day, but during that same time period, 2) he would try to put them out before he passed the half way point on the cigarette. The dialogue that follows occurred in the next session.

Helper: Well, tell me how did the plan work?

Tom (trying to be very controlled): GREAT! No kidding! I can't believe it! I know it probably doesn't mean anything to you, but I really made progress.

Helper: Actually, it does mean a lot to me to see you so encouraged. Would you tell me what you mean when you say "made progress"?

Tom: Well, I still averaged almost 40 cigarettes a day (actually, I counted and it was 38.6). But with the exception of the first day, I stopped every cigarette after smoking only one-half of it. So it is really like I cut my smoking in half! You don't know . . . I've never . . . never . . . been able to do anything like that.

Helper: It sounds like you are pleased with your first attempt. That's good. I assume you want to keep working on our goal, however.

Tom: You bet!

The clearly set baseline and identification of quantifiable goals assisted this helpee in feeling much more optimistic and encouraged about the helping process.

In addition to providing encouragement about progress, a summative evaluation can also be used to define that point at which the helping relationship can terminate. When the initial problems have been eliminated or sufficiently reduced, and the helpee is currently coping better with these problems, then termination appears appropriate and the termination process can begin.

PREPARING FOR TERMINATION

The thought of terminating the helping relationship often evokes strong, ambivalent feelings on the part of both the helper and helpee. This is especially true for those forms of helping which may have encouraged the helpee to be overly dependent on the helper, or in which the helping relationship has developed over a greater length of time.

In the more formal, and generally longer, forms of helping, such as may be the case in psychotherapy or counseling, the helpee often experiences anxiety when considering termination. The helpee may experience termination as a loss (Lacoursiere, 1980), with sadness (Cohen & Smith, 1976), and with grief (Ward, 1982). He or she may wish to "hold on", even though the original concern which brought them to the helping relationship has been addressed, and the helpee is much better able to meet similar concerns in the future.

Brief helping relationships usually do not result in the formation of a lasting bond between the helper and helpee. Even so, the manner in which the relationship is terminated is both important and delicate, and may be met with some resistant on the part of either the helpee or helper. If the relationship has been positive and growth-filled, both the helper and helpee may wish to see it continue. Or, there may be times when the helpee, although well on his or her way to resolving his or her difficulty, may experience some anxiety and concern over the possibility that he or she may not be able to continue the action plan without the helper's aid.

One special area of concern, even for brief helping encounters, is that of dependency—a condition wherein the helpee has come to rely too much on the helper, rather than becoming more self-reliant. Often the helpee's relief at receiving support and intervention ideas during the helping process results in a feeling of dependency on the helper—the helpee may begin to believe that he or she needs the helper, and may begin to doubt his or her own ability to cope and resolve his or her problems without the ongoing support of the helper. The alert helper must be sensitive to this possibility.

Dependency interferes with the educational and preventive goals of helping. Not only is the helper attempting to assist the helpee with this particular problem, but also to assist him or her to function independently as a problem solver in the future. Therefore, even when such anxiety and emotional concerns exist, termination must occur if the helpee is ever to feel competent and independent.

The helpee needs to understand the source of these feelings and concerns, but at the same time understand that he or she is prepared to begin to address his or her problem on his or her own. Thus, in addition to confronting the helpee about his or her ability to handle this and future problems, the helper may start to "wean" the helpee, by scheduling appointments less frequently and with larger blocks of time separating them.

The helpee may be more receptive to the idea of ending the relationship, if he or she understands that such an ending is neither final nor irreversible. Terminating the helping relationship is not an absolute, black or white issue.

The concept of termination may be more pallatable to the helpee, if he or she is are involved in the termination planning. It is useful to discuss with the helpee which approach to termination may be the best for him or her. For example, the helpee could suggest the manner in which termination should occur. Should the relationship be ended all-or-none, tapered off, or even using a trial break? The helpee needs to contribute to the termination plan, just as he or she has been actively involved in the other stages of helping.

TERMINATION

Ideally, termination comes about as a result of the helpee attaining his or her original goals. Sometimes, however, the helpee may wish to terminate the process because he or she does not feel goal attainment is possible. Similarly, there may be times when the helper wishes to conclude the relationship, feeling the work has been done, when the helpee is not so sure. Under these conditions, the helper and helpee must share their feelings, and try to come to mutual consensus and a reasonable plan for termination.

Termination should not be a surprise. It should be part of the helping process. Therefore, the helpee should be aware of it, even from the beginning stages of helping. As part of the helping process, it is not something "done" to the other, but a process to which both the helper and helpee contribute.

The process of termination is made much easier if the helping encounters have been focused on problems and problem solving, and not on simply building a connection between the helper and helpee. When the helpee has made progress toward the attainment of his or her goal, he or she will feel less need for helping. There may even be little hints suggesting this. Perhaps that helpee cancels a session, or asks if he or she could miss next time. As a helper, you need to hear and interpret these signals as suggesting that it may be time to terminate this helping relationship.

The Process of Terminating

The process of termination actually involves a series of tasks to be achieved.

Task 1.   Review the specific conditions which brought the helpee to the helper. Together with the helpee, the helper should review the nature of the helpee's original problem or concern. This review sets the reference point against which progress can be defined.

Task 2. Define the current situation. After reviewing the original presenting complaint, the helper and helpee need to assess the helpee's current situation. At this point, the helper and helpee need to identify the amount of progress which has been made toward goal attainment. This review will serve to highlight the amount and type of work the helpee and helper have accomplished, and also identify the specific gains which have been made. Further, such a review provides an opportunity for highlighting the competence which the helpee is exhibiting in coping with his or her problem.

Task 3. Review strategy. A third task to be accomplished is for the helper and helpee to review the various processes and strategies which were employed and the new learning and coping which has taken place. Reconsidering the procedures employed for problem identification and resolution can serve an educational function. Reviewing the specific procedures and processes used in helping not only serves to reinforce the positive effort and outcome of the helping encounter, but it also assists the helpee to learn these procedures as an approach to problem solving. This learning will foster his or her independent functioning and problem solving in the future.

Task 4. Answer any questions. In the process of reviewing the use of these procedures, the helper needs to be alert to answer any questions, concerns, or misunderstandings the helpee may have about the various techniques.

Task 5. Transfer the learning. It is also useful to have the helpee identify other areas of his or her life where these procedures may have value. The aim is to assist the helpee to transfer what he or she has learned in this specific helping encounter to the more "typical" experiences of his or her life. Such facilitation of the helpee's generalization from this specific situations to others will assist him or her in incorporating these procedures into his or her overall coping style.

Task 6. Transfer support. In order to insure that the helpee maintains his or her progress toward his or her goal, the helper should assist the helpee in identifying other resources available for his or her ongoing support (e.g., friends, family, colleagues, church members, other helpers in the community, etc.)

Task 7. Explore feelings. As one of the final tasks in the terminating process, the helper needs to assist the helpee to explore his or her feelings, or reactions, to the ending of this helping encounter. As noted previously, the helpee may experience some anxiety, sadness, or general concern. These feelings need to be expressed and discussed.

Task 8. Say goodbye. If both the helper and helpee can mutually agree that additional work sessions are not needed at this point, the helper can suggest his or her availability in the future, should additional questions or concerns arise. After this open invitation for renewal of contact, the helper needs to conclude the contract with the appropriate farewells.

The helpee also needs to be made to feel comfortable with the fact that termination does not mean that he or she cannot resume helping, if the helper is available and the helpee chooses. Often the helpee resists concluding the relationship because of concerns that he or she may have difficulty reconnecting should he or she feel like further support or additional help is needed. The helper needs to demonstrate, verbally and nonverbally, his or her availability to negotiate future contracts, while at the same time encouraging the helpee to attempt independent steps toward goal attainment.

Termination is not always a simple lock step process. The tasks identified are often accomplished in what appears to be random order and may be revisited more than once during the termination process. Exercise 10-2 provides you with a sample of a termination session. Your task would be to read the dialogue and identify the processes/tasks which are being demonstrated.

EXERCISE 10-2
A Look at Termination

Directions: This exercise may prove most productive if it can be done with a colleague or classmate. Review the above description of the various tasks to be accomplished during the process of termination. Next read the following exchange and identify the places where the various tasks are being accomplished. Remember that the tasks need not be accomplished in order, nor only once.

Helper: It is kind of hard to believe that we have been meeting for a month now. But it seems like we have accomplished quite a bit. How do you feel about what we have done?

Helpee: Yeah, I think it has been good. I feel better about my relationship with my parents, and I think that I have learned some new ways to communicate with them.

Helper: That's a good point. When you first came to me, your concern was that your parents were always bugging you. As we talked, we both began to realize that it wasn't always, and that most of the time, it was probably that your parents really didn't understand what you were feeling or what you wanted from them. How's my memory?

Helpee: You're right on target. I guess one of the things I really became aware of was, that it really wasn't all their fault, that some of the responsibility rested with me. I had to learn to express myself!

Helper: That's super! And it seems that once we set the goal of having you learn how to identify your feelings and begin to

Continued

EXERCISE 10-2 *Continued*

concretely express yourself toward your parents, you really
began to get enthused.

Helpee: Well, not quite . . . it was a little scary. But I did enjoy
learning those assertiveness techniques that we practiced.
They seem to help. But I know I still have a lot to learn!

Helper: I agree there is still much to learn, for you and me. I guess,
as humans, we will never be able to get it perfectly, but you
certainly have taken some giant leaps forward!

Helpee: I guess. It still feels kind of strange when I confront someone or express my feelings . . . I just hope I can keep it up.

Helper: It is a bit strange when we try some new behaviors, but with
practice they begin to feel more natural. It sounds like you are
practicing your communication skills with other people, in addition to your parents. That's a real good way to keep developing!

Helpee: Yeah, it's funny, some of my friends have even made statements like "who's the new guy?" and "look at Mr. Assertive!"
It makes me feel really good.

Helper: Well, as you know, we originally planned to meet for about
5 sessions in hopes of reducing the tension between you and
your parents. It seems that not only has the tension between
your parents and yourself been reduced, but that the skills you
are learning are enabling you to continue to develop better
relationships with a lot of people in your life.

Helpee: Really . . . it is helping, but I'm still concerned that I will
blow it, or get lazy, or something.

Helper: Well, I can appreciate your concern, that you don't want to
go backward. You know, the university counseling center offers assertive training courses each semester. I have heard they
are very good in that you get a lot of opportunity to practice the
skills. I also heard that they are a lot of fun. That might be a
way to get a refresher.

Helpee: That's interesting. I'll look into it.

Helper: And you know that if you want to talk to me or if something
else comes up, I would be happy to schedule an appointment.
In fact, if you wouldn't mind, I would like to call you, let's say
after Thanksgiving break, to see how it's going.

Helpee: Oh, that would be great. I would even get a chance to tell
you how it went at home over Thanksgiving.

Helper: Well, I've really appreciated all the work you have done,
and I feel good about what we have been able to do together.
Before we end, do you have any questions or anything you
wish to share?

EXERCISE 10-2   *Continued*

Helpee: No, I'm pretty good. I really want to thank you. As you know
I came here feeling a bit defensive . . . a little nervous. You really helped me to relax and feel comfortable and I am really
excited about these techniques you have taught me. Thanks.
Helper: You are welcome. (getting up, extending hand in gesture of
saying goodbye). Don't forget . . . practice, practice, practice
(laughing) and I'll contact you after Thanksgiving. See you!
Helpee: Take care, bye!

FOLLOW-UP

As evidenced in the above dialogue, the helper established a point of follow-up (calling after Thanksgiving). While it is much more preferable for the helpee to find
support and encouragement from those in his or her day-to-day living experience, a
follow-up contact from the helper, even if it is as brief as a phone call or note, may
serve two useful functions.

First, a follow-up to the work already completed will provide the helper an opportunity to support, encourage, and reinforce the helpee's continued use of his or her
new skills developed as part of the intervention plan. As with any new behavior or
skill, the initial implementation of an approach may be less than perfect, thus the
follow-up affords the helper an opportunity for some final fine tuning. Secondly,
follow-up will also highlight the real sense of care and concern the helper has for the
helpee, as well as announce to the helpee that while this particular contract for helping
may be terminated, the helper is available for future contact, should it be desired.

WHAT NEXT

The process of termination is a very important facet of any helping relationship. It not
only prevents dependency and encourages independent application of learned principles and strategies, but also provides the helpee with a sense of closure and achievement in an area, that, until this point, has been confusing and frustrating. One thing
that is important to remember before moving on is that concluding a relationship,
which has been positive and supportive, can be difficult, even anxiety-provoking for
a helpee. As helpers, we must be sensitive to the concerns and anxieties a helpee may
be experiencing in anticipation of ending this relationship. Before we move on it,
would be helpful for you to become more aware of the troublesome and anxious
feelings which often accompany the termination of a positive, supportive relationship. Exercise 10-3 will help you increase your awareness of these troublesome feelings, while also encouraging you to identify ways to reduce such feelings when
ending your helping encounters.

EXERCISE 10-3
The Good and Bad of Endings

Directions: This is a four-part exercise which will require personal reflection.

Part 1: Generate a list of individuals with whom you have had close, caring, positive relationships which are now ended. Allow yourself to think back to friends, family, other significant adults, etc. you may have encountered through your childhood, adolescence, current life, etc.

Part 2: Review the list and place a (*) next to the name of the person with whom the ending of the relationship was particularly painful, scary, or in some way negatively experienced. Next, place (x) next to the name of the relationship for which the ending was least painful or negative.

Part 3: Identify the factors which distinguished the endings of these two relationships. What contributed to the negativity of the one ending versus the other?

Part 4: What might you learn from your own personal experiences about

1. what a helpee may experience in terminating a very positive, supportive relationship with you; and
2. what you can do to reduce the potential negative experience of such an ending?

REFERENCES AND RECOMMENDED READINGS

Cohen, A.M., & Smith, R.D. (1976). *The critical incident in growth groups: Theory and technique.* LaJolla, CA: University Associates.

Hackney, H., & Cormier, L.S. (1991). *Counseling strategies and interventions* (3rd edition). Boston, MA: Allyn and Bacon.

Kanfer, F.H., & Schefft, B.K. (1988). *Guiding therapeutic change.* Champaign, IL: Research Press.

Lacoursiere, R.B. (1980). *The life of groups: Group developmental stage theory.* New York: Human Sciences Press.

Nicholson, R.A., & Berman, J.S. (1983). Is follow-up necessary in evaluating psychotherapy? *Psychological Bulletin, 93,* 261–278.

Parsons, R.D. (1985). The counseling relationship. In R. Wicks, R. Parsons, & D. Capps. *Clinical handbook of pastoral counseling* (pp 97–115). Mahwah, NJ: Paulist Press.

Ward, D.W. (1982). A model for the more effective use of theory in group work. *Journal of Specialists in Group Work, 7,* 224–230.

Ward, D. E. (1984). Termination of individual counseling: Concepts and strategies. *Journal of Counseling and Development, 63(1),* 21–26.

▶ 11

Special Concerns
for Helpers

From start to finish, the helping process can be a draining, yet rewarding, experience. Helping is not simply an automatic, cold, and distant process of problem solving. It is truly a human encounter, one engaging the helpees' and helpers' feelings as well as their minds.

As noted throughout the previous chapters, effective helping requires the presence of facilitating attitudes and the utilization of helping skills. Sometimes, the feelings experienced in the helping encounter may distort the helper's or helpee's objectivity and interfere with the effective utilization of these helping attitudes and skills. These feelings can oftentimes be quite subtle in their development and thus can go unrecognized until they have done their damage.

The current chapter will address two processes in which either the helper's or helpee's emotional reactions may prove not only counterproductive to the helping process but even detrimental to those involved. Specifically, the chapter will:

1. provide a brief overview to the process known as transference;
2. describe the conditions leading to the experience of burnout;
3. discuss steps to be taken to avoid, or at least reduce, the negative effects of either experience.

TRANSFERENCE/COUNTERTRANSFERENCE

In Chapter 1, we discussed a number of conditions which could interfere with the helper's ability to remain objective within the helping encounter. One of these conditions was termed transference.

Transference

Transference is the unconscious process by which the helpee places onto the helper past feelings or attitudes that he or she actually holds for or toward other significant people in his or her past. Transference is a process which oftentimes goes unnoticed, and yet can effectively impede the objectivity of either person experiencing it.

For example, one helpee, James, constantly sought reassurance from the helper that the helper would continue to work with him. In the process of describing his past history, James realized that as a child he often feared abandonment. This same childhood fear of abandonment was acting as a filter through which he interpreted his current relationship with the helper. As such, he was motivated to constantly find evidence that such abandonment would not occur.

As evidenced by the example of James, helpees experiencing transference have lost their objectivity. They are not accurately or objectively processing events as they are actually occurring. Rather, their reactions are tinted or filtered through these earlier emotional events or memories. For example, they may be distorting a current experience as result of their unfinished business with significant people in their life (e.g., parents), and not in response to the here-and-now interaction with the helper.

Transference can be either negative or positive. For example, helpees may exhibit inappropriate anger with the helper, express unrealistic demands of the helper (i.e., negative transference), or begin to demonstrate extremely positive, affectionate feelings toward the helper (i.e., positive transference). Such positive transference was found in the case of Ms. L.

Ms. L. came to counseling as a result of feeling unhappy and disenchanted with her marriage, complaining that her husband never gave her the attention she needed or was used to getting. In the process of meeting with her counselor, she soon began to experience a strong attraction to him. She would attempt to prolong the sessions in order to ask him about his personal life. Ms. L. began to call the counselor, often only to share some minor point or experience. All in all, Ms. L. began to display a liking for the counselor and an interest in his personal life which were beyond the bounds of this professional relationship.

Such a loss of objectivity and blurring of professional lines may be indicative of transference. Or, as reported by Pietrofesa, Leonard, and Van Hoose (1978), transference may be indicated by the presence of any of the following signs:

1. The helpee displays likes or dislikes out of proportion to the situation.
2. The helpee shows too much interest in the helper or overemphasizes a helper trait.
3. The helpee may not be able to focus upon any concern. He or she may continually misunderstand what the helper is saying.
4. The helpee engages in attention-seeking behaviors (e.g., excessive calling, continual lateness, etc.).

These distortions, or losses of objectivity and experience of unrealistic and often exaggerated reactions on the part of the helpee, pose both a special problem and a unique opportunity for the helper. The problem is that the helper needs to remain objective and not be seduced into seeing the helpee's reactions as appropriate. Reviewing the specific conditions which the helpee feels have stimulated these feelings can assist both the helpee and the helper to determine if the response is realistic and appropriate to the encounter, or if the response may be suggesting something about the helpee's past relationships which need to be addressed.

We must be careful not to discount the helpee's feelings as always reflecting transference. Sometimes, the helpee is angry at the helper . . . and nothing more. Understanding the concept of transference, or the possibility that transference may be operating in a relationship, does not provide a helper a license to ignore or discount the helpee's concerns or feelings. It is essential to respond to the feelings—as they reflect either the actual relationship or dynamic between the helper and the helpee, or as they reflect an important part of the helpee's past experience. In either case, the analysis of the reaction can provide the helper and helpee with significant insight into both the nature of their relationship, and the significance of the previous relationships to the helpee.

Countertransference

Transference happens to helpers as well as helpees. Helpers, like helpees, may experience unresolved needs which may be acted out in the relationship with the helpee. Often these needs get exhibited in the helper's unrealistic expectations and reactions to the helpee—reactions and expectations which interfere with the helper's objectivity. When a helper experiences such a loss of objectivity, or transference, it is called *countertransference.*

Countertransference significantly effects the objectivity of the helper, and thus presents a serious concern. With countertransference, the helper's feelings and actions are not responsive to the events of the helping encounter. Even though the helper may be prompted to respond because of a particular event in the helping relationship, his or her response is primarily based on past significant relationships and events of his or her life. Thus, the helper is acting to primarily satisfy his or her needs and not those of the helpee. Consider, for example, the scenario presented in Exercise 11-1.

In a now classic work, *Theory of Psychoanalytic Technique* (1958), Karl Menninger provides a succinct listing of ways to quickly recognize the possible existence of countertransference. An adapted version is listed below.

1. The helper experiences persistent drowsiness during the helping encounter.
2. The helper repeatedly experiences affectionate feelings or erotic fantasies involving the helpee.
3. The helper avoids addressing certain helpee concerns, since they touch on the helper's own concerns.

EXERCISE 11-1
Countertransference

Directions: After reading the background experience of the helper:

1. Identify the emotional theme, or area, which may be so active in the helper that it blocks his objectivity;
2. Suggest one way this countertransference may negatively impact the helping relationship.

Helper: The helper is a 43-year-old male psychologist. The helper has been divorced for 5 years. The divorce was a very painful and costly process for the helper. The experience was painful in that he did not want a divorce, and even to this day desires to be married. Further, his wife's lawyer was extremely aggressive and negative. As a result, he lost a lot of money and property when it came to the property distribution.

Helpee #1: A man having a custody battle with his ex-wife.

Helper's Emotional Issue: _____

_____

Negative Impact: _____

_____

Helpee #2: A young, attractive female who is somewhat socially shy and feeling a bit lonely.

Helper's Emotional Issue: _____

_____

Negative Impact: _____

_____

Helpee #3: A young couple coming for "pre-marriage counseling". They are very much in love, and simply would like to learn some communication skills in order to make their good relationship better!

Helper's Emotional Issue: _____

_____

Negative Impact: _____

_____

Helpee #4: A female experiencing marital difficulties. Her husband, a lawyer, wants a divorce, and she is afraid of being left alone. She has come to the helper to find ways to try to save the marriage.

Helper's Emotional Issue: _____

_____

Negative Impact: _____

_____

4. The helper cultivates continued dependence by the helpee.

5. The helper becomes careless or forgetful in terms of keeping the helpee's appointments, being late for the appointment, or letting the appointment extend longer than was intended.

In each of these situations, the helper may be reacting to his or her own needs rather than the needs of the helpee. For example, if the issues being presented by the helpee cause the helper some personal discomfort, the helper may psychologically attempt to avoid that personal discomfort by withdrawing from the topic by becoming drowsy, or from the helpee by missing the appointment. In these situations, the helper's desire to meet his or her own need will interfere with his or her ability to remain objective.

Reducing Countertransference

One way to prevent or reduce countertransference is to increase our own self-awareness and understanding. Clearly, increasing our own awareness of our actions, our intentions, our motivations, will help us to recognize when our objectivity is being distorted.

A helper seeking to become more self-aware of his or her motivations and actions as a helper will find it much easier to do if he or she has developed a relatively consistent style in dealing with helpees. When the helper employs a stable and consistent style of helping, he or she will be more aware when this normal style and procedure changes. Such a variation from what he or she does "typically" needs to be questioned. A variance may be a clue that the helper is responding from his or her need, rather than in response to the needs of the helpee. For example, assume that a professional psychologist schedules people for 50-minute sessions, and typically does not see people on Fridays. Should that psychologist become aware that he or she has made a recurring exception to either of these standards in the case of one particular helpee, such variation from his or her typical style may be a signal that countertransference is operative. It may suggest that it is the helper, who "wants" or "needs" to see the helpee for longer times, or on "special" days, rather than the helpee, who needs this type of attention.

Because it is not always easy for us to truly monitor our own actions or our own motivations, it is essential that we develop a system of collegial consultation and supervision. Whether the helper is a novice or a highly trained, seasoned veteran, all helpers benefit from professional dialogue and supervision. Meeting on a regular basis with our peers, or those more highly trained and experienced than ourselves, to discuss our reactions and decisions in current cases, invites these others to listen for distortions in our professional behavior or objectivity. The use of case supervision, in which the supervisor not only provides suggestions to the helper for working with the helpee, but can also be a "third ear" listening to the helper's own feelings, intentions, and reactions to the helpee, is a useful tool for identifying signs of distorted objectivity.

Quite often, a loss of objectivity not only interferes with the efficiency and accuracy of the helper's intervention, but may begin to overload the helper with the emotional burden of the cases, and result in what has been termed helper *burnout*. Burnout is a second major concern of those in the helping field and is discussed below.

BURNOUT

Consider the case of Adam. Adam is a social worker working for a local county agency. He has worked for this agency as an intake worker and home visitor ever since receiving his degree 5 years ago. Adam always wanted to be a social worker and was enthusiastic about his ability to be of assistance to those in need. Lately, however, Adam has felt apathetic at work. The joy and excitement just doesn't seem to be there any more. He has trouble concentrating and reports that he has a great deal of trouble becoming motivated to do his rounds. Adam's friends have noted that he generally doesn't want to do anything any more, that he is always complaining about being tired or having headaches, and often he is simply too short-tempered to want to be around. Adam is exhibiting signs of burnout!

Helpers of all sorts often experience emotional stress and even depression as a direct result of their involvement, or perhaps more accurately stated, overinvolvement with their clients, and client problems. One author (Gill, 1980, p. 21) has highlighted this potential danger by noting: "helping people can be extremely hazardous to your physical and mental health".

The research (Freudenberger, 1980; Edelwich & Brodsky, 1980; Gill, 1980; Kottler, 1986; and Maslach, 1982) describes burnout as an experience marked by the progressive loss of idealism, energy, and purpose. While there may be subtle differences in both the experience and definition of burnout, most agree that it is an ongoing process of depletion of energy, increased fatigue, and a general debilitation of one's functioning. Clearly such an ongoing experience can jeopardize the helper's own emotional well-being.

In order to prevent burnout, or reduce the negative effects of burnout, it is necessary to understand the various causes of burnout—the warning signs and symptoms, and even the changes and processes which characterize the development of burnout.

Causes

There appears to be no single cause for burnout. Each helper may be impacted by any number of factors or conditions which elevate his or her stress. For example, when helpers feel overworked, professionally and socially isolated, and underappreciated, the seeds of burnout may be laid. Further, when helpers have limited or no opportunity, either through supervision or collegial exchange, to express their professional and personal frustrations, concerns and questions, they may begin to experience the effects of burnout.

While no one single cause has been identified, each of the following factors has been found to contribute to the occurrence of burnout.

1. Unrealistic expectations: When confronted by a helpee who has been experiencing a problem for a long time, it may be unrealistic to assume that significant changes can occur within a few helping sessions. The helper who has unrealistic expectations about what can be done to help a helpee, and the speed with which it can be done, is at risk of burnout.

2. Overpersonalization: When a helper starts to take too much personal responsibility for the actions or experiences of the helpee, he or she is increasing his or her risk of burnout. Further, a helper who begins to take all of the blame for the lack of progress or the limited success of the helping encounter may be overpersonalizing the situation, and may again be increasing his or her risk of burnout.

3. Loss of objectivity: The helper who too closely identifies with the helpee and the helpee's problem loses the ability to view the situation and process objectively. This is not to say that a helper does not care. Helpers do and should care, but care professionally. Thus, for example, if the helpee is living in a very bad environment or is socially isolated, that does not mean that the helper should not, or cannot, enjoy his or her own surroundings and social contacts without feeling guilty. While it is important to be empathic, the helper must keep a professional distance, recognizing that it is the helpee's problem and not his or her own.

4. Task overload: Helpers who experience having too much to do with too little time or energy to do it risk burnout by overload. The reality is that for many helpers, especially those working in community or social service agencies, too many tasks are asked of too few people. Under these conditions, exhaustion results when helpers attempt to perform superhuman levels of work production; burnout will soon follow.

5. Poor organizational skills: Sometimes it is not the actual volume or quantity of work the helper has to do, but the inefficiency with which the helper approaches the work, which causes the problem. The helper who is poorly organized, poorly self-managed, adds to the stress of the helping profession by wasting needed energy on relatively minor maintenance tasks.

6. Failure to care for self: Burnout risk seems to increase for those helpers who do not self-care. Helpers who are unable to say yes to self, even when that means saying no to others, are at risk of burning out. This can be a very common occurrence among helpers, and shows up in very small, yet potentially destructive ways. Helpers who do not schedule break times, lunch time, or even take time off from the job are elevating their risk of burnout.

7. Lack of support: Feeling like one is going it alone, that as a helper you must "shoulder" your own concerns, as well of those of all of your helpees, without the support of others in your life can contribute to the development of burnout. Helpers need both professional (e.g., collegial consultation, supervision) and personal (e.g., friends, family) support if they are to remain personally healthy and professionally competent.

While it is useful to become aware of these possible contributing factors, it is more useful to begin to identify those to which you, as a helper, are particularly susceptible. Exercise 11-2 is designed to help you identify those particular factors.

While the listing of factors found in Exercise 11-2 is not an exhaustive or all-inclusive list, it does highlight the type of factors or experiences which contribute to the development of professional burnout. In addition to understanding how to recognize potential contributing factors, helpers need to be sensitive to the early symptoms and warning signs of burnout.

Warning Signs

Freudenberger and Richelson (1980) offer a "burnout scale" in which a helper can assess him- or herself along a continuum from "doing fine" to "in dangerous place". Exercise 11-3 is a modification of Freudenberger and Richelson's approach. It may be suggested that the greater the number of symptoms you currently experience, the greater your risk of burnout.

The occurrence of these symptoms does not necessarily mean that one is burned out. The frequency of symptom occurrence and the length of time that such symptoms have been continually experienced is also important in defining burnout.

Burnout as Developmental

Burnout is not something that just occurs, or simply happens overnight to a helper. It seems to unfold or develop over time. Jim Gill (1980) suggests that burnout often develops through a series of progressive levels. In the first level, the helpee may note mild signs and symptoms which occur only occasionally and most often last for only a short time. In the second level, these signs and symptoms become more long-lasting and stable. Finally, in the third level, the symptoms become chronic and result in physical or psychological illness.

Obviously, the earlier in the developmental sequence that one can take note of the symptoms or warning signals, the easier the intervention may be.

Prevention/Intervention

Recognizing the onset of burnout is clearly the first step to intervention. But, in addition, there are behaviors which a helper can employ that both function as interventions to stress and burnout reduction, as well as preventive measures, which make burnout less a possibility.

1. Acknowledge onset: As noted, learning to monitor our own experience of stress is important. In fact, Maslach (1982) argues that detecting the first signs of burnout is critical. Helpers cannot wait for the big bang or deceive themselves, believing that it can't happen to them.

2. Attempt to be objective and rational: It is essential to set realistic expecta-

EXERCISE 11-2
Elevating the Risk of Burnout

Directions: After reading each of the factors which have been found to be associated with professional burnout,

1. place an asterisk (*) next those factors which you potentially could experience;
2. re-read those factors which you have identified with an asterisk (*), and place an (X) next to those asterisked items which you are CURRENTLY experience;
3. finally, identify two steps you can take to reduce or remove each of those factors you are currently experiencing.

Factors Associated with Burnout:

1. Unrealistic expectations
   Plan to reduce: _____
   _____
   _____

2. Overpersonalization
   Plan to reduce: _____
   _____
   _____

3. Loss of objectivity
   Plan to reduce: _____
   _____
   _____

4. Task overload
   Plan to reduce: _____
   _____
   _____

5. Poor organizational skills
   Plan to reduce: _____
   _____
   _____

6. Failure to care for self
   Plan to reduce:
   _____
   _____

7. Lack of support
   Plan to reduce: _____
   _____
   _____

EXERCISE 11-3
Personal Signals

Directions: For each of the following, check the symptoms or signals that you have experienced within the last 3 months. Discuss the symptoms you are currently experiencing with a colleague, a supervisor, or another professional helper, in order to develop strategies for reducing such symptoms.

_____ Hoped that the helpee would cancel or not show up.
_____ Feel apathetic and uncaring.
_____ Finding it harder to pay attention in the sessions.
_____ Have been forgetting assignments, appointments, etc.
_____ Don't seem to laugh as much as usual.
_____ Don't seem to find things as enjoyable as usual.
_____ Lost my cool with a helpee.
_____ Find that I am complaining about my case(s) to others.
_____ Feel extremely fatigued at the end of the day.
_____ Feel overly tense when with a helpee.
_____ Experiencing headaches, muscle tension, or stomach problems.
_____ Feel increasingly sad or irritable.

---

tions about what one can accomplish. Helpers must accept that they are not omnipotent. They will make mistakes, and will always be less than perfect. The healthy helper sets realistic expectations for him- or herself, the helpee, and the outcome of any one relationship.

3. Take care of self: As a helper, one must be extra sure to take care of his or her own physical well-being. It is important that the helper eat properly, rest, and exercise. Helping is an energy-draining process, and the healthy helper attempts to stay in shape for the job that needs to be done.

4. Organize and manage: Helpers need to learn to schedule wisely. It is important to schedule variation into one's day. Helpers should be sure to build into their schedules a variety of activities, including sufficient breaks to take care of bodily needs, paperwork, or even time to meditate.

5. Keep personal perspective: In order to prevent burnout or reduce its early effects, the helper needs to establish time and opportunity for personal support and distraction. It is essential that helping remain *part* of one's life, and not become *all* of one's life.

6. Keep professional perspective: As is evident, burnout happens most frequently when one loses his or her professional distance and objectivity. Helpers need to establish mechanisms for ongoing professional support. The use of professional

---

EXERCISE 11-4
Burnout, a Helper's View

Directions: The causative factors, early warning signs, and recommendations for prevention of burnout provided in this chapter can too easily become only words in a text. In order to make burnout a reality for you and not simply a text book description, it is suggested that you find a professional helper to interview, using the following questions. Share your interview data with your colleagues or class-mates, drawing conclusions about the prevalence of burnout, the actual experi-ence of burnout, and what others do to reduce the possibility or effects of burnout.

1. Background information: What does the person do? How was he or she trained? How long has her or she been doing this job?
2. Expectations and realities: What does he or she enjoy most about his or her job? Least? What is the biggest frustration? What was the biggest surprise, in terms of finding a reality different than his or her expectations?
3. Over the course of his or her career, how has (have):
   a) his or her enthusiasm for the job changed?
   b) his or her approach to the job changed?
   c) his or her expectations of his or her impact changed?
   d) he or she personally changed?
4. If this professional has experienced burnout, what symptoms occurred, or what form did it take?
5. What specific activities or ways of structuring his or her job does this helper employ to reduce excessive stress and avoid burnout?

---

supervision, personal counseling, or collegial consulting may assist the helper in retaining his or her professional perspective, or identify the early signs when such a professional perspective is being lost.

WHAT NEXT

Throughout the book, the focus has been on learning how to take care of the helpee. What is highlighted in this chapter is that one of the essential first steps of taking care of a helpee—the caretaking of the helper! Retaining professional objectivity and avoiding stress overload and burnout are not only steps to be taken in caring for the helper, but essential steps if one is to be a truly effective help giver.

As with each of the other chapters in this book, the information presented is only as useful as your ability to personalize it and integrate it into your own day-to-day

---

EXERCISE 11-5
Self-Monitoring/Self-Caring

Directions: As part of your ongoing professional development, it is useful, if not essential, for you to answer each of the following questions on a regular basis. It is suggested that you keep a professional journal, in which you semi-annually (if not more frequently) perform this task of self-monitoring, along with a re-commitment to self-caring by writing your response to each of the following.

1. How do I know I am being stressed? What are my particular signs of stress (physical, social, emotional, cognitive) which could be used as early warning signs of stress overload and possible burnout? How many of these signs am I currently experiencing?
2. What type of situations, conditions, or problems seem to be more than usually stressful for me? Are there types of problems I find extremely hard to deal with? Or are there types of people or people's styles which I find stressful? What characteristics of an organization or a setting may also increase my feelings of stress? How many of these stressful situations am I currently experiencing?
3. In the last several days, weeks, or months, have I devoted as much energy to my own development and enjoyment as I have to my helpees?
4. What three specific things can I do to increase my current self-care, and reduce the possibility of burnout?

   In three to six months, review your original responses to these questions, and re-evaluate your answers at that time. If you find it difficult to move from burnout to self-care, seek support from a colleague, a professional counselor, or a supervisor.

---

helping style. Before proceeding on to the next chapter, complete Exercise 11-5, an exercise also intended to be an ongoing activity throughout your life as a helper.

REFERENCES AND RECOMMENDED READINGS

Edelwich, J., & Brodsky, A. (1980). *Burnout: Stages of disillusionment in the helping professions.* New York: Human Services Press.

Freudenberger, H. (1980). *Burnout.* New York: Anchor Books/Doubleday.

Freudenberger, H., & Richelson, G. (1980). *Burn-out: How to beat the high cost of success.* New York: Doubleday.

Gill, J. (1980). Burnout: A growing threat in the ministry. *Human Development, 1(2),* Summer 21–27.

Kottler, J.A. (1986). *On being a therapist.* San Francisco, CA: Jossey-Bass.

Maslach, C. (1976). Burned-out. *Human Behavior.* Sept., 46–58.

Maslach C. (1982). *Burnout: The cost of caring.* Englewood Cliffs, NJ: Prentice-Hall.

Menninger, K. (1958). *Theory of psychoanalytic technique.* New York: Basic Books.

Pietrofesa, J.J., Leonard, G.E., & Van Hoose, W. (1978). *The authentic counselor.* Chicago, IL: Rand McNally.

Schafer, W. (1978). *Stress, distress and growth.* Davis, CA: Responsible Action.

▶ 12

Crisis Intervention

The previous chapters presented a brief overview of a rather generic approach to the helping process. The model described assumes that both the helper and the helpee have the time and the needed resources to employ the relationship-building, problem-defining and pathfinding strategies suggested.

However, there are times when the nature of the problem places the helpee in a state of emergency. Under these conditions, neither the helper nor the helpee can afford the luxury of a long-term problem identification or pathfinding procedure. Consider the following case illustration.

> Fred called the telephone hotline at 1 AM Sunday morning. The following dialogue ensued:
>
> Fred: I just can't take it any more!
> Hotline Counselor: Take it any more? Tell me, Fred, what has happened?
> Fred: We've been going together for 6 years . . . 6 years! We were planning to get married as soon as we were out of school. 6 years! I can't believe it!
> Hotline Counselor: You sound very upset, very hurt.
> Fred: Hurt! Upset, you bet! I found her in bed with another guy! I've had it, I can't take it! I'll show her! How's she gonna feel if I just cash it in?

Individuals like Fred who are experiencing an immediate crisis in their lives and who may be so devastated that they begin to consider extreme, self-destructive steps, need a quick, accelerated form of helping which leads to immediate stress and pain reduction. Such an accelerated form of helping is termed *crisis intervention.*

This chapter will

1. present a model of accelerated helping to be employed in crisis situations;
2. illustrate the use of force-field analysis as a technique in crisis intervention; and

3. highlight the specific helper skills and knowledge needed to effectively assess and intervene with a suicidal helpee.

THE NATURE OF CRISIS INTERVENTION

A person experiencing a crisis perceives an event or situation as an intolerable difficulty that exceeds his or her resources and coping mechanisms (Gilliland & James, 1988). Gerald Caplan (1964), a pioneer in the area of community mental health, defined a "crisis" as "a short period of psychological disequilibrium in a person who confronts a hazardous circumstance that for him constitutes an important problem which he can for the time being neither escape nor solve with his customary problem-solving resources". According to Caplan, a crisis tends to develop or progress through four phases:

1. There is an rise in tension as typical, habitual problem-solving techniques are unsuccessfully tried.
2. With the lack of success in coping, more discomfort is felt.
3. This increase in tension acts as a powerful internal stimulus which places the individual in an emergency problem-solving state. The problem may be redefined, or the helpee may simply resign him- or herself and begin to give up.
4. If the situation continues and the helpee can neither resolve the difficulty nor avoid it, tension increases and a major disorganization occurs.

In recent years, the helping profession has responded to the increasing need for crisis intervention by developing services such as drop-in counseling centers, hotline services, teenage advocate programs, etc. Generally, such crisis intervention programs display characteristics that distinguish them from other more traditional forms of helping (Parsons & Wicks, 1994).

1. Focus: The focus of crisis intervention is most typically on the helpee's observable difficulties. While it is clear that in most situations the helpee has deeper, more complicated, and long-standing problems, the focus for crisis intervention is on the immediate incapacitating effect of the present situational problem. If longer-term treatment is also needed, referral will be provided following the crisis intervention.

2. Goal: As implied in the focus of crisis intervention, the primary goal is to reduce the immediate stress and incapacitation and either return the helpee to his or her environment with a better ability to cope, or to refer the helpee for additional longer-term support.

3. Nature: Crisis intervention is a short-term form of helping. Because the goal is to provide immediate relief rather than adjust the helpee's personality or general style of living, the nature of the encounter is by definition brief.

4. Multiple workers: Often crisis intervention involves the services of a number of workers; the helpee in crisis may be treated by a team of helpers. Consequently, the emphasis on the establishment of a binding helping relationship is diminished, since all contacts will be problem-focused.

5. Multiple approaches: With the variety of workers often involved in a crisis and the emphasis on immediate reduction of the problem, crisis intervention typically employs multiple forms of intervention. The crisis counselor may solicit the involvement of individuals from legal aid, social services, human/domestic relations, and even various health care agencies, all depending on the nature of the helpee's crisis.

The reader is encouraged to complete Exercise 12-1 in order to appreciate the relatively unique nature of crisis intervention as a form of helping.

A MODEL OF CRISIS INTERVENTION

As suggested, crisis intervention is by definition brief and directive, and by necessity, it is truly an abbreviated form of the helping model presented within the previous chapters. While the specifics of each intervention will vary by the nature of the problem and the person(s) involved, there are three main phases to crisis intervention which appear somewhat generic to most, if not all, forms of crisis work (Parsons & Wicks, 1994). The three main phases of crisis intervention to be discussed are contact/assessment, planning and intervention, and termination.

Contact—Relating/Reassuring

As with many forms of helping, crisis intervention starts with the initial hello. In crisis counseling, the focus is clearly on providing immediate emotional support through the use of close contact, empathic listening, and reassurance.

During the initial contact, it is essential to assist the helpee to ventilate his or her feelings as a way of reducing the pent-up frustration and pain he or she may be experiencing. It is also essential to begin to develop a sense of hope, or hopeful expectation, about this encounter. Such a sense of hope begins to be developed through the process of reassurance, which can take many different forms.

Reassuring the helpee can be achieved by expressing approval for the helpee, and demonstrating a real understanding of the pain and sense of crisis the helpee is experiencing. Reassurance is also provided by pointing out to the helpee that there are steps, processes, and resources available to assist him or her with this problem. Finally, reassurance occurs when the helpee becomes aware of the possibility of gaining personal relief through the helping encounter, and even the possibility of achieving some positive outcomes as a result of working on his or her crisis situation.

EXERCISE 12-1
The Freshman Experience

Directions: You will achieve maximum benefit from this exercise if you can complete it with a small group of your colleagues or classmates.

Step 1: Review the 5 characteristics of crisis intervention presented above.

Step 2: Read the following details of the case of Drew.

Step 3: With your colleagues or classmates, discuss how each of the 5 characteristics presented above could be used to shape the needed intervention, assuming that you were the helper working with Drew.

Case Information

In the first two months of college life, 18-year-old Drew found the unaccustomed freedom more than he could successfully handle. Drew got into the habit of staying out late, missing classes, and was generally not preparing for his studies. Following midterm exams, Drew was notified by the academic dean that he was on academic probation. He was failing 3 of his 5 courses, and receiving D's in the remaining two courses.

Shaken, Drew made a commitment to knuckle down and get serious about school in order to rescue his grades before finals. He decided, however, that prior to this "push" for academics, he would have one last weekend blast. Partying one more time almost became partying one last time.

While at one party, Drew participated in a contest to drink 60 shots of beer in 60 seconds. The end result was that Drew found himself in the emergency room of the local hospital having his stomach pumped out. As he began to come around to what had happened, he was informed by the Assistant Vice President of Student Life, who had been called to the hospital, that his parents were contacted and because of his grades and his underage drinking, his dorm privileges would be terminated at the end of this semester.

Drew began to experience the pressure of numerous demands and stress points. His failing grades, along with the reality that he would have to move back home (off campus), and the fact that he just endangered his life, felt like too much to handle, especially in light of the fact that he was about to face his parents. As a result, Drew began to panic and attempted to leave the hospital unofficially. In a panic, he began to run from the emergency room, only to be stopped a security officer.

Clearly Drew had a number of serious problems to address, but the pressure had mounted to the point where his coping skills appeared insufficient and thus avoidance (running) appeared to be the only alternative. In this case, the hospital social worker was summoned and crisis intervention was initiated.

Assessment

Just like in other, less crisis-oriented forms of helping, the helper engaged in crisis intervention needs to fully explore the nature of the problem, the relevant historical background, and even identify personal disposing factors which may be contributing to the current experience. But unlike other non-crisis forms of helping, the crisis intervention worker will gather this data ONLY AFTER first identifying current issues, potential dangers, and immediate precipitating factors.

Because of the potential danger that a helpee in crisis may engage in self-mutilation, suicide, homicide, and/or become seriously disorganized, the accurate assessment of the here-and-now condition of the helpee provides the data needed for intervention planning, as well as decisions to refer or hospitalize. It is essential that the helper assesses the degree of risk, or danger, that the helpee may be encountering before any intervention or action is taken.

Helpers engaged in crisis intervention experience a unique demand for speed and accuracy in their assessment. Under the pressure of such crisis, the helper needs to retain his or her composure and be able to focus specifically on those areas that most clearly define the nature of the problem and the unique resources of the helpee.

The assessment process will require the helper to identify in clear, concrete terms the form of the crisis being experienced. This will require that the helper continue to focus the helpee on the current crisis and not be drawn off on tangential conversations, since efforts are directed to the most rapid reduction of the current crisis.

In the process of assessment, the helper not only ascertains what is actually happening to the individual (e.g., raped, fired, divorced, etc.), with all of the real and specific consequences of that event, but also begins to identify the meaning or consequences perceived by the helpee. It is essential for the crisis helper to identify the real versus the perceived problem experienced by the helpee. While such a delineation is always important, it is essential in the case of crisis intervention. Individuals in crisis often elevate their real, concrete problems to the point of experiencing them as absolutely intolerable and unbearable crisis. With such a distorted and unrealistic view of the experience, the person in crisis may feel driven to the point of taking any extreme steps (including suicide) to remove the unbearable condition. Thus, while confronted with real problems that do require adaptation and personal cost to solve, the helpee in crisis fails to see the situation as simply problematic, yet solvable, and may react out of desperation.

For example, Ellen, a 57-year-old mother of three adult children was recently abandoned by her husband. Ellen called a crisis hotline exclaiming that her life was over. From Ellen's perspective, it was clear that no one loved her, she was totally alone, and was unable to go on.

With the help of the crisis hotline worker, Ellen was able to separate out the reality of the situation from her initial reaction to it. Ellen was able to identify the fact that while her three grown children lived out of state, none had abandoned her. Further, she was even able to recall how, during the past year, each of her children had actually invited her to consider relocating to his or her area. Ellen also admitted, that while she felt abandoned and all alone, the reality was that there were single women from her church group (widowed or divorced) who would gladly help her to begin to learn all the things she would need to know to run her house and her financial affairs on her own.

Thus, while there were some very real problems facing Ellen, she was able to recognize that 1) they were not as overwhelming as they first seemed, and 2) she had personal and social resources which would prove helpful as she began to confront some of these real problems.

The process of delineating the real from the perceived problem is not only essential for assessment, but actually begins the process of intervention. It is in distinguishing the hopeless, overwhelming perceived nature of the problem from the real, painful, and problematic reality of the situation that resolutions and interventions to the real problem can be found.

Planning and Intervention

Once assessment is made and referral is determined to be unnecessary (see Chapter 14), plans may be made for practical and direct intervention. The actual interventions vary, again, according to the nature of the problem, and the skills and resources of the helper. However, even with such tailoring of the intervention, crisis interventions generally focus on responding to the recent precipitating event and the resultant problem.

The concern is less on identifying the underlying causes or contributing factors to the crisis, and more directly on understanding and intervening with the specific event and resultant problem.

Unlike the more formalized helping process—where time and energy is invested in developing a collaborative plan, with both helper and helpee engaging actively in intervention planning—in crisis intervention, the helper often takes a more active, directive role in the development of the plan to utilize the helpee's personal assets and environmental supports. The crisis nature of the situation often demands that the helper take responsibility for the intervention planning. This is not to suggest that intervention is done to the helpee. The helpee is still an active part of the intervention process and is provided information on what is to be done and how it should help. The essential difference is that the helper relies less on nondirective, reflective methods, and takes a more personally responsible role for directing the intervention plan.

The directive nature is made clear by the following brief exchange between Ted, a 14-year-old runaway who has been living on the street for the past three days, and the youth worker who discovered him.

> Ted: (very upset) I don't know what I'm gonna do, where I'm going to stay. I don't have any money . . . these are the only clothes I got . . . Man, I screwed up!
> Youth worker: Ted, the first thing we want to do is get you to take a breath

and begin to calm down. It seems like you have been through quite a bit in the last 3 days, but between us, we can begin to work this out.

Ted: I hope so—I know my parents are going to be freaked out . . . I mean I took off, they have no idea what happened.

Youth worker: How about if we take a couple of steps? First, I bet you're hungry, so let's go get something to eat. You can use the showers here at the center, if you want, and I can even find you some sweats to change into. Perhaps just getting a bit cleaned up and fed will help?

Ted: You bet, that would be great. I am starving and I am cold as hell in these wet clothes.

Youth worker: Well, let's go grab something to eat and you can tell me why you left home so we can start thinking about a better way to handle the problem. Also, maybe we could even talk about how we want to contact your parents. They probably are worried about you.

In developing the intervention plan, it is important to consider the internal and external resources available to the helpee. The following types of questions need to be considered as the intervention plan is developed: What skills, or personal coping mechanisms does the helpee possess? How might family and friends be helpful? Are other professionals, agencies, or institutions needed to help in this situation?

While the intervention techniques employed will be highly dependent on the resources of both the helper and the helpee, it is generally agreed that the techniques employed will generally assist the helpee to

1. understand the nature of the crisis;
2. reduce the tension he or she may be experiencing as a result of repressed feelings, by assisting the helpee to discuss his or her feelings;
3. identify and implement his or her current coping mechanisms or develop new styles of coping; and
4. expand the social support network available to the helpee.

One technique which proves quite useful at this stage of crisis intervention, and which has previously been discussed, is force-field analysis. Its application as part of crisis intervention is demonstrated below in Exercise 12-2.

While the goal for this or any crisis intervention is clearly on the reduction of the immediate stress (e.g., finding a job), resolution is only part of the overall intervention plan. As with other forms of helping, crisis intervention attempts to remediate as well as provide the helpee with mechanisms which will ensure more successful coping in the future. This focus on preventing future crisis directs the helpee to identify techniques which will help him or her to identify the beginnings of future crises; techniques for reducing precipitating stressful factors, and a plan for increasing his or her successful coping skills.

EXERCISE 12-2
Force-Field Analysis for Crisis Intervention

Directions: Below you will find a brief description of a crisis situation. Next, you will note the steps employed in crisis planning, using a force-field analysis model. For each step, you have been provided an example of the type of data the helper would attempt to identify. Your task is to add two additional pieces of information under each of the steps.

Problem: Ms. E., a 24-year-old mother of 1-year-old twin girls, was just fired from her job as a secretary/typist at a local business. Ms. E. is a single parent, with a high school education with a business focus. She lives on her own in an apartment complex with other young couples and single parents. Ms. E. has been active in her church and is well liked by people in her community. She appears energetic and willing to do whatever is needed to begin to develop a healthy family for her children. She is in good health, has $400 in savings, and a car, which while having over 100,000 miles on it, appears to be in good running order.

Step 1: Specify the goal or objective to be achieved. Attempt to identify the goal in clear, concrete, specific terms. In this case, the goal is for Ms. E. to find a job that provides enough money to support herself and her children.

Step 2: Identify and list all of the personal and social/environmental factors assisting Ms. E. toward her goal.

Example: has good typing skills

(other:) _____

(other:) _____

Step 3: Identify and list those personal and social/environmental factors that are holding Ms. E. back from reaching her goal.

Example: somewhat poor interviewing skills

(other:) _____

(other:) _____

Step 4: List steps that can be taken to increase the positive forces and/or reduce the negative forces.

Example: rehearse interview with friend

(other:) _____

(other): _____

Termination

Many of the same concerns and issues addressed in the termination of any form of helping need to be addressed in terminating a crisis intervention. The helper needs to review the crisis and how the helpee has dealt with it. The helper needs to highlight how the helpee clarified the limits of the difficulty. The helper needs to assist the helpee to remember to separate the actual, real, nature of the problem he or she faced from his or her exaggerated perception of the nature of the problem. Finally, the helper needs to reinforce the positive steps the helpee has taken.

Prior to terminating, the helper should highlight alternative ways for the helpee to avoid such difficulties in the future, and also to note the various forms (people, programs, and agencies) of support available to the helpee, should such a problem arise in the future. Finally, in some cases, the helpee may have been assisted through this particular crisis situation. However, it may be apparent that this encounter was not sufficient to assist the helpee to develop the strategies needed to effectively avoid or resolve similar problems in the future. In this situation, the crisis worker needs to encourage the helpee to seek a longer-term form of treatment (e.g., psychologist, clinical social worker, psychiatrist, etc.) or treatment facility (e.g., hospital). The process of making such a referral is discussed in detail in Chapter 14.

SUICIDE: A CRISIS NEEDING INTERVENTION

When faced with a crisis and a sense that a problem is hopelessly unbearable, a person may conclude that the only "logical" course of reaction may be the termination of pain and life through suicide.

While it may seem easier to the novice helper to hope and pray that a suicidal person will not reach out to them for help, the sad reality is that many who serve in a helping capacity will encounter a person contemplating suicide. It is essential for all helpers to become alert to the early detection signals of suicide, and the processes needed to intervene.

A number of factors or conditions have been found to be associated with the high risk of suicide. People attempting suicide often provide evidence of experiencing pervasive feelings of loneliness, self-defeat, and unbearable pressure. Often these individuals exhibit signs of *haplessness* (i.e., the feeling that fate has turned against them, that all they have is bad fortune); *helplessness* (i.e., the inability to resolve their problems), and *hopelessness* (i.e., not only is their life useless/valueless, but it cannot be reversed).

One of the most important roles a helper can provide is early identification of high-risk individuals. Early detection of suicide potential requires a knowledge of the predisposing factors and precipitating causes of suicide, as well as an openness to subtle communication of thought and feeling.

Warning Signs

One of the surest, most obvious, and yet often most ignored warning signals is the suicide attempt itself. Statistics suggest that over two-thirds of those who committed suicide had attempted it earlier.

A dangerous myth helpers need to dismiss is that those who threaten or talk about suicide won't go through with it. Such is not the case. Helpers must take seriously all suggestions that a helpee may be contemplating suicide. Comments such as: "What's the use?", "I can't take it any more", and "Everyone will be better off without me" must be taken seriously.

Other indications that one may be seriously contemplating suicide are less direct. Often the suicidal individual begins to invest in death or withdraw from life. For example, the helpee may begin to talk about the legal disposal of personal property following death, or may begin to read about death and dying. The helpee contemplating suicide may begin to withdraw from life. He or she may begin to pull back from normal activities or social interactions, or even cancel future commitments and plans. Again these signs need to be noted and taken seriously.

Assessing the Risk

If the helpee does admit to suicidal thoughts or an inclination toward self-mutilation, further questioning to determine the degree of risk is indicated. Assessing the level of risk can be done by asking questions such as:

Have your thoughts about suicide (dying, ending it all) been persistent, or fleeting?

Have you ever fantasized about how you would do it?

Do you have the means at your disposal to fulfill this fantasy?

Have you ever come close to doing it?

Have you actually attempted it?

Has anyone in your family or a friend ever attempted or committed suicide?

The more thinking and concrete planning about the suicide the person has done, the greater the danger, and the more need for an immediate preventive response on the part of the helper.

What to Do

The nature of suicide as a crisis requires a two-pronged approach to intervention. In the first phase, the helper needs to provide crisis intervention. It is essential during this first phase that the helpee provide immediate support in the form of a caring, therapeutic relationship. The helper must literally tune into the helpee's concern and demonstrate empathic understanding of the pain experienced by the helpee. This is no time for a pep talk or lecture. The helpee needs a warm, accepting, and totally attentive helper, who conveys a real interest in him or her and his or her concerns.

In addition to demonstrating a real concern for the helpee and an accurate understanding of the helpee's problem(s), the helper needs to begin to focus the helpee's attention on what can be done. As with any other form of crisis intervention, in working with the suicidal person the helper needs to provide a realistic, hopeful expectation of what can be done to resolve the helpee's concerns. It is not the helper's purpose to provide the helpee with all the needed answers, but rather a sense that answers can and will be found. If possible, it is helpful to provide the helpee with clear, concrete information about what can and will be done. Also, it is useful to begin to identify the specific resources, skills, etc., that the helpee, the helper, and perhaps others who are available to help, possess and can be brought to bear on the resolving of this problem. This resource identification can help to create realistic sense of hope for the helpee.

As the crisis worker continues to develop the helping relationship with the suicidal helpee, it is useful to elicit a contract, that is, a clear statement regarding what both the helper and helpee can expect and require from each other. One very important aspect of this contract is the commitment from the helpee that he or she will CONTINUE TO LIVE.

This is not a legal contract, but a commitment that the helpee will NOT harm him- or herself as the helper continues to work with him or her to obtain the needed help. It is important to convey to the helpee that the helper's position is that life—his or her (the helpee's) human life—is prized and as such he or she **must** live. It is a position, a point, which in the helper's eyes is not debatable.

Thus, the primary tasks of the helper initially confronted by a suicidal helpee are to 1) demonstrate real concern and understanding, 2) provide reassurance and positive expectations, and 3) articulate a firm statement that life must be maintained. This focus is evidenced by the dialogue between Fred and the hotline counselor, which opened the chapter.

> Fred: I just can't take it any more!
> Hotline Counselor: Take it any more? Tell me, Fred, what has happened?
> Fred: We've been going together for 6 years . . . 6 years! We were planning to get married as soon as we were out of school. 6 years! I can't believe it!
> Hotline Counselor: You sound very upset, very hurt.
> Fred: Hurt! Upset, you bet! I found her in bed with another guy! I've had it! I can't take it! I'll show her! How's she gonna feel if I just cash it in?
> Hotline Counselor: You must have cared very much about the relationship, for it to hurt so badly? It seems that right now all you can focus on, all you feel, is the loss of the relationship? *(expressing concern and understanding)*.

(later in the same initial dialogue, after determining that Fred has neither a plan nor the means to hurt himself, and has never thought about hurting himself before)

Fred: I know you don't know me . . . but you've got to understand I've got nothing without her!
Hotline Counselor: Nothing? I'm sure it feels like that. It may seem to you that without her you have nothing, but is that really true?
Fred: Yes, it's true . . . no one could love me like she did!
Hotline Counselor: I think I understand. When you say you have nothing, you really mean, you have no other women in your life? But do you have others who care about you? Who enjoy you, and you them?
Fred: Yeah, I have friends and family . . . but that's not the same.
Hotline Counselor: No, it's not the same, but I'm glad that you do have family and friends who care about you. That's a lot better than having nothing . . . nothing at all.

(a little later in the conversation)

Hotline Counselor: You sound a little more calm now . . . that's good. Fred, I know you are really saddened by the break-up of this relationship, and I can even understand how, when you feel so bad about this one thing, it may interfere with your ability to remember the other people who are still in your life, and maybe even the other relationships that remain to be developed.
Fred: It's hard to keep focused. Sometimes I just feel overwhelmed by what is happening.
Hotline Counselor: Feeling overwhelmed is not unusual when you experience a loss like this . . . but look, as we have talked, you have been able to become calmer, more focused, less overwhelmed and have even shared with me some of the things that are still enjoyable and positive about your life. I really feel that if we could talk a little more, we might be able to find a way for you to feel better. (*reassurance*)
Fred : I don't know.
Hotline Counselor: You don't know . . .
Fred: I know you have helped, even in this little time, but I don't know what to do . . .
Hotline Counselor: Here's what I would like to do. I would like you to promise me two things. First, and this is non-negotiable, I want you to promise me that you will not try to hurt yourself in any way, as long as you and I are working on this plan. How do you feel about that? Can you promise me that? (*contract*)
Fred: Yeah, I'm okay . . . I'm not going to do anything.

Hotline Counselor: Great, because your life is just too important to me . . . and I really believe that we can find our way out of this.

Fred: I hope so.

Hotline Counselor: Now the second part of the agreement requires that you commit to continue to talk with me or someone else who may be able to help. So, how about your coming over to see me, today or tomorrow afternoon, or at least promise me we can talk tomorrow to begin to plan out what we need to do next?

Fred: If it's okay with you, I am feeling better, so I would like to just go over my friend's house to watch the game and try to relax. But I could drop in at the center tomorrow around 4 if that's okay.

Once the helpee believes that the helper is there for him or her, and that there is hope that together they can see the helpee through this crisis, the helper can begin to turn his or her attention to establishing the ongoing needed help for the helpee. The initial crisis intervention has only tapped the surface pain and frustration felt by the helpee. The depth of depression, anxiety, and loneliness which prevail in the suicidal helpee needs much more than that which can be provided in brief crisis intervention.

In the second phase of suicide intervention, the helper will assist the helpee to either contract for ongoing help with this helper (assuming he or she is qualified to work professionally with the helpee), or, as is more typical of a crisis intervention worker, to find ongoing support and assistance through professional services. In this latter case, it is important to find professional assistance as soon as possible. It is also important for those working in crisis intervention to

1. become familiar with the hundreds of crisis intervention and suicide prevention centers in the United States.
2. be aware of 24-hour hotlines which provide back-up professional consultation;
3. have a listing of professionals, agencies, centers, and hospitals in his or her area which are ready and able to provide the professional help needed.

Knowing when, where, and how to turn for other consultation support and professional help is an important ingredient in any helper's repertoire of intervention processes and as such will be discussed in greater detail in Chapter 14.

WHAT NEXT

Crises do occur, and the tragedy of suicide and suicide attempts are realities those in the helping profession do encounter. Yet, over the course of the last 20 years, those in the helping professions have learned a great deal in terms of early identification, prevention, and intervention of crisis. Exercise 12-3 is presented to help you translate the theory of this text to the reality of your community.

EXERCISE 12-3
The Reality of Crisis Intervention

Directions: Using your local phone book, identify one agency, service, or program that is defined as a crisis intervention resource. Arrange to interview a crisis counselor, asking the following types of questions.

- What is the nature of this program/agency?
- What population is this agency/program intended to service?
- How does one request services?
- What are the frequency and nature of crisis contacts you have experienced?
- What is the procedure (steps?) used when intervening with a crisis contact?
- What parts of the procedure/steps are the most (least) effective? most (least) easy to employ?
- What additional resources (people, programs, etc.) do you rely on to help you in your crisis intervention?
- What would you recommend to someone contemplating getting into the crisis intervention field?
- What changes would you like to see in the procedures or policies of crisis intervention?
- (other?)

If possible, share your data with your colleagues or classmates, noting similarities and dissimilarities. It may also be useful to pull together all the data regarding the nature of the different service programs or agencies interviewed and keep this listing as possible referral sources (Chapter 14) which could be used in the future.

REFERENCES AND RECOMMENDED READINGS

Caplan, G. (1964). *Principles of preventive psychiatry.* New York: Basic Books.

Everstine, D., & Everstine, L. (1988). *People in crisis.* New York: Brunner/Mazel.

Gilliland, B.E., & James, R.K. (1988). *Crisis intervention strategies.* Pacific Grove, CA: Brooks/Cole.

Griffin, M., & Felsenthal, C. (1983). *A cry for help.* New York: Doubleday.

Kardiner, S.H. (1975). A methodological approach to crisis therapy. *American Journal of Psychotherapy, 29,* 4–12.

Norris, H. (1987). *The person-in-distress.* New York: Human Sciences Press.

Parsons, R., & Wicks, R. (1994). *Counseling strategies and intervention techniques for the human services.* Needham Heights, MA: Allyn and Bacon.

Slaikeu, K.A. (1984). *Crisis intervention: A handbook.* New York: Allyn and Bacon.

▶ 13

Theories and Models

In Chapter 1, you were introduced to the characteristics of the effective helper. As you may recall, the effective helper is called upon to be an investigator of sorts. Now that you have read through the previous chapters with their various case illustrations and examples, it has probably become clear to you that, as an investigator, the effective helper is called upon to absorb all the data presented by the helpee and then assist the helpee to make sense of the information and develop a course of action. You may even begin to feel, like many new helpers, that the amount of information the helper needs to attend to, along with the speed with which it is presented, can become quite overwhelming. It becomes less overwhelming when the helper has a general framework, map, or model which helps him or her to organize the information and to begin to make some initial sense out of what is being presented.

This chapter will look at a few of the more classic frameworks, or models, employed by helpers as they attempt to understand the nature and meaning of the information provided them by the helpee. Specifically, the chapter will

1. discuss the value of theoretical models to the helping profession;
2. describe and define the major tenets of the theoretical models presented;
3. demonstrate the use of these theoretical models as applied to a case illustration; and
4. assist the reader to begin to articulate his or her own theoretical bias or beginning model.

THE NEED FOR MODELS AND THEORIES

Imagine that you have just been given two jigsaw puzzles for Christmas. While both puzzles are comprised of 10,000 pieces, puzzle A came in a box which provides a picture of the completed puzzle. The picture shows the approximate size, shape, and design of the completed puzzle. Puzzle B arrived in a plain, brown box, with no instructions, descriptions, or pictures. For which of the two puzzles

- would you have the clearest sense of your ultimate goal, of where you wanted to end up?
- would you have a way of assessing whether you were on the right track or not as you assembled the puzzle?
- would you be able to estimate how much more work needed to be accomplished?
- would you be most able to determine that your work was nearly complete?

The helper's use of theories or models is much like the puzzle assembler's use of the picture. A model provides a framework from within which the helper works. The use of a theoretical model or framework assists the helper in gaining a clearer sense of what the goal of helping should be, how well the process is progressing, and how to evaluate when the work has been completed. The helper's theory or model assists him or her in taking information provided by the helpee, which may at first appear somewhat disjointed and disconnected, and weaving a thread of consistency of theme through the information, so that he or she can understand what is "really" going on and how best to approach this particular helping encounter.

A GREAT ARRAY OF MODELS

The helping profession does not lack in the variety of models or theories one could choose. And while the barriers separating the major schools of helping are eroding (Strupp & Bergin, 1969), there remains value in understanding each particular unique emphasis of the major schools of thought. Perhaps you have heard of some of the helping theories, such as behavioral, psychoanalytic, cognitive, transactional analysis, gestalt, reality therapy, etc. These are but a few of the various frameworks employed by helpers. While this chapter will not be able to present each of these various models in depth, three of the more classical approaches are briefly discussed: the psychoanalytic, the client-centered/phenomenological, and the behavioral/cognitive.

For those who may be interested in developing a fuller understanding of these and other theories of helping, it is suggested that you refer to one of the many excellent textbooks written on the theories of counseling/psychotherapy, for example, Gerald Corey's *Theory and Practice of Counseling and Psychotherapy,* or C.H. Patterson's *Theories of Counseling and Psychotherapy.*

Psychoanalytic

For most lay people, the dramatic image of helping is often presented as involving a couch, the bearded helper, and the patient, who discusses early childhood experiences and recent dreams. Such a dramatization is very loosely founded upon a model developed by Sigmund Freud. The model, psychoanalysis, may be argued to be the beginning of modern day helping models.

Traditional psychoanalytic thought posits a generally negative and deterministic view of humans. It is assumed that humans are generally motivated by the need to meet their own selfish drives. It is further assumed that a person's early childhood experiences and history are central to the development of the adult personality and style of functioning.

Understanding the helpee's early life history and internal, intrapsychic conflicts is essential to the psychoanalytic model of helping. Thus, the helper employing this model would focus much attention and energy on understanding the ways in which the helpee's early childhood experiences have contributed to his or her current adult personality and experience.

In addition to understanding the concept of psycho-history and the influence of early childhood experience, the psychoanalytic approach emphasizes the power of the unconscious. Freud believed that the unconscious—that is, all that is beyond both our awareness and our control—serves as the primary source of motivation for our actions. Thus, in order to help another person, the helper must uncover the unconscious conflicts, concerns, or feelings which are interfering with the helpee's healthy functioning.

The psychoanalytic model, with its emphasis on understanding early childhood experiences and unearthing unconscious material, is a long-term model of therapy. This, coupled with the many years of unique and extensive training required, limits the use of the model.

However, even though psychoanalysis in its pure form may not be appropriate for use by all helpers, as a model it has made a number of significant contributions to the helping field. One contribution which may prove useful for many helpers is the concept of *ego defenses.*

The psychoanalytic view suggested that oftentimes a person placed in a state of distress may exhibit difficulty coping or adjusting to the situation as a result of an experience of psychic tension coming from within (e.g., feeling guilty over having done something he or she feels is wrong) or from without (e.g., being threatened by another). Further, this theory suggests that we have developed processes, *defense mechanisms,* which we use in order to reestablish internal stability and reduce the experienced tension. For example, often when people are confronted by the reality that they did something they should not have done, they may attempt to reduce the tension by excusing themselves from the responsibility. One defense often used for this purpose is *denial,* a process of simply stating it wasn't my responsibility, I didn't know, you never asked, etc. Another psychological defense employed in situations where one has made a mistake is *rationalization.* Rationalization is the process by which we attempt to offer a "reasonable" explanation to justify our actions. For example, consider the following the case of Tina:

> Tina promised her father that she would be home on time to pick up her brother
> at the bus stop. Tina decided to stay at school instead, and as a result her

brother walked home. Tina was confronted by her father and punished by being grounded (EXTERNAL THREAT). In the midst of the dialogue, Tina kept insisting that she was never told to pick up her brother (DENIAL) and that even if her dad had asked her, it would have been impossible since she HAD to stay after school to do an important project (RATIONALIZATION).

Sometimes the psychological threat is internal, for example, when a person is placed in psychological discomfort as a result of becoming aware of painful memories. When memories are causing the discomfort, that person may employ another ego defense called *repression*. Repression is the process of moving painful memories from conscious awareness and placing them in the unconscious. While repression may remove the person from the immediate painful memory, it does not help the person to resolve that memory. Material which has been repressed may find other avenues of expression, avenues which may prove dysfunctional. This was the case for Robert.

Robert was horribly abused as a young boy, often being confined for hours in a small, locked storage cabinet. While Robert did not remember any of these childhood experiences, he manifested an intense and exaggerated fear of closed-in spaces, including fear of being inside spaces even as large as an elevator, a bathroom, or a subway. In the process and safety of therapy, Robert began to remember some of these early childhood experiences. As he recalled the events, and he became free to express both his fear and his anger, Robert's symptoms (his irrational fears) disappeared.

The psychoanalytic approach involves a very complex set of assumptions and structures. Because of this, a brief description such as the one presented here truly does not do it justice. Further, because of the complexity of the theory, helpers interested in employing this model must undergo long and demanding training.

Client-Centered/Phenomenological

A second approach to helping, which has both historical roots and contemporary value, is the humanistic, client-centered, or phenomenological approach of Carl Rogers (1980). Rogers' perspective is in many ways the antithesis of the Freudian viewpoint.

The client-centered/phenomenological model (Raskin & Rogers, 1989) focuses on the uniqueness of each helpee's perception of reality, and assumes that humans are rational and positive. This approach places emphasis on the here and now, rather than the what was, or the individual's psychohistory, as did Freud. For Rogers, human beings, when functioning as they should, are constructive in their decisions, trustworthy, and growth-oriented. The client-centered approach assumes that when clients are in touch with their own potential and value, the decisions they make will be healthy, helpful, and growth-filled. It is assumed, therefore, that people who are experiencing emotional problems are somehow blocked from getting in touch with their potential and natural tendency toward healthy, growth-filled decision making.

Since, according to Rogers, the directions and resources for growth are "naturally" within each individual, the role of the helper is one of non-direction. The helper is not there to tell the helpee what is wrong or what to do, nor is the helper there to provide instruction or insight. From the client-centered perspective, the role of the helper is simply to create the psychological climate, or environment, that encourages the helpee to get in touch with his or her healthy tendency toward growth.

The helper with a client-centered approach is a facilitator, not a healer. The helper attempts to create an environment in which the helpee experiences the helper to be genuine, understanding, and accepting. From the client-centered perspective, these conditions are not only essential for helping, but are in fact sufficient for the helpee to free him- or herself to explore and discover what is right for him- or herself. From the client-centered frame of reference, emphasis is given to the nature of the relationship. It is not what the helpee does to the helper, nor the interpretations or insights the helper provides; rather, it is the helper's ability to provide the helpee with a genuine, non-judgmental, and open encounter that is the core of the helping process.

Behavioral/Cognitive

As with all of the previous models, behavioral approaches, while starting with a strict focus, have been modified and expanded. From an original emphasis on the objective observations of behaviors and the influence of the helpee's environment in the creation of the helpee's current functioning, behavioral approaches have evolved and expanded to include a number of less than directly behavioral focal points (i.e., thinking patterns, cognitions, images, etc.).

The primary focus for behavioral/cognitive approaches is on the degree to which learning and learning mechanisms are held to be of primary value to understanding both the helpee's current level of functioning and the process of change. For many who take a behavioral perspective, emphasis is placed on the function of the environment, with its rewards and punishments, as a source of shaping a person's style of acting. Thus, if one wishes to change a behavior or to develop a certain way of acting, one needs to manipulate the consequences, or reinforcers, following that behavior as the important therapeutic step.

Contemporary behavioral approaches and models are founded in a scientific view of human behavior. Proponents of the behavioristic/cognitive model take a systematic, directive, and structured approach to counseling. While there exists a great deal of variation among those who hold a behavioral viewpoint in terms of the emphasis on learning and their view of the helpee as either a passive creation of environment or an active and interactive agent in their own experience, etc., the behavioral/cognitive approaches in general emphasize

1. the identification of the current influences on the helpee, rather than the historical determinants;
2. the specific identification of problem and goals for helping;
3. the importance of observable, behavioral change as the goal of helping;
4. a scientific, empirical approach to helping.

Many behavioral approaches emphasize the use of teaching techniques (e.g., modeling, practice, conditioning, etc.) for the modification of behavior or the development of new response styles (Wilson, 1989), whereas others focus on identifying and challenging dysfunctional thinking patterns and relearning more functional cognitive patterns (e.g. Beck, 1991; Ellis, 1991; Meichenbaum, 1991). For those behavioral helpers who stress the importance of the thinking process, emphasis is placed on assisting the helpee to

1. understand the connection between the way he or she thinks about him- or herself and his or her world, and the way he or she acts and feels;
2. identify when his or her thinking is based on faulty logic and faulty assumptions; and
3. learn to challenge and correct the distorted, faulty thinking.

A Case Illustration: Three Perspectives

While the brevity of this chapter prevents a complete presentation of each of the theories, the above descriptions of each, along with the following case illustration, should help you to begin to understand the essential differences between these approaches.

Russell, or Russ, as he likes to be called, is a 26-year-old single white male who is currently experiencing some anxiety and even mild depression because of "his difficulty with girls". According to Russ, he came to counseling "... because (I) choke every time I try to ask a girl out."

Russ described his personal history as follows. Russell's father had died when Russ was two, and he was raised by his mother and an elderly aunt. Russell described his home environment as being very religious and strict, and in which all discussion about girls, dating, or sexuality was avoided. Russ was taught "to always respect women." He remembers being told that "women are fragile, and need the males' protection". All of Russ's sex education came from what he picked up from his peers or read in adult magazines, and he remembers his aunt telling him that "sex was something we had to do in order to create babies . . . ."

Throughout high school Russ rarely dated and generally found himself becoming anxious around girls, fearing he would not know what to do and therefore they would think he was weird or something. The one early experience with dating which Russ could remember came when he was in 11th grade. Russ had a friend "set him up" with a girl in his class for the junior prom. Russ recalls the evening to be an "absolute disaster". As he describes it: "I did everything wrong, starting with sticking my date with a pin as I tried to put the flowers on her dress, through literally knocking over a coke at dinner, and staining her dress." "But the actual highlight," he continues, "was near the end of the evening, she finally convinced me to dance (up to that point we had just been sitting at the table). I was so nervous that when we began to dance, I stepped on her foot and we both fell to the floor! I felt like dying—and I am sure she was totally humiliated." Russ had mixed feelings about the experience. On one side he felt happy about being able to go to the prom, but on the other side, he felt "like such an absolute idiot, a real nerd". Russ has had a few dates since then, most often set up as blind dates by a friend. With each of these dates, his memory of the night of the prom comes back "loud and clear". In fact, his most recent date was again a blind date set up for the office Christmas party. According to Russ, it was almost an instant replay of the prom. " Even though we didn't dance or I didn't trip her, I did almost everything else. I did spill a drink. I stammered and stuttered all night and generally acted like a real fool! There is no way she would ever . . . ever want to go out with me again. In fact, I don't think anyone at the party would risk dating such a nerd."

Psychoanalytic Perspective

The psychoanalyst would be very interested in hearing more of Russell's early childhood experiences. The overly strict and puritanical environment may have led Russell to repress his normal sexual urges. Further, the fact that Russell never knew his father, or had the opportunity to identify with a male figure, would be a point the psychoanalyst would seek to pursue.

As Russ's early psychosexual and developmental history unfolded, the reasons for his current anxiety around women would become clear. Most likely, his lack of a male figure with whom to identify, and the somewhat "idealized" and "detached" experience with women, along with his image of sexual activity as "filthy", would all be contributing to his current difficulty.

Client-Centered Perspective

The fact that Russell was experiencing such anxiety and depression, reflective of his inability to accept and love himself, would become a central focus for the client-centered helper. The helper would employ active listening and reflecting skills to demonstrate to Russell that he was not only understood but also valued and accepted. While Russell may begin to discuss his early childhood experience, as if relating a there-and-then story, in the process of client-centered helping, he would soon move to the here-and-now. Russell would relate his unacceptance of himself. He would talk about his fear of being unacceptable to others and feeling like "a nerd".

As the client-centered helper reflected Russell's expressed confusion (between wanting to love and accept himself, and yet feeling like he needed others to approve of him first), Russell would begin to see that he was unconditionally valued. He would accept that he was lovable and valuable, even if he had limited social skills or acted somewhat awkwardly in social settings. As Russell increased his own self-acceptance and truly embraced the sense of being worthwhile and valuable, independent of his skills or achievements, he would experience a reduction in his anxiety about being himself around others.

Behavioral/Cognitive Perspective

The behavioral helper would want Russell to be concrete about what is was he wished to develop as a result of this helping encounter. Was Russell interested in being less anxious around women? Did Russell want to develop better social skills?

The behaviorist would hypothesize that the early experiences with his mother and aunt "taught" Russ to see women as if they were unapproachable and on a pedestal. Further, the behaviorist would see Russ's early experience with the prom and subsequent similar unsuccessful dating experiences as ones in which Russ learned to anticipate failure in these social encounters. It would further be hypothesized that such anticipation of failure increases Russ's anxiety, which in turn interferes with his being relaxed enough in social settings to enjoy them, or even to function "appropriately". Thus, anxiety continues to create a situation where failure is likely. This continued failure reinforces the initial belief and anticipation of failure, and thus the cycle continues.

Once the goal was established, for example, to decrease the anxiety associated with socially engaging with a woman, a directed, systematic program would be developed. The program might include having Russell learn relaxation techniques to control his anxiety, develop positive self-talk to counteract his negative self-concept, and participate in a program to teach and practice social, conversational skills.

TECHNICAL ECLECTICISM: AN ALTERNATIVE APPROACH

Many helpers will argue that they like a little bit of this theory and a little bit of that. They may even call themselves "eclectic". But eclecticism is more than taking a piece of this or that. Eclecticism is the process of selecting methods, tenets, and assumptions from a variety of sources and systems. When a helper consciously and deliberately attempts to *integrate* a variety of concepts, terms, techniques, strategies, procedures, and assumptions into an approach which meets the needs of the client, such a helper could be considered eclectic in his or her approach.

Too often, eclecticism is used to mean that one indiscriminately and arbitrarily chooses a part of this theory and a part of that theory. For eclecticism to be of value as a model, it must have as a base the helper's consistent philosophical beliefs about the nature of human functioning, the causes for dysfunctioning, and the factors or variables required for correcting the problem. When the helper has a firm set of operational assumptions, and finds that many techniques, derived from a variety of schools of helping, fit into this framework, then that could be considered *technical eclecticism.*

As previously noted in Chapter 7, one theory model which exhibits such technical eclecticism is the multimodal approach offered by Arnold Lazarus (1981, 1989). As you may recall, Lazarus' model focuses on seven interactive modalities of human functioning. The seven modes are **b**ehavior, **a**ffect (feelings), **s**ensations, **i**magery, **c**ognition, **i**nterpersonal relationships, **d**rugs/diet, yielding the mnemonic acronym BASIC ID. Lazarus employs these seven modes as diagnostic, or problem identification reference points, as well as targets for possible intervention. Further, given the broadness of his model, Lazarus is able to integrate many of the techniques and strategies developed by the other more restrictive models. For example, consider the following application to the case with Russ.

Modality	Focus	Intervention Strategy
Behavior	Fails to make eye contact, low voice volume, and very limited self-disclosure.	Undertake social skills training program with instruction, modeling, and practice.
Affect	Anxious	Help him to recognize and express his anxiety using a gestalt therapy technique called "empty chair".
Sensation	Jittery	Teach behavioral technique of deep muscle relaxation.
Imagery	Negative self-image in social circumstances	Use cognitive approach of guided imagery
Cognition	Belief that he must be perfect to be liked.	Undertake rational-emotive training
Interpersonal	Withdrawn	Assist him to understand his childhood injunctions against approaching women and against viewing sexual desires as normal, using transactional analysis process called re-scripting.
Drugs/Diet	Too much caffeine	Employ a biochemical approach including switching to decaffeinated coffee and reducing chocolate intake.

WHAT NEXT

Employing a theoretical model or theory to guide your process of helping requires that you gain a fuller understanding of the various models currently employed. Further, in addition to understanding the theories, you, as an effective helper, need to discern which models, or which aspects of models have empirical support. It must be noted, however, that since there is no one model which has up to this point been demonstrated to be totally adequate and factual, you will be left to decide which theory in your estimation not only has the most support, but which blends with your own thoughts, feelings, and philosophy.

As to where to go next, a three-pronged attack is suggested. The *program outline* is an approach which you should begin now, and continue throughout your years of effective helping.

1. Read! Throughout this book suggested readings and references have been supplied. New research information is always being published. It is important to read what others have found about the usefulness and validity of the various approaches to helping.
2. Discuss! Find people in the helping professions and discuss their experiences, the pros and cons of various models, concepts, techniques, and strategies.
3. Reflect! As you engage in helping, continue to reflect on your own decisions and processes. Ask yourself, Why did I do this or that? What guided my decision making? What information do I seek, or ignore? How do my various decisions reflect those of other helpers and how might they reflect my model?

REFERENCES AND RECOMMENDED READINGS

Beck, A. (1976). *Cognitive therapy and the emotional disorders.* New York: New American Library.

Beck, A. (1991). Cognitive therapy: A 30-year retrospective. *American Psychologist, 46,* 368–375.

Corey, G. (1991). *Theory and Practice of Counseling and Psychotherapy* (4th edition). Belmont, CA: Brooks/Cole.

Ellis, A. (1991). Using RET effectively: Reflections and interview. In M. Bernard (Ed.), *Using rational-emotive therapy effectively.* (pp 1–33). New York: Plenum.

Ellis, A., & Harper, R.A. (1975). *A new guide to rational living.* North Hollywood, CA: Wilshire Books.

Karoly, P., & Kanfer, F.H. (1982). *Self-management and behavior change.* New York: Pergamon Press.

Lazarus, A. (1989). *The practice of multimodal therapy.* Baltimore: Johns Hopkins University Press.

Lazarus, A.A. (1981). *The practice of multimodal therapy.* New York: McGraw-Hill.

Meichenbaum, D.H. (1977). *Cognitive-behavior modification: An integrative approach.* New York: Plenum.

Meichenbaum, D.H. (1991). Evolution of cognitive behavior therapy. In J. Zeig (Ed.), *The evolution of psychotherapy II.* New York: Brunner/Mazel.

Parsons, R., & Wicks R. (1994). *Counseling strategies and intervention techniques for the human services.* Needham Heights, MA: Allyn and Bacon.

Patterson, C.H. (1986). *Theories of counseling and psychotherapy.* New York: Harper and Row.

Patterson, C.H. (1989). Values in counseling and psychotherapy. *Counseling and Values, 33,* 164–176.

Rogers, C. (1980). *A way of being.* Palo Alto, CA: Houghton Mifflin.

Raskin, N.J., & Rogers, L.R. (1989). Person-centered therapy. In R.J. Corsini (Ed.), *Current psychotherapies* (pp. 154–194). Itasca, IL: F.E. Peacock.

Strupp, H.H., & Bergin, A.E. (1969). Some empirical and conceptual bases for coordinated research in psychotherapy: A critical review of issues, trends, and evidence. *International Journal of Psychiatry, 7,* 23–115.

Wilson, G.T. (1989). Behavior therapy. In R. J Corsini & D. Wedding (Eds.), *Current psychotherapies* (4th ed.) (pp. 241–282). Itasca, IL: F.E. Peacock.

Wolpe, J. (1973). *The practice of behavior therapy* (2nd edition). New York: Pergamon Press.

▶ 14

The How and Why of Referral

There are times when the best way to be of help to someone is to recognize when our own helping skills and abilities are simply not enough. There will be situations where our skills of listening and problem solving, while being comforting, may fall short of the type of assistance the helpee needs.

It is at these times that we must be able to call upon the professional resources and services around us, and assist the helpee in his or her transition to another source of helping. This chapter will discuss both the need for and process of making a referral. Specifically the chapter will

1. assist the reader to recognize when someone needs additional assistance;
2. assist the reader in increasing his or her familiarity with the resources and professional services available in his or her community; and
3. provide a set of steps and procedures involved in making a referral.

KNOWING WHEN TO REFER

If seeking a simple answer to the question "When should a helpee be referred?" one could posit, "Any time they ask to be!" or *Any time the helper has doubts.* But the reality is that knowing when a helpee needs another form of professional assistance is not an easy process, nor is it cut and dried.

Since a person seeking help is often unclear about both the actual nature of his or her problem or the appropriate resources needed for meeting that problem, it will be rare to find a helpee specifically asking for a referral. Although the helpee may not directly or specifically ask for a referral, there will be subtle signs exhibited in the helping encounter which suggest that referral is desirable. It is incumbent, therefore, upon the helper to identify these signs and decide what may be the best route for the helpee.

In general, it appears that the helper's decision to refer a helpee to another source of helping should reflect the helper's own awareness of his or her skill limitations, as they come to bear on the unique needs of the helpee, especially in light of the alternative resources and services available. Such self-awareness would include

1. knowing his or her own areas of expertise;
2. being aware of the kind of support and supervision available to him or her which can be called upon in this case;
3. having an accurate sense of his or her own time, energy, and availability to take on this particular case.

In addition to having such self-awareness, the helper must be aware of the various dimensions of the case being presented when considering making a referral. Specifically, when attempting to decide whether to continue to work with a helpee or refer him or her to a different source of helping, the helper should take into consideration: 1) the severity of the problem, 2) the helper's sense of clarity about the cause of and solution to the problem, and 3) the degree and direction of change currently experienced.

The Severity of the Problem

A helpee is certainly free to seek additional assistance and professional support any time he or she desires, and referral should be considered any time the helper feels unsure about his or her ability to assist a helpee. But as a general rule, a person feeling a bit down or confused about a specific time-related issue may not be a cause for alarm, in and of itself, nor should it signal a need for referral. For example, a student who is upset about a poor grade on a test, or an individual "grieving" about the break-up of a relationship, or even one experiencing anxiety about an upcoming event such as a job interview, may simply need an objective and caring person to help clarify his or her concern and identify a strategy for coping with the situation. Such situational, time-limited concerns generally do not require professional assistance.

However, if the helpee's reactions to these problems appear to be more severely impacting—affecting more and more areas of his or her daily functioning, and extending for longer periods of time—then perhaps referral to professional help is in order. The focus here is on *severity and duration* of the helpee's symptoms and dysfunction.

When the reaction appears out of proportion to the actual cause or event, in either degree of severity or duration, then perhaps professional assistance is warranted. For example, consider the following case illustration.

> Helen came to her local minister in her own words, ". . . feeling very sad". In the initial encounter, the minister discovered that Helen had broken up with her boyfriend of three years. The two of them had been dating throughout college and even for the past year after graduation. However, last October (five months ago), he announced that he met someone at work and that he wanted to see other people. Helen stated that she ". . . was devastated". She

reported feeling like the world had been turned upside down, that she didn't know what she was going to do, and that since that time (five months ago), she has had difficulty sleeping or eating, is unable to concentrate at her work, and has withdrawn from social contact.

While the loss of a meaningful relationship would most often result in an experience of sadness and even grief, the extensiveness of the effect of this loss (i.e., affecting her health, her work, her social life), along with the length of impact (five months), seem to suggest that this is more than a normal reaction of sadness, and that, in fact, Helen may be experiencing a depressive reaction. Under these conditions, should the minister feel ill-prepared or untrained to work with depression, referral would be appropriate.

Other situations are by their very nature severe and would typically require the skills and competency of a trained professional helper such as a psychologist, psychiatrist, clinical social worker, etc. These situations, while not limited to the following, would include:

- helpee's expressing "bizarre" symptoms such as

  hallucinations (experiencing things not present in reality)
  delusions (systematizing false beliefs, such as believing he or she has special powers or that people are plotting to get him or her)
  poor reality checks (not knowing who he or she is where he or she is, or even the date, year, or other time references)
- persistent severe depression, including symptoms such as

  poor appetite or significant weight loss
  difficulty sleeping or trouble staying awake
  loss of interest or pleasure in usual activities
  feelings of worthlessness or excessive guilt
- expressed and planned desire to hurt him- or herself or another
- excessive drinking, drug use (prescribed or illegal), gambling
- frequent loss of self control (anger outburst)
- engagement in illegal or antisocial behaviors
- extreme sense of anxiety/fear
- ongoing and repetitive sleeping or eating problems
- extreme risk-taking behavior to the point of endangerment
- a repeating pattern of interpersonal problems (including marriage, family, and work relationships)
- serious work-related or school-related problems

The Helper's Sense of Clarity

Another situation in which referral appears necessary is when the helpee has no, or only a very limited, sense of understanding about the nature of the problem or the needed steps of helping. Clearly, if the helper is clueless as to what is happening or what should be done, he or she can be of little assistance to the helpee. This is not to suggest that a helper must be completely clear about all the elements of the problem and the exact steps to take in helping, right from the point of initial contact. Obviously, clarity comes with ongoing contact and work with the helpee. What is being suggested is that when the helper, after working with the helpee, is still unsure about the nature of the helpee's concern, the direction to be taken, or what to do with the helpee and as a result doubts the efficacy of this helping encounter, referral to another professional appears appropriate.

A helper's lack of clarity and direction may be a result of the complexity of the problem at hand. It can happen that the presenting complaint is so intricately tied with many other dimensions of the helpee's life that the helper may feel overwhelmed by the intricate and interdependent web of problems and simply not know where to start. It is possible that even when the cause or causes is (are) evident, the helper may still be unsure how to proceed. Consider the situation discussed by one counselor in training.

Maria was a graduate student in counseling currently working in the local high school as part of her professional training. As an intern in the high school, Maria was asked to work with an 11th grade student, Nina, who was sent to the counselor because of her excessive absences. As the counselor and the student began to meet and discuss the why's and what-to-do's of her absenteeism, the counselor soon discovered the following.

1. The student was the oldest of 8 children;
2. Her father abandoned the family, and her mother was an alcoholic who worked in the evenings and often would not come home after work;
3. This student took "parenting" responsibility for her 7 siblings, including cooking, cleaning, and getting them off to school;
4. The student had been diagnosed as having juvenile diabetes and was very inconsistent in watching her diet and insulin injections;
5. The student was working part time (9 PM to 11:30 PM) cleaning offices to make money to purchase her own clothes.

As the story continued to unfold, the young counselor-in-training recognized the vast array of problems—medical, social, financial, etc.—confronting this teen. However, even in recognizing the many contributing factors or causes for the student's poor school attendance, the young counselor had no idea of what to do or even where to begin. Under such circumstances, seeking additional professional assistance and referral is clearly warranted.

A helper's lack of clarity and direction can occur even when the problem is not that big or complicated. A helper's ability to clearly understand the nature of the problem at hand, along with the direction and steps needed to be taken, can be blocked by a number of sources of interference, such as those previously discussed (e.g., lack of objectivity, burnout, etc.).

Regardless of the reason for the helper's lack of clarity about the nature of the problem or the direction to take, when a helper continues to feel unclear and directionless, referral is suggested.

The Degree and Direction of Change

One final indication that referral is required is when the helper notices that the problem is getting worse, or the helpee is making little or no progress. While it would be nice to assume we could provide the helpee with immediate relief and resolution, such is not usually the case. Quite often the problem has evolved over time, oftentimes quite slowly and subtly. Similarly, resolving the problem may take time, and occur, at least initially, in small steps. But, when helping is taking place, movement in the desired direction should be expected.

Again, this is not to suggest that one expects immediate resolution. However, progress in terms of forming a helping relationship, identifying problems, or establishing goals should be expected, and once this foundation has been established, it is reasonable to expect some movement in both the implementation of the intervention plan and the effect of that plan. With these milestones (i.e., making a helping relationship, identifying problems/goals, creating an intervention plan, implementing that plan, demonstrating progress) as our reference point, helpers who find the movement blocked, stalled, or regressing may start to consider referral as the next logical step as an alternative approach to helping.

AVAILABLE RESOURCES

Many new helpers (and even some not-so-new helpers) may be unfamiliar with the resources available to which they could refer. Exercise 14-1 will begin to test your own current knowledge of resources available.

It is essential that as a helper you become familiar with the resources available in your community or college campus. In fact, according to one group of helpers, the American Personnel and Guidance Association's Code of Ethics, it is incumbent upon the counselor to be knowledgeable about referral resources so that a satisfactory referral can be initiated (Nugent, 1981).

The effective helper, therefore, builds a referral system branching through the surrounding geographic area (Cunningham, 1985). The referral system should include psychologists, psychiatrists, social workers, ministers, physicians, clinics, social service agencies, etc. There are a variety of professional helpers found in most communities. A psychiatrist is a physician who has had additional training, beyond his or her general medical training, in the area of psychology. As physicians, they can prescribe medications where such may be indicated. A psychologist is an individual with a master's degree, or most often a doctorate (Ph.D., Ed.D., Psy.D.) degree. While referred to as "doctor" these individuals cannot prescribe medication, but will work with a medical doctor if such medication is required. Mental health counselors, social

EXERCISE 14-1
Where to Turn?

Directions: This exercise is best done with a number of colleagues or classmates.

Step 1: As a group, share your current knowledge of persons, agencies, programs, or services you could use as referral sources for helpees experiencing each of the following:

eating disorder
spiritual crisis
career indecision
suicide
drug and alcohol addiction
run away
test anxiety
financial problems
abused
academic difficulty

Step 2: Contact one professional helper and ask him or her to identify where he or she would turn if seeking assistance with helpees with each of the above described problems. Share the results of this interview with your colleagues/classmates.

Step 3: After completing Exercise 14-1, individually redo Step 1 of this exercise.

workers, and pastoral counselors are additional professionals who may have special training in the areas of counseling and psychological services.

The more knowledge the helper possesses about the purposes, functions, and procedures of the various individuals, programs, or agencies available to provide professional help, the more effective he or she can be in assisting a helpee to find the needed assistance. One way to begin to develop such a knowledge base is to become personally familiar with the various helping professionals and agencies in your local community (see Exercise 14-2). Further, a listing of social service agencies in your community can be obtained by contacting the local county government or mental health/mental retardation agencies which are listed in your phone book. These numbers should be easily and rapidly accessible.

But in addition to simply knowing the name, location, and phone number of a particular professional or service, the effective helper needs to identify the specific nature of the services offered and the process and procedures required. Questions such as "Whom do we contact?", "How much will it cost?", "What can I expect?",

"How do I begin?" need to be answered. Unless the helper has had personal or professional contact and experience with the various people, services, or agencies he or she will not be able to assist the helpee in answering these questions.

The effective helper will know more than simply the title or degrees of the persons being referred to. The title of the individual may be less important than his or her educational background, training, and experience working with various age groups and problem areas. It is important to have a feel for the "person" of the helper, as well as his or her credentials, when attempting to connect a helpee with one of these professionals.

MAKING A REFERRAL

Recognizing that a person who came to you for assistance may need to be referred is only the first step. The real challenge is to convey this awareness to the helpee in such a way that it will embraced by the helpee. Often helpees interpret the suggestion that they may be more efficiently helped by going to another as a sign of rejection, or as evidence that they are beyond help. The effective helper will present the idea of referral in a way that it understood as a continuing, productive step in the helping process. For example, consider the following brief dialogue between a counselor in a displaced women's center and a new client.

> Counselor: Tina, I am very happy that you have been so open and honest with me.
> Tina: It has been easy, you are a very good listener.
> Counselor: Thank you. But as I listened to you, I started to realize that of all the things you are concerned about, the one thing which seems to need some attention is helping you with your housing problem.
> Tina: Yeah, I don't have any money or anything.
> Counselor: Yes, I remember you saying that you really didn't have any place to go or any resources, such as money. But Tina, this is an area where I am not completely familiar with all the possible resources available.
> Tina: Oh, no . . .
> Counselor: No, it's going to all right. Even though I am not aware of the resources available, I know of someone who can really help us. So what I would like to do is call Ms. Albertson over at Community Service Center, and set it up so that you can talk with her. This would be a really good step in getting the help you want. How do you feel about me calling for you?

As evident in the brief exchange, making a referral needs to be presented the helpee as the hopeful first step of intervention. For some people, being told that they need help from a mental health professional (such as a psychiatrist, psychologist, etc.), may be interpreted as evidence that they are "sick" or "crazy". They may fear that this recommendation will act as a stigma, characterizing them for life. Again, the helper making the recommendations needs to present the information in the light that this is an opportunity to develop the helpee's potentials and strengths, and that recognizing the value of working with another professional is a good step toward problem resolution.

It is also important that the helpee accept that the helper will work with them, actually walk with them (if need be), as the initial contact with the referral service is made. This is not a rejection, but a continuation of their work together. More specifically, when preparing a helpee for referral the helper should:

- Be clear and direct about the goal and the expectation for seeking professional assistance; assist the helpee to understand why the helper feels referral is desirable.
- Clearly confront what referral is NOT. Be sure the helpee understands that making a referral is not the helper's way of rejecting the helpee, nor is it a statement that he or she is hopeless or unabled to be helped.
- Share information about the referral source, the nature of the service, the various details of costs, location, etc.
- Discuss the helpee's feelings and concerns about the referral.
- Answer all questions from the helpee.
- Reassure the helpee about the value of this recommendation, the qualifications of the resource, and the helper's expectations of a growth-filled outcome.
- Assist the helpee in preparing for the initial contact. What would he or she like to ask? What does he or she want to know about the resource? What does he or she want to achieve? What role, if any, would he or she like the helper to play?
- Establish a means of follow-up with each other. Encourage the helpee to let the helper know how the initial visit went. This will assist the helpee to understand that the helper is not abandoning him or her.

After the contact has been made, it is important for the helper to back off from the treatment, unless requested to stay involved by the attending professional. Sometimes, a helpee who experiences some anxiety with the referral source may "run" back to the original helper. It is important to redirect the helpee back to the professional, and encourage the helpee to share his or her concerns directly with the new helper.

WHAT NEXT

Perhaps more than any other aspect of helping, making a referral requires that the helper possess a well-developed knowledge base. Thus, the next step in developing your own professional abilities and skills is for you to increase your knowledge and

---

EXERCISE 14-2
Learning about Community Resources

Directions: In order to develop the information and awareness needed to have a competent resource base, begin to develop a referral database by answering the following questions about the services in your community or on your campus.

Name: _____

Address: _____

Phone: _____

1. What is the purpose or mission of this agency or professional service?
2. What type of people (age, gender, socioeconomic position, race, etc.) are best serviced by this source?
3. What type of difficulty, problem, or concern is most often addressed by this service?
4. What resources are available (24-hour hotlines, medical facilities, housing, educational materials, etc.)?
5. What is the procedure or process for seeking assistance?
6. What is the general model, theory, or approach to helping which is used?
7. What are the training levels of people who work there?
8. Are there fees involved? How much? Payment plans? Sliding scales? Do they take insurance, etc.?
9. Who is the contact person?
10. Other related or special services?
11. Other impressions or information?

---

familiarity with the services available in your local community. Exercise 14-2 is designed to assist you with the development of your own referral data base. This can be an extension of the data you collected in Exercise 14-1.

REFERENCES AND RECOMMENDED READINGS

Cunningham, M.M. (1985). Consultation, collaboration, and referral. In R. Wicks, R.D. Parsons, & D. Capps, (Eds.), *Clinical handbook of pastoral counseling* (pp. 162–170). Mahwah, NJ: Paulist Press.

Nugent, F.A. (1981). *Professional counseling.* Monterey, CA: Brooks/Cole.

Parsons, R.D., & Wicks, R. (1994). *Counseling strategies and intervention techniques for the human services* (4th edition). Needham Heights, MA: Allyn and Bacon.

▶ 15

Helping: Opportunities and Responsibilities

This text has attempted to describe and operationalize the steps, procedures, and techniques employed in helping so as to demystify the helping process and make it comprehensible. While just as a demystifying and operationalizing process is necessary if one is to develop the knowledge and skills needed to become an effective helper, this process does bring with it a caution.

The effective helper will understand and continue to appreciate the fact that helping is not simply the sterile application of techniques or procedures. The process of helping another human being, who is in pain, is an intense, responsible form of human encounter. Thus, while it is important for the helper-in-training to not be intimidated by the invitation to help another, it is just as important for the helper to never lose the sense of awe for the power and responsibility of the helping encounter.

THE NEED FOR GUIDELINES

Helping is a powerful, awesome process which carries with it equally powerful and significant responsibilities. Sadly, it is all too easy to find examples of helpers who have abused this power and responsibility.

One need only to turn on a television talk show to find examples of unethical therapists who have sexually abused their clients, counselors who have ignored their clients' suicidal pleas for help, or even medical and social service workers who have personally gained from the misfortunes of others. As helpers, we are given the responsibility to care for individuals, who, by the definition of needing help, are often those who are most vulnerable to manipulation.

Helping is surely a powerful and awesome process, and helpers who take their responsibilities seriously need guidelines for protection and care of those seeking their help. Some of the commonly accepted guidelines, which should serve as ethical beacons for helpers throughout their careers, are:

- Ethical helpers are aware of their own needs and how these may be active in the helping relationship.
- Ethical helpers do not meet their own needs at the helpees' expense.
- Ethical helpers appreciate the power of the helping relationship and use it for the benefit and care of the helpees.
- Ethical helpers employ techniques, models, and frameworks of helping which are recognized and accepted within the profession.
- Ethical helpers are aware of the boundaries and limits to their own competence and training, and do not seek to practice outside the limits of their competence.
- Ethical helpers continue to develop their professional skills and knowledge through formal training, professional membership, and peer consultation and supervision.

PROFESSIONAL STANDARDS AS GUIDELINES

Professional organizations, such as the American Counseling Association (formerly the American Association of Counseling and Development, AACD), the American Association of Marriage and Family Therapy (AAMFT), the American Psychological Association (APA), and the National Association of Social Workers (NASW) all provide more specific statements of guidelines for ethical practice and help giving. The ethical helper needs to become aware of these standards of ethical practice by becoming involved with the organization that represents his or her profession. Even helpers-in-training need to become aware of their profession's guiding principles. The names and addresses of these national organizations can be found in Appendix A.

While each specialty in the helping field may emphasize one or another ethical principle of practice, two guidelines focusing on helper competence and care-giving for the helpee appear common and fundamental to all professional groups.

Helper Competence

A fundamental ethical principle to which all professional groups subscribe is that a helper must be aware of the limitations of his or her own professional competence, and not exceed those limitations in the delivery of his or her service.

It is all too easy for a helper to find him- or herself alone in an office, or in the field of practice, without teachers, mentors, or supervisors looking over his or her shoulder, and assume that he or she can try this or that new technique or approach, or deal with any and all problems or situations presented. Such is not the case. New techniques and approaches need to be learned, and practiced under appropriate supervision. Similarly, helpers cannot be everything to everybody.

Ethical helpers do not employ procedures or techniques for which they have not been trained, nor do they extend their helping to those individuals whose problems are well beyond their scope of training and expertise.

Knowing the limits of competence, being willing to seek ongoing training and supervision, and knowing when to seek consultation from a colleague or make referral to another helper, are all characteristics of an ethical helper.

The Care of the Helpee

Among the various helping professions, it is commonly held that the helping relationship exists for the helpee's benefit, for his or her care, and NOT for the personal needs or benefits of the helper.

The helper who uses the helping relationship to make him- or herself feel powerful, important, or needed is placing his or her needs before that of the helpee, and is being unethical. It is in placing the rights and needs of the helpee as primary that the helper begins to establish the general framework for ethical practice. The ethical helper demonstrates this primacy of the rights and needs of the helpee by providing the helpee with *informed consent,* establishing *confidentiality,* and maintaining a *professional relationship.*

Informed Consent

The ethical helper will demonstrate a respect for the right of the helpee to be fully informed. Helpees need to be provided with information that enables them to make informed choices.

Clearly this can pose a challenge in that the helper needs to attain a balance of providing the information needed for informed decision making, at a time and in a manner that the helpee can understand and successfully use that information. Too much information, too soon, can prove overwhelming, anxiety-provoking, and even destructive to the helping process. The goal of informed consent is to promote the cooperation and participation of the helpee in the helping process. Thus, the ethical helper will attempt to provide the helpee with information that can assist the helpee to decide if he or she wishes to enter and/or continue in this helping relationship.

Confidentiality

In seeking help, the helpee should be able to expect a relationship which is trusting, honest, and safe. For helping to be effective, the helpee must feel free to disclose and share private concerns. For such a sense of freedom to exist, the helpee needs to feel that the interaction is one which is confidential.

Confidentiality is both an ethical and legal issue. As with other areas of practice, confidentiality is not absolute, nor are decisions to hold information in confidence always black and white. The maintenance of confidentiality requires professional judgment.

While the situations under which confidentiality must be broken can vary, as a function of age, condition, setting, etc., it is generally agreed that helpers MUST break confidentiality when it is clear that a helpee might do harm to him- or herself or to another, as might be the case in suicide, child or elderly abuse, or homicide. The circumstances that typically dictate disclosure of information should both be understood by the helper and shared with the helpee. For example, it is important to inform a helpee that an ethical helper would have to report material shared by the helpee when:

- the helpee poses a danger to him- or herself or others.
- the professional helper believes that the helpee who is under 16 has been, or is, a victim of sexual abuse, physical abuse, or some other crime.
- the information has already been disclosed, as in the situation where the issue is in court action.

Since the determination of when a helpee is in clear and imminent danger to him- or herself or to another is a professional judgment, the ethical helper will consult with colleagues, whenever possible, to assist in that determination.

Professional Relationship

Finally, it is generally agreed that the helpee has a right to enter a professional relationship with the helper. Relationships in which the helper is using the interaction with the helpee to meet his or her own personal needs, or situations in which there exists a dual relationship between the helper and the helpee—such as may be the case as when the helper and helpee have social and personal relationships—threaten this principle of professional contact. As with all of the ethical guidelines, it is not a simple, cut-and-dried matter. Clearly there are times or situations when a person may be a friend and yet be able to gain the professional objectivity to assist the helpee. Under these situations, it is important for the helper to attempt to define and maintain some control or boundaries on the types of information being discussed, or the nature of the relationship as it may be appropriate to each of the varied roles (e.g., friend or helper).

INCORPORATING GUIDELINES

The standards and concerns expressed in the various organizations' code of ethics are guidelines. As the helper continues to develop increased knowledge and skill, he or she will need to formulate his or her internal values and standards of practice. The ethical helper should be aware of the general guidelines offered by his or her professional organization. But more than simply having knowledge of these guidelines, the ethical helper must be willing to reflect on these guidelines, dialogue with colleagues around the guidelines, and then formulate his or her own values which will then direct his or her helping interactions.

WHAT NEXT

While this is the end of this text, it is really only the beginning of an ongoing and continuing process of becoming an effective, ethical helper. There is much more to be learned, much more to practice, and it will continue to be so, throughout your professional helping career. As researchers document the effectiveness of new methods and new approaches, helpers—both new and seasoned—will need to update their knowledge and skills. Thus, this is truly just the beginning and not the end!

Helping is a very special, responsible, and rewarding experience. It demands much from the helper . . . but gives much in return.

REFERENCES AND RECOMMENDED READINGS

American Psychological Association. (1987). *Casebook on ethical principles of psychologists.* Washington, DC: Author.

Corey, G., Corey, M., & Callanan, P. (1988). *Issues and ethics in the helping professions* (3rd edition). Pacific Grove, CA: Brooks/Cole.

Flores, A. (Ed.). (1988). *Professional ideals.* Belmont, CA: Wadsworth.

Eberlein, L. (1987). Introducing ethics to beginning psychologists: A problem-solving approach. *Professional Psychology: Research and Practice, 18,* 353–359.

▶ Appendix A

Major Professional Organizations

The following national associations may be contacted for information regarding membership, practice standards and ethical guidelines, continuing education, and employment opportunities. Additional information may be obtained by contacting local and state affiliates of each of the national organizations. Names, addresses, and phone numbers for the local, state, or regional affiliates are generally listed in the yellow and/or blue pages of your telephone directory.

American Counseling Association
5999 Stevenson Avenue
Alexandria, VA 22304
(703) 823-9800

American Association for Marriage and Family Therapy
1717 K Street NW, #407
Washington, DC 20006
(202) 429-1825

American Psychological Association
1200 17th Street NW
Washington, DC 20036
(202) 955-7600

National Association of Social Workers
7981 Eastern Avenue
Silver Spring, MD 20910
(301) 565-0333

Index